SLAYING THE DRAGONS

SLAYING THE DRAGONS

21st Century Literacy

Barbara Frandsen

authorHOUSE®

AuthorHouse™
1663 Liberty Drive
Bloomington, IN 47403
www.authorhouse.com
Phone: 1-800-839-8640

First published by AuthorHouse   08/25/2011

ISBN: 978-1-4634-3566-0 (sc)
ISBN: 978-1-4634-3565-3 (ebk)

Library of Congress Control Number: 2011913006

Printed in the United States of America

Contents

Slaying the Phonics Dragon 41

Preface

We know that those fearsome, fire-breathing creatures known as dragons do not truly exist. Yet, in the world of literacy instruction, teachers often feel as though they are battling equally severe and frightening conditions that hinder literacy success. *Slaying the Dragons: 21st Century Literacy* considers several causes of literacy failure. The most severe challenges come from various types of dyslexia and dysgraphia and are the predominant challenges that are considered for remediation in these modules. Research information, suggested strategies and recommended modifications follow the introduction of each "dragon."

The modules are written for pre-service teachers attending four-year universities, alternative certification programs, elementary in-service teachers and home school parents. Straight-forward wording, bulleted items and short lines of print create a text that is easy for the eyes to follow. In addition to strategies, suggested modifications for ELL students (English Language Learners), gifted and talented students and students who learn differently are added.

Acknowledgments for Cover Design

Lane Williams designed and implemented front and back covers for *Slaying the Dragons: 21st Century Literacy*. A younger Lane and his brother, Dalton provided examples of developmental art when they were small boys. As young men, they continue to be an inspiration and source of joy to me.

Acknowledgments

A special thanks goes to Dr. Frank Guszak, former professor from the University of Texas in Austin, Texas who spent time consulting with me. Later, Dr. Guszak invited me to observe as he initiated reading instruction to a group of kindergarten children. Students at St. Edward's University who have worked with me to identify ways to benefit beginning readers also deserve acknowledgement. The quest to teach well, which is frequently seen in novice teachers, provides fuel for motivation and continued study.

Introduction

How many times have teachers felt their abilities called into question while facing the challenges of teaching literacy? Although many children and adults learn to read easily, others seem to defy all approaches. Only the bravest teachers dare to face up to the *dragons*—those obstacles that delay or even deny literacy success. Although this text includes a variety of challenges, the major dragons presented in this book represent types of dyslexia

What are the most daunting dragons confronted in *Slaying the Dragons: 21st Century Literacy?*

- One dragon emerges in students who puzzle teachers by mastering phonics and sight words without gaining adequate understanding when reading. Lack of **comprehension** presents the first dragon.
- Another dragon comes in the form of students who have good comprehension but need help when reading orally. Poor oral **fluency** presents a second dragon.
- When teaching **phonics**, teachers sometimes face the enigmas of children who over-use phonetic generalizations as well as those who seem incapable of discriminating between auditory differences in the sounds of letters.
- Learners for whom English is a second language present yet a different dragon in areas of **vocabulary** and **spelling** as well as fluency and comprehension
- A different dilemma occurs when students who can discuss concepts verbally discover a setback when putting pen to paper. This **writing** dragon can impede both the mechanics of scripting letters as well as the ability to express ideas in a written format.

Throughout the text, vocabulary words, necessary to understanding, are typed with a bold font. When modifications are appropriate, you will find ideas beside the main content. All five of the components of literacy recommended by the National Reading Panel are included in addition to other areas of instruction. A variety of strategies follow explanations of research in each area.

Slaying the Dragons: 21st Century Literacy, provides a series of nine modules. Each module offers new ideas as well as strategies with proven histories of demonstrated value. This text stimulates the intellect by facing common dragons and invites academic engagement through the presentation of alternative proposals.

Begin at the Beginning:

Ages 4-40

Beginning At the Beginning in Reading

What Is Reading?

Many diverse ideas can be found about reading. Initial definitions of reading from the Google Dictionary *http://www.merriam-webster.com/* on the web include the following.

- "Reading is a complex cognitive process of decoding symbols for the intention of deriving meaning (reading comprehension)."
- "Reading involves construction of the meaning represented by printed symbols."

Roe, Smith and Burns claim that all of the processes below contribute to reading and are necessary for success.

- Sensory input begins the process with visually seeing letters and words and by hearing **phonemes (sounds)** that accompany the **graphemes (symbols)**.
- Not only must the reader have adequate **visual and auditory acuity** (physical ability), but perception is also needed. **Perception** involves taking the sensory input and interpreting it for the brain. Students with **visual discrimination** problems lack the ability to discriminate between subtle differences in letters. Those with **auditory discrimination** challenges do not hear subtle differences in sounds. All areas should function for successful reading.
- Sequence is important in English language. For example, readers must sequence **directionality** from top to bottom and from left to right. In addition, English language involves a sequential pattern of grammar.
- Students who come to school with many life experiences will be able to link ideas from reading with life concepts. This background knowledge is known as **schema**.
- Thinking about the context of reading is critical for understanding. Not all students realize that they should be actively thinking about meaning as they decode words.

Decoding implies breaking the code made by the squiggles we call letters.

- **Affective aspects** of reading include interests and attitudes. Thus, motivation plays a key role in successful reading.

Decoding print, gaining understanding, and identifying feelings are all part of the reading process. According to Rose, director of CAST (Center for Applied Special Technology), reading involves brain activity related to seeing (visualizing), hearing (reacting to the words), and emotionally responding to the author's message. View videos on the following web site:

http://www.youtube.com/watch?v=yETeE.

Yet another basic definition states that reading includes decoding the symbols in order to gain meaning by cognitively and emotionally interacting with text and with the author. Without the basic combination of decoding and understanding, there is no reading.

Research about Technology and Reading

New research indicates that in addition to visual and auditory processing, reading also involves feeling emotions. According to David Rose, a developmental neuropsychologist and educator, PET scans and MRI's indicate that glucose burns in one part of the brain when hearing words. When seeing words, glucose burns in a separate, frontal section. In addition, reading involves an affective area, which runs through the middle of the brain. The more glucose that is being used, the more the brain "lights up." Although new learning requires a lot of glucose, once a skill is mastered, glucose levels are reduced. Glucose will fail to burn if the task if so difficult that the student feels frustrated. According to Rose, "Learning is not one thing. There are many different kinds of learning and different kinds of learners." Language uses many parts of the brain. It is possible to have a disability in one part of the brain but function well in other centers. See the video at: *http://www.youtube. com/watch?v=yETe92mwoUE.*

Students with dyslexia use different parts of the brain from typical readers. Maturity also adjusts areas in the brain where glucose is burned due to changing emotions.

Print Disability and the NIMAS Center

Typical instruction does not work for students who learn differently. A problem arises when we teach reading the same way to all students because students learn in vastly different ways. Rose calls this a disability of instruction. He also prefers the term **print disability** (PD) instead of referring to a learning disability. The problem comes from the print, not the individual.

For students who can't decode print, books are miserable. Also, there are many types of learning that work better with hands-on experiences than with print. Books no longer prepare 21ˢᵗ century students for future jobs. Rose suggests that instead of getting an easier book (a way to dumb down a learner), we must create smarter books by using technology.

The National Instructional Materials Accessibility Standard (NIMAS) was commissioned by the federal government to provide technology materials to replace all textbooks for children with special learning needs. The Center for Applied Special Technology (CAST) is a nonprofit center that works to improve learning opportunities and materials for students with disabilities. In addition, CAST allows any teacher to transform a regular print book into a technology version with electronic features.

Beginning from Zero

There are as many ideas about how to teach **emerging literacy** (beginning literacy) as there are ideas about defining reading. In *Teaching Reading in Today's Schools*, the authors state, "There is no one correct way to teach reading." The authors continue by suggesting that reading should be taught to each child in a way that brings success and pleasure. We can all agree to the previous statement, but the question remains, "How do I begin with a nonreader? How can I get the process started?" Below, you will read diverse views about how to get started. The first begins with assessing and applying scientifically researched strategies.

Traditional Approach

Whether you teach a four-year old child or a 40-year old non-reader, you face similar questions. Do you start with the alphabet, the individual's name, by matching letter names and sounds, or by memorizing a list of sight words? Research indicates that the best predictor of successful reading is phonemic awareness, the understanding that sounds make up words and words are made of sounds. Is phonemic awareness appropriate for both learners?

Similarities and Differences in Ages

Assessing phonemic awareness in the child is appropriate but may not be wise for the adult. Most adults, even those who do not read, realize that sounds are used to compose words. A second disparity is the different levels of sophistication between the two non-readers. The adult will be insulted by reading material that looks immature. One of your greatest challenges for teaching an older child or adult to read will be locating age-appropriate material that is written at a beginning level.

Young children usually begin with early basal readers called **primers** (prī-mər). Most series begin with PP1 (pre-primer one) and proceed to PP3 before moving into the first grade book. Hopefully, these beginning readers use **decodable text**, which is based on word families or phonograms. A few sight words are included in order to make the story flow. A teacher's edition guides daily instruction. See Approaches to Reading for more information on basal readers. These early books will not be useful for older children and adults.

Both the non-reader who is a child and the one who is an adult need to know the letter names and sounds. Both learners need to master the alphabet along with the most common alphabetic principles. After laying a foundation, both learners will need to read connected print with understanding. Project Read® suggests a logical starting place by suggesting the steps below.

A Starting Place

- Begin by identifying the vowels as the star letters. Every syllable in English must include at least one vowel. Both the child and the adult non-reader need this information.
- If you are using a traditional approach, teach three to five consonant letter names and sounds.
- Teach at least one vowel. The name of the vowel is considered the vowel's long sound. Each vowel also makes a short sound (a) in cat, (e) in pet, (i) in pig, (o) in hot, and (u) in up.
- Blend the consonants and vowel into various words. Arrange the words into sentences by adding a few sight words such as "the," "and," or "said."
- As quickly as possible, begin to create multisyllabic words such as "remember" or "attention."
- Continue to add additional consonants and each of the remaining vowels.

Teaching Language Experience Approach

A **Language Experience Approach** (LEA) can be combined with a traditional reading method or it can be your total literacy program. Both the child and the adult will enjoy an experience you provide or will be able to recall an event experienced recently. This approach is student-centered.

Language Experience Approach (LEA) has been around a long time as both a reading and a writing strategy. Language Experience Approach started as a formal reading/writing program in Harlingen, Texas. R. Van Allen explained the value of the strategy in the following way.

> *What I can think about, I can say.*
> *What I can say, I can write or someone*
> *can write for me. What I can write, I*
> *can read.*

If possible, use a computer for the writing step. You can take dictation much faster and make revisions much easier using a computer. As students begin to write their own stories, the computer will support their early efforts also. For the student with **dysgraphia** which is a disability with physical writing, the computer opens the gateway to expressive communication that otherwise may be closed.

If you have poor handwriting and there is no computer available, the story can be hand written quickly and copied after the students leave. The neatly written copy will be ready for the next day. Show both the original and the corrected copies to the students so they will see the value of first draft writing and revising. As the story is read and reread each day, students may think of new ideas. Keep all drafts to document progress and to demonstrate revising and editing changes.

Try to include one language experience approach each week. Use the process to indicate similarities and differences between oral and written language and to connect oral language with writing and reading. Use the student's words (including dialect differences), but spell words correctly as you take dictation. The following steps indicate the sequence of LEA.

Steps of LEA

- Offer your learners an *exciting experience* (field trip, story, art, music, or a memory of an exciting experience).

- Spend time encouraging students to *verbalize* about the event. The chart below shows one possibility for developing vocabulary after a field trip to a bakery.

What did we see?	What did we touch?	What did we smell?	What did we taste?
flour	flour	vanilla	raw sweet cookies
sugar	sugar	yeast	raw rolls
salt	salt	cooked cookies	cooked cookies
	raw dough for rolls	cooked rolls	cooked rolls with butter

- Ask questions to elicit verbal responses from the students. Extend thinking by asking, "What else . . ."
- Take dictation. Younger students can dictate the story to you. Older students and good writers may write their own stories.
- Read group stories *to* and along with the students. During reading, let your hand flow under the line of print.

Reading Material and Skill Lessons from LEA

Type stories in an appropriate font size for the age. Young children need an equivalence of Times 22. After fourth grade, drop to Times 16 or 18. For adults, use Times 14 to 16. Ask the students to read the story together or to read the story with you if you are working with an individual. Encourage students of all ages to re-read a story until it becomes independent reading material.

If you find yourself in a situation without resources, LEA can provide an entire curriculum for reading and language arts. This was the case for a Native American school. Reading and writing were developed through students' life experience stories. All additional language arts skills such as spelling, vocabulary, phonics, punctuation and grammar were built from skill needs derived from the stories. Even if you have adequate curriculum, plan to develop a collection of stories based on students' experiences.

Examine each LEA story for possible follow-up activities. For example, the text may contain suitable vocabulary for sight word study. Other possibilities include creating phonic lessons, Develop skill lessons on an "as needed" basis depending on evidence from stories produced by students. You can also use LEA stories for identifying the main idea, cutting text into separate sentences to sequence, and sequencing words within one sentence.

Age Similarities and Differences

Young children, older students and adults benefit from Language Experience Approach. Because it is challenging to locate reading material at the easier reading levels for older students and adults, LEA provides a way to provide reading material that is interesting to the learner and is based the student's vocabulary. Using their words and their sentences avoids insulting them with materials that look too immature.

With older students and adults, you will probably rely on their personal experiences rather than the field trips and types of experiences provided for young children. Often, "What did you do last weekend?" brings enough thoughts to create a story.

Individualized Reading Approach

During the spring of 2011, Dr. Frank Guszak, former professor from the University of Texas in Austin asked me to observe and video a beginning reading lesson to a group of kindergarten children. The lesson began with Dr. Guszak showing the children his name and asking them to call him "Mr. G." Individual word cards were placed in a pocket chart that read, "I see Mr. G."

I		see		Mr. G.

After modeling by reading the cards, Dr. Guszak substituted a few of the children's names for his own. The word "not" was introduced and added so that the sentence could be manipulated. Children who attempted to sound out words were encouraged to think about what would probably fit in the sentence. Once most of the children could read the cards, Dr. Guszak invited them to come to the front of the room and choose a book to read. Many books, differing in levels of difficulty, were available and the children were instructed to stand and try reading a book before returning to their tables.

A few books were hand made and included the exact words Dr. Guszak had used on the sentence chart. The easier published books also used the same words but added additional ones. As children returned to their tables to begin reading, Dr. Guszak moved from child to child. On a few occasions, he suggested that the child return the chosen book and pick up one of the hand made copies, which were easier.

Each time a child encountered an unknown word, Dr. Guszak encouraged thinking of a logical word rather than sounding out. By the end of the lesson, each child was reading. Dr. Guszak's fundamental belief is that "reading is caught; not taught." *In Reading for Students With Special Needs*, Guszak states the following basic principles.

"Reading is caught, not taught.
Reading is caught principally from books.
Reading is caught from books that fit.
Reading is caught when books that fit are read regularly.
Reading is caught when books are shared." (Guszak, 31)

Catching Reading

According to Guszak, books fit when they are at a child's instructional or independent reading level. He believes that fluency is a better measure of fit than word recognition. Reading is also caught when children read regularly. In addition to reading at school each day, the children who read at home usually make more progress than children who do not like to read. In a study with second language reading in Fuji, the children who engaged in Sustained Silent Reading and those who participated in Shared Reading outperformed children in a control group, which followed a normal structured English language program with little connected reading.

Recommended Books

Books recommended by Guszak include predictable books such as Martin's *Brown Bear, Brown Bear, What Do You See*. **Predictable books** repeat a phrase or sentence, which your beginning readers can quickly recall and read with you. **Build Up Readers, basal readers** from the 1900's, and carefully chosen **trade books**, which are library books are also included. The following lists are taken from *Reading for Students With Special Needs*. All books listed below are **decodable texts**, which build on **linguistic patterns** (phonograms) and repetition of sight words. Repetition of words and text using phonograms make beginning reading easier than books with many new and different words. Early Scott-Foreman books also work well.

Houghton Mifflin, 1986
PP1   Bells
PP2   Drums
PP3   Trumpets
P   Parades
1 - 2 Carousels
2 - 1 Adventures
2 - 2 Discoveries

Harcourt Brace Jovanovich Reading, 1986
PP1   New Friends
PP2   Mortimer Frog
PP3   Mr. Fig
P   Wishes
1 - 2 Smiles
2 - 1 Streamers
2 - 2 Stairways

Teachers create **Build Up Readers** (BUR's) from vocabulary in the PP1 book. Only one new word is introduced on each page. Each day, the child begins on page one of the build-up reader and rereads all previously introduced pages.

Creating Build-Up Readers

Keep the following guidelines in mind when you create build-up stories.

Include one new word on each page. A page is called a story.

- Write in complete (and simple) sentences.
- Use correct grammar, spelling, and punctuation.
- Include previously introduced words.

Format

Always type build-up stories in a primary font (approximately Times 22). Apply the following suggestions.

- Leave one-inch margins or more.
- Use the new word as the title. Type the title word with both upper and lowercase beginnings (See, see).
- Underline the title.
- The line of type should be approximately three inches across.
- Double space between lines of print.
- Number each story (*1. Go go*).

Sample beginnings that introduce one word at a time include sentences such as the following.

<u>*1 See see*</u>
See (name of child).
See, see (name).
(Name), see, see, see.

<u>*2 Go go*</u>
See (name) go.
Go, (name), go.
Go see (name).
See (name) go, go, go.

<u>*3 It it*</u>
Go see it.
See it go, (name).
It sees (name) go.

<u>*4 Can can*</u>
Can (name) go?
Can (name) see?
Can it see (name)?
Can it see (name) go?

How to Use Build-Up Readers

In the beginning, tell the child each title word. Later, after the child develops appropriate decoding skills, you may choose to allow the child to sound out new words with your assistance.

Repeat stories as many times as necessary for mastery. Avoid overloading the child with too many new words at one time. Students with weak skills usually learn one new word at a time. Children with more advanced skills may master as many as five words each day. Gifted readers do not need to use BUR's.

After you are confident that a child can read a build-up reader, send the stories home for additional reinforcement with parents. Never assign any homework that causes frustration and struggle.

Time Needed for Connected Reading

With the emphasis on learning to read by reading instead of completing workbook pages, Guszak recommends that children rehearse or practice reading **connected text** (paragraphs and stories) a minimum of 30 minutes a day at school in addition to time at home. Children who experience difficulties with reading connected text need increased time. Research also shows that children read with improved oral fluency after reading silently first. Rehearsals using recorded texts provide even greater benefits for struggling readers.

Guszak also avoids round robin reading in which children wait their turns to read orally. Instead, he recommends that as all children read silently (or mumble read), the teacher moves from child to child to listen and ask questions. Phonics and structural analysis are taught at a separate time from connected reading.

Similarities and Differences in Ages

Regardless of age, Dr. Guszak recommends providing a large array of reading material and allowing each learner to self-select. Books for younger children should be included in the collection. However, a variety of content, format and readability will be necessary. Teacher prompts will focus on content rather than on letter-sound recognition. Elmhurst Public Library on the Internet <*http://www. elmhurstpubliclibrary.org/*> lists high interest books using Lexiles, DRA levels and grade levels. Each **high interest book** is written with an easy vocabulary, many phonograms, and a few sight words that are repeated often. Stories are aimed at older students and are too mature for young children. Another source of high interest—low vocabulary books is High Noon Books. These books restrict the number of sight words and develop stories using as many **decodable words** (words that follow the phonics rules) as possible. Your best source of reading material for older students and adults will be the LEA stories written by the learners.

Beginning at the Beginning in Writing

Emerging Writers

Several thousand years ago, beginning writing probably started with pictures. Today, we call this type of activity pictographic writing. Emerging writers usually begin writing by using pictographic writing. Initially, you will see little or no difference in art and writing. Only when the child begins naming scribbling will you begin to discern a difference. During this time, it is important to avoid asking, "What is it?" The question is inappropriate for children who are simply scribbling for the joy of doing it. For those who realize that the marks can represent a thing, your question may be insulting. Instead, make the following types of statements.

- "Tell me about your work." (Use *work* if you don't know whether the piece is art or writing).
- "Tell me about it."
- "What's happening?"

The value of inviting the child to talk about the art/writing, is that you are encouraging oral language. When the child talks, the child is engaging in **expressive language**. When you talk and the child understands your requests, the child is practicing **receptive language**.

Initial scribbles may seem unimportant. However, those scribbles signify pretend writing and suggest an important understanding; marks on paper represent words and thoughts. Encourage **pretend writing**, which is called **approximation**.

Each day, point to the alphabet and say, "These are letters and this whole set makes up our alphabet. Letters make words. Words create messages that we share with one another."

Each time you write directions, names, dates, or notes, share your thoughts aloud in order for children to benefit from your cognitive patterns. For example, when writing the date, you might say, "September is the name of a special month. I must use an uppercase letter." From your modeling, children learn the importance of paying attention to print. Instead of teaching skills in isolation, teach writing skills within

Modification
When teaching young children and those with dysgraphia, use large chart paper and markers. Encourage the child to use gross motor movements before graduating to regular paper.

the context of real writing as often as possible. Guide children with comments and questions such as the following.

- "Find a word that begins with _____."
- "Point to all the periods."
- "Can you find a question mark?"

Kindergarten or first grade teachers use finger plays, songs, and games to help students get ready for fine motor activities. If you teach an older student who is not yet developmentally ready for fine motor skills, ask the student to use a hole punch to strengthen and develop hand muscles.

Students learn to read by reading and to write by writing. They do not develop these competencies by filling out skill pages. Standardized test scores indicate that in classes where students are encouraged to write regularly, **connected writing** scores improve. Connected writing involves sentences and paragraphs in which words come together to create meaning. However, many of these same students score poorly on the mechanics sections of the same test. How can a classroom teacher win?

Although variations occur, children go through predictable stages in acquiring writing skills. These stages include: letter formation, word writing, sentence construction, spelling, punctuation, and grammatical expression. The answer lies in achieving balance. Definitely spend brief time each day directly teaching skills. Preferably, teach skills such as capitalization within the context of a story. Validate skill instruction with *application* of skills through writing opportunities.

Tools for Emerging Writers

To begin actual writing, first use crayons, then introduce markers, and eventually, use pencils for writing activities. Even after letting students write with pencils, allow them to take tests with crayons or markers. Any time you begin a new writing skill, initially teach the skill with crayons.

Young children have difficulty seeing the light blue lines found on commercial notebook paper. Purchase tactile paper with raised lines (Meade). You may also want to fold primary paper along lines to give a tactile as well as a visual reference for writing.

Emerging writers benefit from using large muscles for gross motor activities. Work at chalkboards, whiteboards, or large charts helps develop large muscle movement. If children have difficulty moving from gross motor to fine motor, which is required for paper-pencil writing, help them make the transition. Take a large piece of chart paper and divide it into four rows. Use the folds as lines so that the child can form large letters.

```
-------fold----------------------------------------------------------

-------fold----------------------------------------------------------

-------fold----------------------------------------------------------
```

If a child ignores the lines (or folds), be patient and initially say nothing. Continue to model and the time will come to encourage the concepts of lines and spaces.

Begin With Correct Letter Formation

In *Nurture Shock*, Bronson and Merryman recommend teaching emerging writers to use self-talk when learning to form new letters. "When the kids are learning the capital (C), they all say in unison, 'Start at the top and go around' as they start to print. No one ever stops the kids from saying it out loud, but after a few minutes most students cease verbalizing directions. A couple of minutes later, a few kids are still saying it out loud—but most of the kids are saying it in their heads."

Naming the letter strokes by chanting and repeating the steps may avoid the frequent problem of children learning to form letters incorrectly and from incorrect starting places. Once a child establishes a habit of starting the C at the bottom of the page, it is hard to re-establish a different behavior.

Writing Concepts

The following print concepts are being developed.

- Reading and writing are ways to communicate.
- Messages can be understood through labels, signs, logos, and other forms of environmental communication.
- Letters are different from numbers.
- Pictures add meaning but are not the same as print.
- Marks on a page (letters) create words that match the words I say.
- Others can read these words to me or I can read them myself.

Beginning Journal Writing

Journal writing in prekindergarten and kindergarten usually begins with scribbles. A good way to start is to follow the sequence below from Art and Scaffolding Journal.

- Read a short story to or with a child.
- Ask the child to draw a picture about the story. For some children, you will need to set a time limit on the drawing.
- Monitor and assist as each child plans a story (one sentence long) about the picture. Ask, "What would you like to write about your picture?"
- Invite oral language by asking, "What is happening?" Tell me about your picture.
- As a child describes the art, place sticky notes naming the people or items in the picture.
- Ask the child to write a story below the picture. Encourage the child to use the words you wrote on sticky notes but do not require this.
- Encourage the child to repeat the sentence from the art—scaffolding journal several times before beginning to write.
- As the child writes, ask questions such as, "Can you spell _____? If not, can you find that word on one of the notes? What letter do you hear at the beginning?" As you assist, you gain opportunities to teach and explain literacy concepts.

Composition Sentences

- If the child scribbles, say, "Good job! I will show you a *different* way to write what you wrote in your journal."
- As you listen and observe, write the child's exact words on a sentence strip. Say, "Another way to write what you said looks like this."
- Read the sentence (from your copy) several times.
- Help the child read and re-read your copy of the sentence.
- Say, "I'm going to try to trick you." As the child watches, cut your copy of the sentence into individual words (include the period with the last word).
- Scramble the words. Ask the child to place the words in the correct sequence. When the child can sequence correctly and read the sentence, you have made the connection between the scribbles and writing and between writing and reading.

Save for Future Reading

On the outside of a small envelope, write the child's entire composition sentence. Place the individual words inside the envelope for future independent reading experiences.

- Follow up the next day by pointing to the sentence the child wrote in the journal and asking, "Can you read what you wrote in your journal yesterday?"

- Present the individual words from the envelope and ask the child to organize the words into the original sentence.
- Repeat the same composition sentences many times during independent reading times to build confidence and fluency.

Authentic and Individualized Writing

When children use crayons, markers, and a variety of paper sizes and types, they engage in authentic writing. The child's attempt at creating connected print is real—**authentic.** Concepts develop from observing as you model and think aloud. Actual writing develops from spending time writing.

Regardless of what books, charts, or doctors say, each child progresses at his or her rate. Children must be allowed to determine when, how, and what to learn. Trying to force a child to learn a concept before the child is ready is frustrating to the adult and cruel to the child.

Bibliography

AIMSweb. "Assessment and Data Management for RTI". *PsychCorp a PEARSONbrand.2010.* <http://www.aimsweb.com/>

Allington, R. "What At-Risk Readers Need." E.L. Educational Leadership. Mar. 2011 Volume 68 number 6.

Anderson, Wilson, and Fielding. "The Effects of Independent Reading on Reading Achievement." Houghton Mifflin Col: Boston, MA. 1997. <http://www.eduplace.com/rdg/res/literacy/in_read1.html>

Atwell, N. "The Pleasure Principle" *Scholastic Instructor.* Edgecomb, Maine. 2011. <http://www2.scholastic.com/browse/article.jsp?id>

Coyne, M.D., E.J. Kami'enui, and D.W. Carnine. Research on Beginning Reading. Pearson, Allyn Bacon, Prentice Hall. 2006-2011.

Elmhurst Public Library. High Interest Low Vocabulary Books. Elmhurst, IL 2011. <http://www.elmhurstpubliclibrary.org/Kids/High InteresLowVocabBooks.php#Grade_One_Lexile_100_400>

Fitzsimmons, Mary. "Beginning Reading." Education.com. 2006-2011.

Frandsen, B. and S. Smith. *Dyslexia Analysis.* Education Analysis. 1989.

—*Yes! I Can Teach Literacy.* Family School: Austin, Texas. 2006.

Guszak, F. *Reading for Students with Special Needs.* Kendall Hunt: Dubuque, Iowa. 1997.

"High Noon Books" Academic Therapy Publications. 2009. <http://www.highnoonbooks.com/HNB/samples-hnb.tpl>

Barbara Frandsen

Irlen, H. "The Irlen Method." *Irlen*. 1998.
  <http://irlen.com/index.php>

McCardle, P., Vinita Chhabra. *The Voice of Evidence in Reading Research*.
  Brooke Publishers: Baltimore, MD 2004.

Oney, Banu. "Reading: Beginning Reading." Education.com.
  2006-2011.
  <http://www.education.com/reference/article/reading-beginning-
  reading/>

Peacock, G., R. Ervin, E. Daly, K. Merrell. *Practical Handbook of School
  Psychology*. Guilford Press: New York, NW. 2010.

Rich, M. *A New Assignment: Pick Books You Like*. The New York Times:
  Jonesboro, GA. 2009. <http://www.nytimes.com/2009/08/30/
  books/30reading.html?_r=2>

Roe, B, S. Smith, and P. Burns. *Teaching Reading in Today's Elementary
  Schools*. Houghton Mifflin: Boston, MA. 2005.

Rose, David. *Dr. David Rose on Universal Design for Learning*. You
  Tube. 2007.
  http://www.youtube.com/watch?v=yETe92mwoUE

Rose, D. and B. Dalton. "Learning to Read in the Digital Age".
  *iGeneration: How the Digital Age is Altering Student Brains, Learning
  and Teaching*. Public Information Resources, Inc.: Needham, KMA.
  2011.

Stahl, Skip, D. Rose, G. Goldowsky, J. Zabala. "About NIMAS Center"
  National Center on Accessible Instructional Materials at CAST, Inc.:
  Wakefield, MA. 2010. <http://aim.cast.org/learn/policy/federal/
  what_is_nimas>

Wassermann, S. "Déjà vu All Over Again: Individualized Reading
  Resurfaces as Reading Workshop." *Larry Cuban on School Reform
  and Classroom Practice*. WordPress.com. 2009.

Phonemic Awareness and Emerging Literacy

Phonemic Awareness

What Is Phonemic Awareness?

The following quotation is taken from "Explicit Systematic Phonics," a website by Scholastic, Inc. According to the authors, "**Phonemic awareness** is the understanding or insight that a word is made up of a series of discrete sounds (phonemes). This awareness includes the ability to pick out and manipulate sounds in spoken words." In *Words Their Way*, the authors state, "This ability to divide syllables into the smallest units of sound is called phonemic awareness." Guszak claims that phonemic awareness allows children to differentiate individual sounds. It is important to realize that phonemic awareness has nothing to do with seeing, touching, or saying the names of letters. Phonemic awareness activities are carried out with only auditory prompts. No letters are seen at this time. The focus remains on developing and locking in the concept of sounds and words.

The National Reading Panel explains that approximately 41 **phonemes**, which are the smallest sound units in English, make up syllables and words. According to the panel, "Phonemic awareness refers to the ability to focus on and manipulate these phonemes in spoken words."

Phonemic Awareness Activities

A few ways to help children develop sound awareness include the following ideas.

- Read nursery rhymes and other poems with rhyming patterns. After reading a rhyme aloud numerous times, ask children to supply missing words. For example:

  Jack and Jill went up a _____.
  Little Miss Muffet sat on a _____.

- Encourage word games and use of books that demonstrate both real and nonsense words, such as Dr. Seuss collections. Point out sound similarities of words being read.

- Play a game called, "I Spy" to stress beginning *sounds* (instead of letter names) by saying, "I spy something in our classroom that begins with the sound (make the sound of a letter)."
- Play a similar version of "I Spy" by asking children to locate everyone whose name begins with a certain sound.
- Introduce children to the concept of initial sounds in words by using tongue twisters and alliteration stories in which all words begin with the same sound.
- Ask children to sort toys or pictures into categories with identical initial or final sounds.
- Sing the tune of *If You're Happy and You Know It Clap Your Hands,* and use the words, "If you know a word with /t/, say it now." When you sing the song, be sure to make the sound of the letter instead of the name. Pause to call on individual children to name words, such as *toy, top,* or *Texas.*
- Collect animal and insect puppets such as butterflies, caterpillars, or bears. Each puppet asks children to change initial sounds in their names to match the first sound of the puppet. For example, when using the butterfly puppet, *Mary* becomes *Bary, Juan* becomes *Baun, Aidan* becomes *Baidan.*
- Create a sound chain by asking one child to think of a word. Each child must add a new word using the same beginning sound. To challenge children, play the same game repeating ending sounds such as *bat, hit, toot.*
- When lining up, ask children whose names begin with the /m/ sound to get in line first. Continue by stating different sounds until all children are in line.
- Teach children to count or segment individual parts of words by sounding out easy words such as hot or hat, and asking, "How many separate sounds do you hear?"

Reading Recovery, a program from New Zealand, provides one-on-one tutoring to the low performing first graders for approximately 16 weeks. The purpose is to reduce the number of children requiring special education or other long-term remedial programs. Although a few children continue to exhibit problems with reading and writing, approximately 75% reach grade level expectations. Each session lasts 30-minutes and is taught by a teacher who has received extensive education in the Reading Recovery methods.

A phonemic awareness memory game uses a game called "**Push-a—Penny**" in which you create a row of boxes, each containing a different letter sound. Say one word at a time, stressing individual sounds within the word. Ask the child to listen, repeat the word, and push a penny or token representing each sound into one of the boxes.

It is important to note that some words have more letters than sounds. For example, "Pete" has four letters but only three sounds.

When counting blends, push a token for each letter in the blend. For example, the blend /sm/ would separate the /s/ and the /m/ with a token for each. Blends include combinations such as the /dr/ in *draw*, /bl/ in *blind*, and /sn/ in *snap*.

Ending blends also use a token for each sound in a blend such as the /-ng/ in *king*, /-sk/ in *risk*, /-nd/ in *grind*, /-ft/ in *left*, /-sk/ in *ask*, /-sp/ in *rasp*. The word *blind* requires five tokens (two initial and two final).

Digraphs /ch/, /sh/, /th/, /wh/, or related combinations of /ph/ and /gh/ have two letters but only one sound and therefore, require only one token each. In digraphs, you do not hear any of the individual letters as they form a totally new sound. For example, the word "she" requires only two tokens

Push-a-Penny
Directions: Listen to one word at a time. Repeat each word. For each sound you hear, push a penny (or token) into one of the boxes.

Sequence of Phonemic Awareness

Awareness of the importance of sounds and speech precedes learning letter names and sounds and is the most important concept needed for reading and writing. The goal is to develop the ability to manipulate sounds into meaningful speech. According to many reading experts, a child who cannot detect and analyze sounds in words will fail to read by the end of first grade.

Phonological and phonemic awareness are not the same as phonics but form the foundation for phonics. Phonics, a system designed to teach a correlation between letter names and sounds, includes and is based on phonemic and phonological awareness.

Phonemic awareness skills listed in the sequence of difficulty include understanding the following concepts.

- First of all, even babies can participate in **nursery rhymes**, riddles, songs, poems, and read-aloud books that manipulate sounds. Children born into families that talk to them (from before birth), look at them and respond to their babbles are fortunate little learners. Recent research indicates that responses such as facial expressions, gestures and even words from adults and older children help develop the concepts of communication and therefore, language.
- Pre-school children can be led to pay attention to and to **substitute initial sounds** such as beginning sounds in bet, met, or net. Once children can substitute initial sounds to create new

25

words or **pseudowords** (nonsense words), they understand the concept of phonemic awareness.

- Listening for and **substituting final sounds** is more advanced. Guide children to pay attention to ending sounds such as final consonants in bet, bed, or beg. Nonsense words might include bem, bej, beb.
- You can begin to show children how to **blend sounds** into words by saying, /h/ + /o/ + /t/ = *hot*. At this time, you are only using sounds; no printed or plastic letters allowed.
- A higher-level task is to **add or delete phonemes** to create new words (e.g., by removing the /th/ in *mother*, you create the sound *mu-er*).
- To **segment** means to count or to separate. You can segment (count) the number of sounds in a word. "How many sounds do you hear in hot?"

What Is Phonological Awareness?

The Scholastic web site states, '**Phonological awareness** is an umbrella term that includes phonemic awareness, or awareness of words at the phoneme (sound) level. It also adds an awareness of word elements that are larger than a phoneme. Therefore, phonological awareness includes the following understandings:

- words within sentences,
- rhyming units within words,
- syllables within words,
- phonemes, or sounds, within words (phonemic awareness),
- features of individual phonemes such as how the mouth, tongue, vocal cords, and teeth are used to produce the sound.

Phonological Awareness Activities

Notice that like phonemic awareness, phonological awareness does not involve seeing letters or stating letter names. Like phonemic awareness, phonological awareness is a totally auditory activity. No visual clues involved.

- Sing the Bingo song using syllables in children's names. For example, "There is a student in our class, Fernando is his name. Fer-nan-do, Fer-nan-do, Fer-nan-do, Fernando is his name." Children with one-syllable names require only one beat.
- Ask children to draw self-portraits and write their names under their pictures. On the back of the portraits, ask children to divide their names into syllables. Connect to math by filling in a teacher-made graph indicating the number of syllables in

each child's name. At the end of the activity, count the number of names with one syllable, two, three, or more.

- After reading 'Pinocchio' from Shel Silverstein's book, *Falling Up*, ask students to say their names with the "eo" sound added at the end. Bob becomes Bobeo, Mary becomes Maryeo.

Emerging Literacy

What Is Emerging Literacy?

Emerging literacy encompasses all experiences with language and print beginning at or even before birth, including the non-conventional reading and writing done by many preschool children. Emergent literacy includes phonemic and phonological awareness as well as an involvement with print. From early experiences with print, such as seeing others read, being read to, watching a parent create a grocery list, and seeing names of favorite places, the young child learns many literary concepts. For those children fortunate enough to enjoy rich language and literature experiences before entering school, learning to read usually comes easily. Areas that form emergent literacy include:

- oral language,
- phonemic awareness,
- phonological awareness,
- concepts about print,
- alphabet letter names,
- letter sound-to-symbol recognition,
- beginning sight vocabulary.

Although individual variations occur in literacy, acquisition develops in predictable patterns by moving from pre-reading (emerging literacy) to conventional literacy. Children who come to kindergarten or first grade (or even later grades) without adequate background must be **immersed** (surrounded) with letters, sounds, and books embedded into and linked to the literacy program. For children lacking early literacy experiences that provide the background for phonemic awareness, a phonics lesson on any particular letter must seem like total gibberish. To reach these children, you must gather them around you on the carpet and create the early literacy environments that will enable them to absorb ideas about what reading and writing are all about.

An examination of practices of loving parents suggests the following ideas for emerging literacy classrooms. Parents do not read books with carefully controlled and sequenced vocabularies such as those found in basal reading series. Favorite books, loved by children and adults alike for their richness, become primary reading sources in emerging literacy classrooms as well as at home.

An important aspect of early childhood reading includes sitting close to a parent or sitting in a parent's lap. Teachers who promote shared learning have an opportunity to bond reading and writing with the kind of pleasure and motivation found in homes where parents lovingly read to children on a daily basis. There is hope that with time, modeling, and positive experiences, children will develop their own strategies for acquiring vocabulary, decoding print, and using clues to derive meaning. In many cases, the children who enter school without early literacy experiences remain behind throughout their school experience.

Although much research has been done on various literacy programs—all claiming to be the one best approach—the simplest and most natural way to get children ready to succeed in reading continues to be reading to them. Across the world, across cultures, and across generations, those precious moments of closeness and shared language become the most important of all for preparing lifelong readers.

Actions to Support Emerging Literacy

The activities that lead to language development are the same when developing emerging literacy. To be successful in oral language as well as literacy, children must be immersed in print experiences. Surround young children with books, magazines, newspapers, lists, signs labeling objects, and cartoons. In addition, children learn by observing others. As a teacher, you will **model** reading, writing, **expressive oral language** such as speaking, and **receptive language** when you listen and understand. You are the expert—the model. Children will learn by copying you.

It is more important for you to have positive **expectations** than you may realize. Research studies have demonstrated that if a teacher believes a child is hopeless, the teacher will unconsciously think differently about the child who will live down to the low expectation. Children need teachers who will believe in them, regardless of their situations. Not all children will go to college. All children can learn. You must realize that children learn and improve at individual rates (amounts of time). Although each child goes through predictable stages of development, each does so at an **individual pace.**

Children learn to read by holding, examining, and attempting to read real books. Likewise, they learn to write by holding pens, pencils and markers and making strokes on paper. This is **authentic learning** with real books and materials. Children will not learn to read or write by completing workbook pages.

Approximation involves pretending to read and pretending to write. You must validate pretend or practice reading and writing and recognize the behavior as important in the learning process. In both language development and in reading/writing, approximation involves practicing literacy. In reading, approximation takes the form of talking like a book.

Emerging literacy occurs with **feedback** from adults who answer unspoken questions such as, "How am I doing? What should I do next?" Responsive feedback must be relevant, honest, and non-threatening in order for learning to ccur.

Concepts All Beginning Readers Need to Have

All readers must gain the following concepts in order for reading to make sense. Older students and adults have probably gained the concepts, but you will want to informally assess to be certain.

Print Understanding

As phonological awareness is becoming secure, the child's skills expand into an understanding of print by emphasizing each of the following ideas.

- Reading and writing are ways to communicate.
- Messages can be understood through labels, signs, logos, and other forms of environmental communication.
- Letters are different from numbers.
- Pictures add meaning but are not the same as print.
- Marks on a page (letters) create words that match the words I say.
- Others can read these words to me or I can read them myself.

Concepts about Books

Children whose lives seem devoid of reading experiences may have difficulty with the most basic ideas about books. Concepts concerning books include understanding the following actions:

- ways to handle, carry and store a book,
- how to hold the book for reading,
- the front and back covers of the book,
- a book has an author and a title,
- how to turn pages of a book,
- letters are grouped to form words,

- words are separated by spaces,
- there is an association between spoken and written words,
- different texts have different purposes (lists, recipes, newspapers, letters, and stories).

Directionality

In addition to knowing how to handle a book, children must understand the following:

- the top to bottom movement required for reading,
- that reading begins at the top and left side of each page,
- the concept that spoken words have a one-to-one correspondence to printed words,
- that movements made by eyes (and fingers) follow print from: left to right, word to word, down the page, and include a return sweep.

Letter and Word Knowledge

As children begin to grasp the concept that the words one says can be written down and read back again, letters and words begin to take on meaning. Children will soon be able to:

- recognize letters by their shapes,
- locate beginning letters in familiar words,
- identify environmental words such as "Taco Bell®, McDonald's®, STOP,"
- identify one or two words learned at school,
- point to a specific word, such as the child's own name,
- identify matching upper and lowercase letters,
- make some associations between letters and sounds,
- identify a few high-frequency words.

Writing Concepts

Pre-kindergarten children begin to explore writing for themselves. They also begin to ask adults to write messages for them. As the concept of writing unfolds, the child will attempt to do the following:

- write messages,
- use known letters along with made up letters,
- begin to connect sounds to letters,
- dictate words and phrases to adults.

Higher Level Concepts

As children add reading vocabulary to their repertoires, more sophisticated concepts become relevant parts of the reading process. Some of the higher-level concepts in reading include understanding these specifics:

- ending punctuation marks,
- quotation marks,
- the importance of using initial (beginning) letter sounds as clues to word identification,
- the importance of final (ending) consonant sounds as clues to word identification,
- the use of pictures as clues to story understanding,
- the importance of structural clues such as configuration (the shape of a word), prefixes, suffixes, and endings to decode unknown words,
- the importance of memory aids for recalling a story.

Children with reading difficulties commonly identify the initial letter of a word but fail to decode the middle and ending letters.

Teaching the Alphabet

Alphabet Sequence

Teaching the alphabet is usually attempted through the well-known alphabet song. Although music is a wonderful way to teach, relying on the song creates a problem. In order to make use of this memory aid, children often have to begin at the beginning and sing their way through until they get to the letter needed. This is a slow process for a skill that is very important in literacy.

In addition to teaching the song, you can greatly strengthen alphabet recognition by adding a visual component. Originators of the Multisensory Teaching Approach (MTA) suggest creating an alphabet rainbow of letters. The goal is for children to begin to visualize letters in small clusters and to see the way the sequence comes together.

Teaching Sequential Letter Placement

Teaching alphabet sequence requires a set of plastic alphabet letters for each student. Although the plastic letters may seem too immature for older students, the activities soon become challenging and fun.

Initial activities require placing letters in the formation of a rainbow with A in the lower left corner, MN at the top of the arch and Z in the lower right corner.

It is important for the teacher to model the creation of the rainbow of letters. Model the position of each letter before asking students to place letters in their own sets. Allow approximately two feet for the width of the semicircle (A to Z) and approximately a foot for the highest point of the arch (MN).

Modification
Younger children and those with learning differences should begin with the first fourth of the alphabet, increase to the first half, and continue. Sometimes, the entire alphabet is too overwhelming.

MN

A   **Z**

33

Before beginning, designate the needed space for each student's rainbow and locate a flat surface for each student to use. Ask students to keep sets of letters together in plastic bags.

- Following your example, students position A, Z and MN in the beginning, end, and middle of the designated rainbow space.
- Students verbalize, "A is the initial letter, Z is the final letter, and MN are the medial letters."
- Model by sequentially naming and filling in the letters between A and M.
- Continue to name and model placement of letters until the alphabet is complete.
- Students name each letter while placing the letter in the proper position.
- After all letters are arranged in the rainbow arch, students recite the names in sequence, touching each letter as the name is stated.

Teaching Random Placement

Random placement provides a more challenging task than arranging letters in sequential order. The goal is to place letters in their correct locations in the rainbow arch by estimating. Each child will need a complete set of plastic alphabet letters.

- Students follow your model by placing the letters A, MN, and Z are in their initial, medial, and final positions.
- Randomly name a letter and estimate placement in your own rainbow arch.
- Students name the letter, locate the letter, and estimate its placement within their own rainbows.

When their rainbows are complete, students name and touch each letter in sequence.

Teaching Missing Letter Decks

Materials needed include sequence cards.

- Create (or purchase) cards with missing letters. Notice the following examples.

Modification
Children who are only mastering the first fourth or half of the alphabet for sequential placement will use the same sections for random placement.

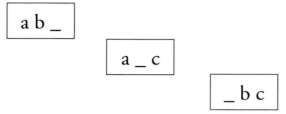

- Introduce three cards at a time.
- Students practice each set of three cards until knowledge of the missing letters becomes automatic before beginning the next set.
- A new set of three letters would consist of:

b, c, _
b, _, d
_, c, d

Stop after three sets of letter cards during one lesson (nine cards). It is preferable to master a few sets of missing letter cards rather than cover more than students can assimilate. This is a case when "less is more."

Teaching Alphabet Battle—The "After" Game

Alphabet Battle is a departure from the previous activities. It is a game that students of all ages enjoy. Materials needed include a written desk copy of the alphabet, two paper bags, and one set of plastic letters for each *pair* of students.

- Pairs divide one set of plastic alphabet letters into two equal parts and put each half into one of the two paper bags.
- When you say, "Go," each player reaches into his or her bag and selects one letter. Each player places the letter on the desk at the same time.
- The player who has the letter closest to Z collects both letters and adds them to his or her individual pile.
- Players must verbalize, "I win because M is closer to Z than C."
- Continue until all letters have been played. The player with the most letters is the winner.
- A variation is to see who gets the letter closest to A. This would be the "Before" Game.

Developmental Reading

Sequence of Reading Development

Reading instruction begins early and is directly related to oral language development. Before jumping into the academic side of reading, you may be comforted to know that reading occurs naturally in the following sequence.

Body Reading

The reading process begins with body reading, the identification of ears, eyes, nose, and other body parts Between birth and six months, talk to your baby and begin teaching body parts by saying, "This is your eye." Later say, "Point to your eye." Around 18-months to a year, touch the child's eye and ask, "What is this?" Once you grasp the difference in difficulty between: "point to _____" and "what is_____," you will be a better teacher. Use this sequence of steps when teaching any new item or word.

- First, tell the child the name of the item or word.
- Next, say, "Point to _____." The child will point to the item or word.
- Only after practice and success ask, "What is this?" Following this final question, the child will state the name of the item or word being learned. Naming is much more challenging than pointing to something you name.

Environmental Reading

Environmental reading (often referred to as **logographics**) emerges when the child identifies symbols such as those used for McDonald's®, Toys-R-Us®, or Taco Bell®. Recognition of logographics occurs when a child is very young and should be acknowledged for what it is—reading.

Labeling Objects for Reading

Once a child begins to read logographics, you can begin placing written names on items in the child's environment such as chairs, tables, walls, floors, and doors. Print using lowercase letters. Make the letters approximately two inches tall. Signs on familiar objects provide opportunities for informal learning but should not be used for drill or memorization.

Language Experience Approach

Use a Language Experience Approach (LEA) to demonstrate to children that what one says can be written down and what one writes can be read. LEA offers a wonderful opportunity to build on children's cultural and home backgrounds, to facilitate their oral language development, and to connect the skills of speaking, listening, writing, and reading.

> Begin by giving one student an exciting experience. Encourage the child to talk about the experience and ask the student to dictate a story to you. Write down exactly what the child says and read the story back to the child. Dictation helps develop a connection between language and print.

> For the next level, take dictation from two or more students and read the story to the same small group. The language/print concept now extends to include, "What others say can be written down and read also."

> Arrange for half the class to be out of the room while you take dictation from remaining students. When the other students return, read the story to them. The expanded concept includes, "It isn't necessary to hear the story to be able to read and understand it."

Sight Word Reading

You may now begin whole word/sight word reading from words in the LEA. Without sounding out letters, begin to teach students to visually recognize words.

Linguistic Reading

The next level of reading, called **linguistic reading**, builds on word patterns such as, "The fat cat sat on the mat." In this particular pattern the **rime** or **phonogram** *at* is changed by using different beginning consonants or **onsets**.

When using linguistic reading, you will often create nonsense words, called **pseudowords**, by repeating the same word phonogram rime and changing the onset.

Phonics

The final developmental step for teaching reading is phonics. Begin with single vowels and single consonants. Next, teach sound patterns for consonant, vowel, consonant /cvc/words such as cat, hat, or mat. The child is now ready to learn the structure of language that is comprised of alphabetic principles.

Bibliography

Adams, M, B. Foorman, I. Lundbert, and T. Beeler. *Phonemic Awareness in Young Children*. London, England: Brookes Publishing Co., 1998.

Bear, D., M. Invernizzi, S. Templeton, F. Johnston. *Words Their Way, 4th Edition*. Upper Saddle River, NJ: Pearson, 2008.

Berk, Laura. *Infants, Children and Adolescents*. Boston, MA: Allyn and Bacon, 1993.

Child Development Institute, LLC. *Language Development in Children*. 2000. <http://www.childdevelopmentinfo.com/development/language_development.shtml>

Clay, Marie. *Reading Recovery*. Auckland, New Zealand: Heinemann, 1993.

Crawley, S. *Remediating Reading Difficulties, Sixth Edition*. New York, NY: McGraw Hill, 2012.

Cunningham, James, P. Cunningham, J. Hoffman, H. Yopp. *Phonemic Awareness and the Teaching of Reading*. (International Reading Association, April, 1998.

Ekwall, E. and J. Shanker. *Teaching Reading in the Elementary School*. Columbus, CO: Merrill Publishing, 1989.

Fox, B. *Phonics and Structural Analysis for the Teacher of Reading, 10th Edition*. Boston, MA: Allyn and Bacon, 2010.

Frandsen, B. *Yes, I Can Teach Literacy*. Austin, TX: Family School, 2006.

—*Diversified Teaching: An Anthology of Teaching Strategies*. Austin, TX: Family School, 1993.

Gambrell, L., L. Morrow, and M. Pressley. *Best Practices in Literacy Instruction*. New York, NY: Guilford Press, 1999.

Gunning, T. *Creating Literacy Instruction for All Students 7th Edition*. Boston, MA: Allyn and Bacon, 2010.

Guszak, F. *Reading for Students With Special Needs*. Dubuque, IA:Kendall/Hunt Publishing Company. 1997.

—*Diagnostic Reading Instruction in the Elementary School*. New York: NY: Allyn and Bacon, 1978.

Hittlemann, D. *Developmental Reading, K-8*. Columbus, OH: Merrill Publishing, 1983.

Wilson, K. G., and B. Daviss. *Reading Recovery: Basic Facts*. New York, NY: Teachers College Press, 1994.

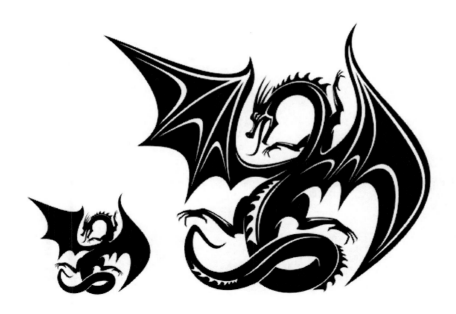

Slaying the Phonics Dragon

Two types of children struggle with phonics. Both types lack the ability to discriminate between similar sounds. Children with **Deep Dyslexia** do not "sound out" words easily. In addition, children with **Phonological Dyslexia** (pho-no-logical = sounds are not logical) fail to hear subtle differences in sound-to-symbol combinations.

Children with **Surface Dyslexia** over-use phonics and attempt to match sounds to letters in words that are irregular and do not fit the rules of our language. This module will focus on Deep and Phonological Dyslexia

Phonics Principles

What is an Alphabetic Principle?

Phonics instruction matches the sounds of letters to the written symbols (**sound to symbol,** also called the **phoneme to grapheme**). When discussing the written symbol, the letter will be enclosed in parentheses (b). When referring to the sound of the letter, you will see slashes such as /b/. The generalizations/rules of the English language are referred to as **alphabetic principles**. The term "alphabetic principle" means, "Words are composed of letters that represent sounds." Refer to the web site:

<http://reading.uoregon.edu/big_ideas/au/au_what.php#>

Children often discover exceptions to the phonics rules/ generalizations. Although exceptions occur because of the many languages that influenced the development of English, one constant insists that every syllable in the English language must include at least one vowel.

What Does Research Indicate?

The National Reading Panel supports phonics as one of the five essential components in teaching children to read. In **synthetic phonics**, the focus is on individual letter sounds, which are blended into words. For example, if you know the sounds /b/, /a/, and /t/, you can say them together and pronounce the word "bat." In **analytic phonics**, children are initially shown a word and are then asked to analyze the sounds within the word. An example of analytic phonics might start with the word "crown" and then ask children to identify the letters that make the /ow/ sound. Research favors synthetic phonics although there are benefits to all approaches.

Another important requirement found in research is "explicit systematic phonics." Explicit means that the sound-symbol connections must be taught directly by the teacher. Research shows that children do not discover the sound-symbol connections or derive understanding from reading texts or stories. The word "**systematic**" means that phonics generalizations should be taught in a correct sequence with frequent reviews.

Research further indicates that phonics instruction provides greater benefits and gains with younger children. A very structured and systematic phonics program is believed to help children with **dyslexia** (disability with reading letters). According to research, phonics instruction becomes less effective as children grow older. A summary of the research guidelines includes: 1) start in pre-kindergarten and kindergarten, 2) use **direct instruction**, instruction provided by the teacher, to inform children about sound and letter connections, 3) maintain a sequential and systematic program with frequent reviews.

Do Individualized Programs Teach Phonics?

Practices used to recognize words, include context clues, phonics, sight words and structural analysis and are considered **word recognition skills**. In individualized programs, skills are usually taught indirectly by prompting a child to figure out an unknown word by using information surrounding the word. Often, as children begin to read, they develop structural analysis independently. The following phonics skills are generally taught indirectly or through inquiry experiences.

- Sound-to-symbol for consonants,
- Initial consonant substitution using **onsets and rimes**. (initial consonants and rhyming patterns such as *can, fan, man*),
- Final consonant substitution such as *can* to *cap*.
- Medial vowel substitution such as *bat* to *bit* or *bet* to *but*,
- CVCe patterns such as *bit* to *bite or hop to hope*,
- Multisyllabic words such as attack.

Vowel Strategies and Modifications

Each strategy presented below will be preceded with an adult **generalization** (a rule that is usually true). These generalizations are also referred to as **alphabetic principles**. Alphabetic principles form the basic structure of our language. Therefore, you will learn the generalization/alphabetic principle and then consider a method to teach the principle.

Most of the strategies in the following sections originated with Project Read®, which is a company formed by two teachers. In order to make learning more entertaining and memorable, the teachers implemented stories and movements. Many of these strategies include integration of various sensory modalities including vision, hearing, touch, and large movements called **kinesthetic** or **gross motor** movements. Songs and puppets supply additional appeal. In many cases, the teaching strategies provide their own modifications.

Introducing Vowels

Each short vowel sound is accompanied by an action that becomes a mnemonic device. Movement is powerful for tactile and kinesthetic learners and adds enjoyment for all students. Tactual learners enjoy touching and feeling objects. Kinesthetic actions use large muscle movements.

- Begin by showing students an alphabet chart with stars above each of the five vowels.
- Tell students that the vowels are starred because they are very important.
- Each word must have at least one vowel (star letter).
- With young children, write vowels on students' fingers, beginning with (a) on the thumb and ending with (u) on the smallest finger.

Dyslexia Modification
Any time you add stories, songs movements, or puppets, you help diverse learners.

Teaching Actions for Each Short Vowel

Materials needed include the following items: pictures to represent a concrete object for each vowel, large copies of lower case letters for each vowel, and letters for children to trace (called puffy paint letters because thick paint or glue creates a raised surface).

As you teach each vowel sound, complete the following steps: 1) Teach a motion or story for each vowel (movements and stories below). 2) Show a picture or object, and ask students to make the sound and the movement with you. 3) Ask children to trace puffy paint (raised) copies of the vowel. 4. Say, "The name is _____ and the sound is _____," as the children trace the raised letters. Actions and stories for vowels are suggested below.

ELL Modifications
Pictures and real objects—*realia*—help ELL children as well as those with learning challenges.

Short A

A = Ask children to locate their Adam's apples in their throats. Tell them to bring their hands straight out from their throats as they say the short /a/ sound (as in apple).

Dyslexia Modification
Provide additional sensory strength for short (a) by touching, smelling and tasting real apples.

Short E

E = Show students a puppet representing Mr. Ed, the horse. Pull back on his reins as you make the short /e/ sound (as in Ed). Teach children to use their own reins by pulling back on the corners of their mouths.

Short I

I = Using your thumb, touch the bottom of your chin and with your first finger, dot your nose you make the short /i/ sound (as in Icky). Tell the children that when (i's) mother wanted him to eat something he did not like, he said, "This is icky."

Short O

O = Show students a puppet of Ms. Odd, the opera singer as you make the short /o/ sound (as in odd). Demonstrate how to form your mouth into a circle as you sing the /o/ sound. Ask children to form circles with their mouths as they sing /o/.

Short U

U = Push an imaginary barbell from your chest to above your head as you say /u/ as in up. Another option is to open an imaginary umbrella as you make the sound of a short (u) (as in umbrella). Use realia, real objects.

Is (Y) a Vowel or Consonant?

The letter (y) is actually a vowel more often that it is a consonant.

- (Y) is a consonant at the beginning of words as in yes.
- (Y) is a vowel when it sounds like either (e) or (i) at the end of syllables. In *baby* (y) replaces (e). In *my*, (y) replaces (i).
- (Y) is a vowel when it acts like a silent (i) or (e) as in may.

Ways to Create Long Vowels

Each vowel follows three basic generalizations for making its long sound. A few long sounds have additional letter combinations.

- Each vowel becomes long when the syllable is **open** (only one vowel, which comes at the end of the syllable as in the words *be, my* and *no*).
- A vowel followed by a consonant and a silent final (e) is almost always long as in *date, Pete, bite, mote,* and *brute*.
- Much of the time, the talking vowel in a vowel digraph is long (but not always). Consider *bait, beat, pie, boat* and *true*.

Dyslexia Modification
For additional sensory strength for short (i), bring a food or substance with a terrible smell. Ask children to smell while telling the story of Icky.

ELL Modifications
When teaching (e) and (o), puppets add **realia** (real objects), which helps ELL students.

In addition, sounds for long (a) and long (i) can be created additional ways. For example, the long sound of (a) is made with (ei) in words like *neighbor* or *eight*. The sound of long (i) is made with the letters (igh) as in *high* and *light*. Below, you will find examples of each vowel's long sound combinations.

All Formations of Long /A/

The long (a) sound is created with the following combinations:

- at the end of a syllable as in *a-pron*, or the word *a*,
- followed by another vowel as in *maid* and *may*
- followed by a consonant and silent (e) as in *cake*,
- (eigh) as in *freight* or *vein*,
- (ae) as in *Gaelic*,
- (au) as in *gauge* (there is only one example),
- (ey) as in *they*,
- (ea) as in *steak* and *great*,
- (aigh) as in *straight*,
- (ei) as in *veil* and *vein*,
- (eig) as in *feign* or *reign*,
- (ag-e) in *champagne*.

All Formations for Long /E/

The long (e) sound is created with the following combinations:

- at the end of a syllable as in *be*,
- followed by another vowel as in *meat* or *feed*,
- followed by a consonant and a silent /e/ as in *Pete*.

All Formations for Long /I/

The long (i) sound is created with the following combinations:

- at the end of a syllable as in I or *bi*cycle,
- followed by another vowel as in *pie*,
- followed by a consonant and silent (e) as in *bite*,
- followed by (gh) as in *light*.

All Formations for Long /O/

The long (o) sound is created with the following combinations:

- at the end of a syllable as in *go*,
- followed by another vowel as in *boat*,

- followed by a consonant and a silent (e) as in *rote*).

All Formations for Long /U/

The long (u) sound is created with the following combinations:

- at the end of a syllable as in *u*nicorn,
- followed by another vowel as in *blue* or *Sue*,
- followed by a consonant and a silent e as in *mute* or *brute*.

Schwas

A schwa is an unaccented syllable in which any vowel makes the sound of a short (u). Schwas are coded with an upside down (e) above the vowel. Notice the examples below.

- Denim = the (im) sounds like /um/
- Lemon = the (om) sounds like /um/
- About = the (a) sounds like /u/
- Woman = the (wo) letters sound like /wu/ and (man) sounds like /mun/
- Connect = the (con) sounds like /cun/
- Divide = the (di) sounds like /du/
- Silent = the (ent) sounds like /unt/

The (u) is a schwa in circus. Since the (u) also makes the short sound of /u/, you do not need to treat this vowel like a schwa.

Teaching Schwas

Teach schwas with a story from Project Read®. Tell children that the vowels went for a walk in the forest one day. As they were walking, a giant space ship landed and little aliens began to walk around. The aliens were friendly and wanted to meet the vowels. Unfortunately, the vowels were very frightened. Each time an alien tapped a vowel, it zapped all of the vowel's energy and the vowel could only say /uh/. After modeling, ask children to act out the parts of vowels and aliens.

Schwas often depend on the dialect of the English language and in some cases are the result of sloppy English. Often schwas are debatable. **Code** (mark) schwas with an upside down (e) above the schwa vowel.

Vowels and Syllables

Syllables determine not only where to divide words but how to pronounce them. It is important to remember that **syllables** always focus on the vowels. All vowels (a), (e), (i), (o), (u) and (y) make a sound that vibrates in the throat. If you say the letter name or sound, including (y) copying (e) or (i), you will feel the vibration. Vowels and most consonants make *voiced* sounds. A few letters that do not vibrate in the throat, and are considered **unvoiced** sounds include (c), (ck), (t), (p), (s), (sh), and (ch).

Each vowel is also considered an open sound. **Open sounds** require an open mouth and throat with no restriction on the tongue or teeth. Consonants are **closed sounds** because some part of the lips, teeth, tongue, or throat will close when pronouncing consonant names and sounds.

Dyslexia Modification
Usually, you will not teach students about open/closed letters or about voiced and unvoiced ones. You will use this information to teach students with dyslexia. The added information provides a new and different memory aid.

Types of Syllables

Open Syllables (cv) and Vowels

When a word or syllable ends with a vowel and there is only one vowel, the syllable is **open**. The name of each letter makes the long vowel sound and is **coded** (marked) with a long dash over the letter called a **macron**. Examples include these words: (a) in *apron,* (e) in *me,* (i) in the word *I,* (o) in *open,* (u) in *university* and (y) in *sky* or (y) in *lonely.* Each of the syllables above is called an open syllable because the vowel is open at the end.

Stress that words such as *shape-ly* end with an open syllable. The (y) is the only vowel and is at the end of the word. Other examples of (-ly) open syllables include words such as the following.

rip-ply, on-ly, slow-ly, gig-gly, quick-ly, large-ly

Teaching Open Syllables

When teaching open syllables, provide containers that can open and close. Each time a child reads an open syllable, the container should be opened. If locating enough containers proves difficult, ask children to begin with closed fists and open them each time an open syllable is encountered.

Closed (cvc) Syllables

Almost always, when a consonant ends a syllable, the vowel in front of the final consonant will be short. In many reading programs, short vowels are taught before long sounds. The consonant-vowel-consonant (cvc) pattern is one of the most predictable syllables. The first consonant is not important. It is the final consonant that closes the door on the vowel. Examples include the words below.

bat   bet   bit   bot (as in bottle)   but   byt (nonsense word)

ELL Modifications
Allow yourself to be outrageous and dramatic as you share these stories. The more body movement and facial expression you use, the better.

After modeling, let children repeat the stories with movements.

50

Teaching Closed Syllables

To teach closed syllables, give individual students copies of letters to arrange into words. Begin by asking a child with the letters (m) and (e) to stand side by side to form the word *me*. Sound out and pronounce *me* for children and then again with them. Next, add a (t) to form the word *met*. Once again, sound out and then pronounce *met*. Code closed syllables with a **brĕve**, which looks like a smile above the letter.

Tell children that the final consonant closes the door and frightens the vowel so much it uses its short sound. Emphasize by clapping as the final consonant is pronounced. Once you have taught one vowel and four or five consonants, you can begin finger spelling the sounds into words.

Teaching Finger Spelling With Closed Syllables

Before teaching finger spelling, review individual letter sounds that will be used to form words. Follow the steps suggested below with (cvc) words such as *hat, bit, hot, met,* and *hut.*

Dyslexia Modification
Finger spelling provides a modification for children who learn by moving (and who doesn't find moving helpful?).

- Show one word card at a time with words made up of letters that the children know. Begin with closed syllable (cvc) words. All vowels should make short sounds.
- Say each word and ask children to repeat the word after you.
- Finger spell the **phonemes** (sounds) for words instead of the **graphemes** (letter names). Model the movement described next.
- Raise your thumb for the first phoneme. As you say the other sounds, raise an additional finger for each one. Tapping or lightly pounding the table can be substituted for finger spelling.
- At the end of finger spelling or tapping, make a sweeping motion and say the word.
- Ask students to copy each finger spelling movement with you.

Increase learning by asking children to stand instead of sit while finger spelling.

Finger spelling always uses **phonemes** (letter sounds) rather than letter names, which are called **graphemes**.

Long Vowels—vc

In two syllable words with a vowel and a consonant (vc) pattern, inexperienced readers wonder where to divide the two syllables since the pattern resembles a cvc as in the word *lad*. Experienced readers recognize most cvc words, and by pronouncing the words, know where to divide them. The words below are cvc words that create open syllables by dividing after the vowel.

ba-by,   *la-dy,*   *sha-dy,*   *ra-ting,*
 v c   *v c*   *v c*   *v c*

Short Vowels—vc

Usually, two syllable words with a vowel and a consonant follow the cvc pattern with a short vowel sound. The words below are cvc words that create closed syllables by dividing after the consonant.

liz-ard,   lem-on,   wag-on,   den-im,   win-ning,   in-vite

Silent (e) Syllables

When a silent (e) is added to a closed syllable or word, the silent e causes the first vowel to say its long sound. Begin with cvc words, add the silent (e) and pronounce the new word. Often **pseudowords** (nonsense words) are used. Examples include the words below.

bate   Pete   bite   brute   mote   byte

Teaching Silent (e) Syllables

Tell children that a final, silent (e) is magic. (e's) magic allows the letter to *leap over* the consonant and sprinkle magic dust on the first vowel. When this happens, the first vowel must say its real name (the long sound of the vowel). To teach this concept, give children cards with letters including (c), (a), (p), and (e). Initially arrange the children so that their letters spell the word cap. Sound out and pronounce the word *cap*.

Next, bring an (e) to *cap* and sound out and pronounce the word again as *cape*. As the (a) makes its sound, the (e) must pretend to leap over the (p) and sprinkle magic dust on the (a). Providing a wand or special pencil adds to the drama. It is most important to emphasize that (e) must leap over the consonant. When (e) stands next to a vowel, a vowel digraph is formed (see next section).

Dyslexia Modification
Emphasize leaping over the consonant. The more movement and fun children have, the more likely the lesson will go into long-term memory.

Vowel Digraph Syllables

When two vowels stand side by side in a word or syllable, one vowel makes its long *or* short sound and the second vowel remains silent. In most cases, the first vowel is the one who "speaks" and the second is silent. However, this is not always true. Sometimes the second vowel says its long or short sound and the first vowel keeps silent.

Coding vowel digraphs may use a mācron or a brĕve along with a slash through the silent vowel. Notice that (ee) is a vowel digraph. Examine the common examples below:

- In (mēa̸t), the first vowel speaks and says its long sound.
- In (fēe̸t), there is no way to know which (e) is talking.
- In (trūe̸), the (u) is long and the (e) is silent.
- In (nēi̸ther), the (e) is long and the (i) is silent.
- In (breāk), the (a) is long and the first vowel is quiet.
- In (brĕa̸kfast), the first vowel makes its short sound.
- In (chīēf), the second vowel speaks and makes its long sound.
- In (līe̸), the first vowel is long and the second is silent.
- In (frūi̸t), the first vowel is long and the second is silent.
- In (māy̸), the first vowel is long and the second is silent.

Closer Examination of Vowel Digraphs

In the section below, you will see groupings of additional vowel digraphs. In most cases, the first vowel is long and the second is silent. Watch for exceptions.

Vowel (ie) Digraph

In the vowel digraph (ie) often the first vowel is silent and the second creates the sound as in *chief, belief, relief.*

Vowel (ei) Digraph

The vowel digraph (ei) usually has a long (e) followed by a silent (i) as in *neither, leisure, and seize.*

When the (ei) combination follows (c), the (e) is long and the (i) is silent as in *ceiling, deceit, receive, and perceive.*

Vowel (ea) Digraph

The (ea) digraph can trick you. Usually, the letter (e) is long and the (a) is silent as in *bean* or *each.* However, the (ea) digraph can change the sequence as in *break.* In the words *breakfast* and *meant*, the (e) is short and the (a) is silent.

Teaching Vowel Digraphs

Project Read® refers to vowel digraphs as "vowel teams." The speaking vowel (whether first or second) says, "I'll do the talking but I need your silent support." Link the team concept to a football team in which the quarterback does the talking and depends on the big, quiet linemen to provide support and protection.

To teach the concept, combine individual letter cards to create words such as (dear), (deer), (may), (maid) and (tries). Pass cards out to small groups of children and ask them to arrange themselves to create words. In each case, the child with the talking vowel turns to the silent vowel and says, "I'm the quarterback and I'll do the talking but I need your silent support."

(R) Controlled Syllables

When (r) *follows* a vowel the sound of the vowel is compromised by the sound of the (r). Code the vowel with a squiggle over the vowel. Sample words in which you do not hear the vowel sound include: fär, her, fïr, fŏr, and für. The sound in (far) and (for) are distinct. The sounds in (her) (fir) and (fur) all sound like /er/.

Teaching R Controlled Words

In Project Read®, you tell a story about a mother who tried very hard to teach her son, (r), to be courteous. Mother always insisted that (r) allow the vowels—the star letters—to go ahead of him in line. Although (r) obeys his mother, he is a bossy, grouchy fellow who wants to take control. When standing beside any vowel, (r) will tell the vowel, "I'll let you go first but you have to say _____." In each of these words, the (r) is called a "*Bossy R*".

Create letters to compose words with the Bossy (r). Distribute cards and arrange children to create new words. Each child holding an (r) card will say, "I'll let you go first but you have to say (ar), (or), or (er) depending on the vowels.

Diphthong Syllables

The (ph) in diphthong is pronounced /f/. If you keep this in mind, you will spell the word correctly. All diphthongs are determined by sounds that can be created with various combinations of letters. Although diphthongs often contain consonants as well as vowels, the standard definition states that diphthongs are "gliding vowels" which occur in the same syllable. The tongue moves when pronouncing a diphthong.

Teaching Diphthongs

One easy way to recall the most common diphthong sounds is to memorize the following story in which each diphthong sound is used.

Kinesthetic Modification

Bring a real football to class. Assign a word with a vowel digraph to each child. When all children have a word, stand in a circle and toss the football to one child at a time. The child will answer three questions.

"What is your word?" "What is the letter name of the quarterback?" "What does the quarterback say?"

Dyslexia Modification

Give some children stars and others frowning faces along with letters to create words. As children line up to form words, those with vowels will hold up stars. The children with the (r's) will hold up frowning faces. Act out *Bossy R's* speech to the stars.

Auditory Modification

The "pig" story provides an auditory memory aid for the basic sounds of diphthongs. Some children will also need the visual chart.

When the pig was happy he said, "**Oink**."
One day he hurt himself and said, "**Ouch**."
When he got slops for supper, he said, "**Ew**."
The farmer said, "You won't get anything else." With disappointment, the pig replied, "**Aw**."

These are the basic diphthong sounds. Note that these sounds may be created using different letter combinations. Below, you will see sound patterns in the first chart. The second chart provides additional spelling examples.

Diphthong Sound Patterns

oi = oink	ou = ouch	ew = blew	aw = awe
oy = boy	ow = cow	eu = neutral	al = all
	*ow can have a long vowel sound as in blow.		au = haul
			ought

Diphthong Spelling Examples

point	ouch	blew	ought	slow
soil	couch	threw	awful	mow
coil	around	grew	always	low
boy	bow	neutral	haul	bow (in hair)
toy	brown	neuter	because	crow
Roy	flowers	neutron	also	grow

Diphthongs with Double (oo)

There are two additional diphthongs and both are made with (oo). The long (oo) in bal*loon* sounds very much like long (u) in *u*nion. The short (oo) is heard in the word *took*.

Remember the long and short sounds by saying, "The boy read a *short book* by the light of a *long moonbeam*." Code with a large breve over the (oo's) in book and a long macron over the (oo's) in moon.

A sample of long (oo) diphthong words can be seen below.

loom, swoon, broom, maroon, cocoon, shoot, baboon

Read through the list of short (oo) words below.

rook, nook, shook, wood, cook, book

Final Stable Syllables

There are two types of final stable syllables. One type is made up of word endings such as (tion) that are familiar to most readers. These common syllables cannot be "sounded out." Additional examples are below.

- (-tion) as in station,
- (-sion) as in explosion,
- (-ture) as in picture,
- (-dure) as in procedure,
- (-cial) as in facial,
- (-cian) as in Grecian,
- (-cious) as in gracious,
- (-tial) as in partial,
- (-tious) as in cautious,
- (-cient) as in ancient.

In addition, any syllable ending with a consonant and (-le) is considered a final stable syllable. Notice the differences in words that end with -ly, which are found in open syllables and the consonant (-le) ending in final stable syllables. See examples of final stable syllables listed below.

- bat tle,
- Bi ble,
- cy cle,
- fid dle,
- gig gle,
- peo ple,
- tat tle,
- siz zle,
- nib ble,
- sim ple

Teaching Final Stable Syllables

The following example demonstrates a pattern for teaching the final syllable, *tion*. Write *tion* and ask students to do the following.

- "Spell (tion)." With your lead, children will spell the letters with you.
- "See (tion) in your head." Ask children to close their eyes.
- "Spell (tion) to yourself in your head."
- "Write (tion) in the air." Use both arms and keep hands together to sky write.
- "Write (tion) on your desk with your palm or thumb."
- "Spell (tion) orally." Lead with your voice.
- "Close your eyes and write (tion) on a piece of paper." Model by writing on the board or on chart paper.

Modification
A modification can be as small as doing something a different way to catch the attention of students.

Teaching Multisyllabic Words

Even those who have problems decoding, usually read the beginning syllables correctly. You want to encourage their eyes to see all parts of the word. Introduce syllables in a multisyllabic word from right to left. Then read the word correctly from left to right. The following example demonstrates detailed steps for teaching the word *attention*.

Modification
Teaching (tion) can be very boring. Add colors, actions, and tracing in the memory pan.

- On the chalkboard, write: *at ten tion*.
- Begin teaching the final syllable by saying, "This says *tion*. Say *tion*."
- "You know the word ten. Say *ten*."
- "You know the word at. Say *at*."
- "Now put it together. Say *at ten tion*."

With some students, use vertical spelling to learn a multisyllabic word such as the word *different*.

- Write: *diff*
  er
  ent

- Start at the bottom and say: "This is *ent*, say *ent*. You know *er*, say *er*. This is *diff*. Say *diff*. The word is *diff er ent*."

Teaching a New Way to Read Multisyllabic Words

Guszak offers a way to teach multisyllabic words to students who do not develop their own method. Instead of worrying about syllable division, Guszak places a dash before the second vowel and before every vowel following the second one. He then instructs students to read and blend the parts together. Notice the following words.

remember	re m/em b/er	re mem ber
attempt	at t/empt	at tempt
magnetic	mag n/e t/ic	mag net ic
unintelligent	un /in t/ell /i g/ent	un in tell i gent

Note: the second /i/ in *intelligent* is a schwa.

Teaching a Way to Identify Syllables

An easy way to identify each syllable is to say a word with your chin in your hand. Each time your chin drops, you count a syllable. Usually, words with two consonants in the middle (except for consonant blends or consonant digraphs) divide between the two consonants. Examples include the words below.

Lit tle,   pup py,   bet ter,   com mon,   jum ble,   sim ple

According to "K Smarties", a web site for parents, *http://www. preksmarties.com* you can also determine the number of syllables by following the steps below.

- "Count all of the vowels.
- Subtract silent vowels.
- Subtract one vowel from each diphthong.
- The number of vowel sounds left will be the number of syllables in a word."

Came has two vowels. Remove the silent e. You hear one vowel sound and the word has one syllable.

Outside has four vowels. Subtract the silent (e). Next subtract one of the vowels in the diphthong (ou). That leaves two vowel sounds. There are two syllables in the word.

Using Accents

If you listen carefully when you pronounce a word, you will probably hear one syllable that is slightly louder than the others. The loudest syllable is the one that gets the accent.

- Usually, the accent is on the first syllable as in the word **pre** *fix*.

- If the word has a prefix, the accent will be on the root word as in the word *un **hap**py*.
- If the word has a suffix, the accent will be on the last or next to last syllable before the suffix as in words *suc**cess** ful*.

Irregular Words and Consonants

Irregular Words

Words that do not follow the alphabetic principles are called **irregular** words. In some phonics programs they are referred to as **outlaw words** or **red words**. An example of a word that looks like a silent (e) word but doesn't follow the rule is the word "one." Making the magic (e) leap over the (n) should make the (o) say its name. When the rule doesn't work, you know the word is irregular. Always try the generalization (rule) first. Notice the list of irregular words below.

Word	Looks Like	But is Irregular Because . . .
come	silent e word	(o) does not make a long sound
said	vowel digraph	neither vowel sound is heard
have	silent e word	(a) does not make its long sound
some	silent e word	(o) does not make its long sound
what	closes (cvc)	(a) does not make a short sound
were	silent e word or r controlled	(e) does not make a long sound Without the silent (e) at the end, the word would be pronounced with the /er/ sound. Since there is no need for the final (e), the word is considered irregular.

Teaching Irregular Words

The last thing you want to do with an irregular word is to ask children to "sound it out." Words such as *said* cannot be sounded out and the request will confuse children. To distinguish between phonetically regular words that can be finger spelled and irregular words that cannot use their sounds, you must say the letter names instead of the phonemes (letter sounds).

Letters in words such *said, one,* or *come* that are phonetically irregular are spelled orally by naming the graphemes. With each letter named, the dominant hand taps down the opposite arm starting at the shoulder and ending at the wrist.

Dyslexia Modification
Any additional movement you can add to tapping down the arm will strengthen the activity. Experiment with music or rhythm instruments.

- Show a card with an irregular word such as *said.*
- Say, "This word is said." After saying the word, gesture to guide children to repeat the word.
- Begin at the shoulder and move downward to the wrist with one tap for each letter name.
- After spelling the letter names for the word, make a sweeping motion down the arm and say the word.
- In Project Read®, these words are called "red words" and are printed with red ink.

When spelling words that are phonetically irregular, always say the graphemes (letter names) rather than attempt letter sounds.

Consonant Strategies and Modifications

Letters other than vowels are called consonants. They include the following letters:

b,c,d,f,g,h,j,k,l,m,n,p,qu,r,s,t,v,w,x,y,z,ch,sh,th,ph,wh, ng, and *gh*

Teaching Consonants

After students have learned one vowel sound, introduce three to five consonants. Tell students that by combining vowels and consonants, they can begin to create words. An important aspect of teaching consonants is to encourage students to clip the sounds quickly. If a consonant sound is elongated, a vowel is accidentally added and students miss the true sound of the consonant being taught. For example, instead of saying /b/, you will make the sound of /bu/.

Tactile Modification
Tracing in the memory pan helps with recall. Ingredients can be dry jello, salt, cornmeal, oatmeal or similar textures.

NOTE: Soft flour is so fine that it can cause sneezing problems.

- As you teach each consonant sound, demonstrate clipping the sound by cutting off a corner of a piece of paper as you say the sound.
- As students repeat the sound, ask them to use their first two fingers as imaginary scissors and pretend to cut the sound.
- The **memory pan** (a shallow pan with fine sand) is used for locking in consonant sounds.

  Say, "Make the symbol in the sand as I say the sound."
  Say, "The name is ___. The sound is ___."
  Students trace the letter in the sand as you say the sound.

Barbara Frandsen

- Skywriting is also used to lock in the consonant sounds. Students are encouraged to think of a skywriting plane leaving a trail of smoke behind.

Tell students to use a stiff arm with their first two fingers extended to create a trail of smoke.

As students write in the air, say, "The name is ___. The sound is ___."

Teaching Movements for Consonants

For each of the consonants listed below, an associated movement is suggested. The aids and movements are not from Project Read®.

	Memory Aid	Movements
Bb	bouncing ball	bounce a ball
Cc	counting coins	count money
Dd	digging dirt	pretend to dig dirt
Ff	fanning feathers	pretend to fan
Gg	giving gifts	pretend to give
Hh	holding hands	hold hands
Jj	jumping jacks	jump in place
Kk	kicking kick balls	pretend to kick
Ll	licking lollipops	pretend to lick
Mm	making money	touch play money
Nn	nodding north	nod toward north
Pp	passing potatoes	pass a potato
Qq	quiet quacking	quack very quietly
Rr	running robots	run in place like robots

Dyslexia, ELL Modification
Each of the movements amounts to a modification. You strengthen each memory aid with real objects. For example, bouncing a ball benefits many diverse learners.

62

Ss	slithering snakes	slither like snakes
Tt	ticking time	pretend to be a clock
Vv	view valentines	look at a valentine
Ww	washing windows	pretend to wash windows
Xx	x-ing out X-rays	draw an x in the air
Yy	yawning youth	yawn broadly
Zz	zig-zagging zebras	zig-zag around the room

Consonant Digraphs

A **consonant digraph** occurs when two consonants, side by side, create a *totally new sound*. Individual sounds of each letter disappear as the new sound is formed. For example, in the word (when), the (w) and (h) totally lose their individual sounds. There is not a hint; not a blend; but a totally new sound that is unheard in the English language except when (wh) come together.

Teaching Consonant Digraphs

Project Read® explains consonant digraphs by introducing the "H Brothers." Each brother has distinctive characteristics.

- Ch Brother—This brother wants to become the engineer of a train. He believes that trains say, "Ch, ch, ch, ch." The letters (tch) can also make the sound of (ch). Although there are exceptions, letters (-tch) usually follow a short vowel as in the word "catch."
- Sh Brother—This very polite brother wants everyone to be quiet and is always saying, "Sh, sh, sh, sh."
- Th Brother—This brother is rude to people and sticks out his tongue as he says, "Th, th, th, th."
- Wh Brother—This brother tries to whistle but only blows air.

ELL Modification
Your dramatization and explanation will benefit ELL students as well as those with learning differences.

To lock in each digraph, take the memory pan to individual students and ask them to trace the symbols as you make the sounds. Say, "Make the symbols for the sound . . .
The names are (____) and (____). The sound is /____/."

Ending consonant digraphs include (-nk) as in (sink), and (-ng) as in (king).

Hard and Soft /th/

The (th) can be either voiced, with a vibration in the throat, or unvoiced, with no vibration. Voiced (th) can be heard in the following words.

there   their   this   then   breathe   rather   weather   mother father   either   other   brother   smooth   the

Unvoiced (th) will be noticed as air passing under the tongue in the following words.

tooth   math   bath   mouth   think   thought   north   path forth   healthy   something   anything   Beth

Cousins Ph and Gh

The letters (p) and (h) look like the H brothers but are not a consonant digraph for a very good reason. Each of the H brother sounds creates a totally new sound, which is never heard in the English language except when the two letters come together. The (ph) combination loses the sound of the (p) and (h) but a totally new sound is not created. The (ph) combination copies the letter /f/ sound.

When the (g) and (h) come together as in the word (tough), they also make the sound /f/. Although you do not hear either the (g) or the (h), they do not create a unique sound. Like the (ph), the (gh) combination is not a true consonant digraph.

Consonant Blends

Blends occur when two or more adjacent consonants are said so quickly that although individual sounds are still heard, they seem like a single sound. To show how consonants blend, bring sugar and chocolate powder to school. Allowing students to touch the real items makes a powerful difference.

If you can get children to laugh, you release endorphins which will put information into long-term memory. Examples of initial consonant blends include the following combinations.

bl, br, cl, cr, dr, dw, fl, fr, gl, gr, pl, pr, sl, sk, sl, sm, sn, sp, st, scr, shr, spl, spr, squ, str, tr, thr

Consonant blends can also occur at the end of words. Examples of ending blends include the following letters. The (-) indicates that the letters come at the end of the word.

-ct, -ft, -lt, -nt, -pt, -rt, -st, -ld, -nd, -rd, -lp, -mp, -rp, -sp, -nb, -nk, -rk, -sk, -lb, -lf, -rb, -rf, -rm, -rn, — (sk, sp, and *st* can be either initial or final).

Teaching Consonant Blends

Dyslexia Modification
Allow children who struggle to add taste to the sensory experience.

Initially introduce the concept by putting sugar on one side of a bowl and cocoa on the other. As you stir the two ingredients together, point out that you can still see bits of white and bits of brown, but the two are blended together. When you model, use a real bowl and spoon. Children can pretend but still need to go through the actions.

Following the sugar and cocoa demonstration, show letter blending by following these steps.

* Without letting students see what you are doing, put a card with a consonant blend into a large mixing bowl.

Example: (bl)

* As children observe, put a card with (b) and a card with (l) into the bowl.
* Take a large spoon and stir the letters as you hold the bowl in your other arm.
* Reach into the bowl and pull out the card with the (bl) blend.
* Ask students to create imaginary mixing bowls and spoons and stir pre-arranged sets of cards with blends after you model.

When skywriting blends, use the same wording, "The names are (___) and (___). Their blended sound is /___ /."

Preconsonantal Nasal Blends

According to *Words Their Way*, blends with (m), (n), or (ng) produce subtle sounds. Preconsonantal nasal blends occur before the final consonant in a few words such as the (m) in bump, and the (n) in rink. The final (-ng) in king is also a preconsonantal nasal.

Influences of /w/ and /l/

Much like (r) in r-controlled words, the (l) changes the sound of (a) in words such as *all, ball, wall,* and *mall.* When (w) is immediately before an (a), it changes the sound of (a). Notice that (a) is not long or short in the words *want, was, wash, word,* or *was.*

Teaching Double Final (F), (L), (S), (Z)

There are four consonants that double at the end of a syllable with a short vowel sound. These letters are (f), (l), (s), and (z). The following sentence serves as a memory aid.

Jeff will pass Buzz.

Hard and Soft Consonants

Several consonants have dual sounds.

- (C) followed by (e), (i), or (y) acting like (e) or (i) has the soft sound of (s) as in *cent, city,* and *cycle.*
- (C) followed by (a), (o), (u) or any consonant has the hard sound of (k) as in *cat, cot, cut,* and *clue.*
- (G) followed by (e), (i), or (y) has the soft sound of (j) as in *gem, giant,* and *gym.*
- (G) followed by (a), (o), (u) or any consonant usually has the hard gargling sound of (g) as in *gap, got, gut,* and *glue.*
- (S) at the beginning of a word has the soft sound of (s) as in *snake.*
- (S) at the end of a one-syllable word has the hard sound of (z) as in *has.*

Dyslexia Modification

When introducing the soft and hard sounds, ask children to whisper all words with soft (c) or soft (g) sounds. When saying words with hard (c) or hard (g) encourage children to say words in a louder voice.

Teaching Hard and Soft Consonants

Although the National Reading Panel recommends teaching phonics with **direct instruction** (instruction delivered by the teacher), you may want to deviate at times. Use your own judgment. If students can discover patterns, they will recall them more easily than if you simply tell them. For this reason, you will sometimes use an **inquiry** or **discovery** approach in which children determine a rule by considering the examples. There will be times when you need to use both approaches.

When introducing soft (c) words, ask children to touch a soft cotton ball. When teaching hard (c), ask children to knock on their desks each time they hear a hard sound. Repeat for hard and soft (g).

Letter (c)

The letter (c) actually has no sound of its own. The (c) will either copy (s) or (k). Show a list of words with hard and soft c such as the following:

city, cat, cent, copy, cycle, cut, car, cite, cope, crash, cute, circle

- Ask children to help you find all of the words that begin with the soft (c) sound that sounds like /s/. Create a new list with the soft (c) words, including: *city, cent, cycle, cite, and circle.*
- Guide children to locate all the hard (c) sounds that copy /k/. This list will include the following: *cat, copy, cut, cope, crash and cute.*
- Guide children to discover that all of the (c) words with a soft /s/ sound include (ci), (ce), or (cy).
- In the hard (c) words, the /k/ sound is usually followed by (a), (o), (u) and all consonants. Another way to word the generalization is to say that hard (c) is followed by any other letter in the alphabet except (e), (i), or (y).

Letter (g)

The letter (g) has its own hard sound that imitates gargling. Soft (g) uses the same generalizations as (c). When (g) is followed by (e), (i), or (y), it copies the sound of the letter (j). The challenge is that soft (g) often does not follow the rules. Notice the following words with (gi) or (ge) that do not make the sound /j/: *give, girl, get, and gear.*

Use the same inquiry approach that was used for (c) to teach the generalizations for hard and soft (g). List the following words and ask children to separate the words into two lists.

Gay, gentle, grass, gym, glass, gain, goofy, gut, George, guppy, gigantic, grab

- Help children identify the hard (g) words, which are: *gay, grass, glass, goofy, guppy, grab.*
- Create a second list with the soft (g) words including the words: *gentle, gym, George, and gigantic.*
- Indicate that there are many (g) words that should make the soft (g) sound but do not.

Modification

Because (g) has several exceptions to the soft (g) generalization, consider creating a "jail" for these deviant words. Emphasize why the word is in jail. Ask the word to make up a defense.

Letter (s)

The letter (s) has totally different generalizations for determining whether it is soft or hard. When (s) comes at the beginning of a word, it is usually soft and makes the sound of a snake hissing. At the end of syllables or words with a short vowel, (s) usually copies the sound of (z). Create the following list and ask children to discern when (s) makes its own soft sound and when it copies (z).

soft, his, snake, so, sad, as, has

Dyslexia Modification

When teaching hard and soft (s), ask children to whisper when saying words with the soft sound. Exaggerate the /z/ sound at the end of words.

- Guide students to discover that the words with the hissing snake sound place (s) at the beginning of the word, such as in: *soft, snake, so, and sad.*
- Words that end with (s) following a short vowel, usually sound like /z/ as in the words: *his, as,* and *has.*

In order to make (s) at the end of a word make its own soft sound, double the (s) as in the words: *miss, hiss, sass, bass, and lass.*

Three Ways to Make the Sound /j/

There are three ways to make the /j/ sound.

- The first way to make the sound /j/ is to use the letter (j) as in *jug, judge, jump,* or *joy.*
- A second way to make the /j/ sound is to use words with (ge), (gi), or (gy). Refer to soft (g) above.
- A final way to make the /j/ sound occurs at the end a word with -dge. Notice that the word judge demonstrates two ways to make the /j/ sound. Examples of -dge endings include these words: *Madge, judge, lodge,* and *hodge.*

Kinesthetic Modification
Every time children hear the /j/ sound, ask them to jump. The physical movement will help retain long-term memory.

When to Use (k) and When to Use (c)

Due to the fact that hard (c) copies the letter (k), it is challenging to know when to use each one for spelling. The key is that when the /k/ sound is followed by (e), (i), or (y), the (k) is used. Notice the following list of words including:

make, sketch, poker, kind, risky, skin, token, skill, keep, like, flaky

Use the same discovery method as suggested above for separating hard and soft (c) and (g).

Additional Information about (k) Sounds

There are four possibilities for making the sound /k/.

- One method involves (k) followed by (i), (e) or (y). Examples include words below:

kite, make, like, kind, keep, kyphosis, kylix, keratosis, and dyskinesia.

- Hard (c) followed by all consonants and (a), (o) or (u) also make /k/ sound. Examples include *cat, corn, victim, pecan, and bacon.*

- A third method for the /k/ sound is with (ck), which always follows a short vowel in words such as *luck, pick, rock, truck and Dick.*
- Finally, /k/ can be made with (cc) as in *mecca, occupy, raccoon, and succulent.* In two-syllable words, (c) often doubles to protect the first short vowel.

Silent Consonants

Silent consonants are tricky because they look like consonant digraphs (H brothers) as well as consonant blends. In order to separate silent consonants from consonant digraphs and consonant blends, you must say the word to yourself. If the letter combination makes a totally new sound, you know it is a consonant digraph. If you hear a little of each letter sound, it is a blend. If you only hear one of the two consonants, you are dealing with a silent consonant word. Study the list of words below and determine which ones fall into the silent consonant category.

when, dumb, crash, know, that, write, blank, gnat, church, ghost

Additional words with silent consonants are included the list of words below:

- K̶new = the (k) is silent,
- W̶rote = the (w) is silent,
- G̶naw = the (g) is silent,
- Lig̶h̶t = the (gh) combination is silent
- Chick̶ = the (k) is silent (also truck̶, flick̶, Rick̶)
- Bomb̶ = the (b) is silent

Three Sounds for Past Tense Verbs

You may have wondered why some past tense words sound like /ed/ at the end while others may sound like /d/ or even /t/. Answers you have longed for are below.

- When the last sound your hear in a base word is voiced, the past tense will be pronounced /d/. Examples include the following words:

  roared, gagged, played, maimed, willed, named, restored, scorned, stored, sobbed, sneered, rained.

- When the last sound you hear in a base word is unvoiced, the past tense will be pronounced /t/. Consider examples:

Modification
Provide letters to spell words with silent consonants. Students holding silent consonants will wear gags and remain silent as words are spelled phonetically.

Modification
When teaching a word with a voiced ending, ask children to pronounce the base word very loudly before adding the equally loud /d/ sound. Base words that end with unvoiced sounds will be whispered softly before adding the soft /t/ sound.

hissed, kissed, flashed, clicked, rocked, clashed, typed, laughed, worked.

- When a base word ends with (t) or (d), the past tense will be pronounced /ed/. Consider these words:

rented, dented, ended, breaded, instructed, granted, worded, sleeted, spaded.

Configuration Clues

Children who process visually benefit from instruction in configuration clues, which focus on the figure or shape of the word. Not all words take on interesting shapes. Others offer excellent visual clues. The shape of the word includes:

- the length of the word and the height of the letters (for example, configuration):

c o n f i g u r a t i o n

- ascenders—tall letters such as (b), (h), (k), (l),
- descending letters—letters that hang below the regular line of print such as (g), (p), (q), (y),
- double letters such as in moon or balloon.

Kinesthetic Modification
Use hands and arms to indicate the shape of a word. Teach ascenders by stretching arms as high as possible. For descending letters, bend over and touch the floor. Demonstrate length by opening arms horizontally.

Summarizing the Phonics Dragons

Phonological Dyslexia and Phonics

One of the most bewildering types of dyslexia is Phonological Dyslexia (phone NO logical = sound is not logical). Children with **Phonological Dyslexia** have good comprehension and master sight words through memorization of flash cards but are unable to distinguish subtle differences in letter sounds. Elephant /e/ and igloo /i/ require **auditory discrimination**, which is the ability to hear small differences in the sounds. The subtle differences are lost on the child with Phonological Dyslexia as well as children with Deep Dyslexia.

Phonics strategies from Project Read® offer excellent methods of teaching phonics to children with Phonological Dyslexia because movements and pictures serve as reminders of sound differences. Because children with Phonological Dyslexia usually memorize flash cards easily, the Memory Strategy works well when mastering sounds.

- Introduce a letter name and sound that you want children to remember.
- During the introduction of a letter name and sound, provide a picture along with a kinesthetic memory aid to match the strong visual skills of children with Phonological Dyslexia.
- After introducing and providing memory aids for three letter sounds, stop and review. Check for understanding as you review.

Deep Dyslexia and Phonics

Many of the suggestions for children with Phonological Dyslexia fit the child with Deep Dyslexia. The major difference is that in addition to auditory problems, children with **Deep Dyslexia** display characteristics that are similar to a child with poor vision. With weakness in both auditory and visual processing, children will need to include movement, touch, taste and smell. Dropping to easier levels of phonics will not help the child with Deep Dyslexia. The characteristics will continue no matter how easy the phonics task. Two important ideas to remember about a child with Deep Dyslexia are 1) the child is probably very intelligent and must be taught at his or her thinking ability 2) incorrect answers and responses should always be dignified.

Children who continue to struggle with sounds through second grade will probably struggle in middle school. You will be faced with the decision to 1) continue work on mastering sounds or 2) give up efforts to teach sound-to-symbol matching. It is probably best to de-emphasize oral fluency, phonics and memorization of sight words and be thankful for the good comprehension.

Help for Phonological *and* Deep Phonics

Movement and touch will be helpful for children with either Phonological or Deep Dyslexia.

- Tell the child to trace the letter while repeating, "The name is _____ and the sound is _____."
- Trace a letter in a memory pan (Project Read®) filled with salt, dry corn meal, or sugar. Avoid flour, which is so fine it may cause sneezing.
- Sky write the letter with the child while saying, "The name is _____, the sound it _____."
- Children with Phonological or Deep Dyslexia often require integration of taste and smell.

Word Deafness (Phonological and Deep)

Although the suggestions above may provide adequate help for most children with Phonological or Deep Dyslexia, a few children may require more extreme measures. A more dramatic procedure builds on the concept of "word deafness." Because children with Phonological and Deep Dyslexia do not hear subtle differences in sounds, the concept of "deafness" may expand understanding. Consider, "How would I teach a deaf child?"

Touch the child and say or indicate, "Look at me. Look at my mouth and notice the placement of my tongue and teeth when I make this sound." (All vowels are made with an open mouth, tongue and teeth and are called "**open sounds.**")

- Give the child a mirror and say, "Make your mouth, tongue and teeth look like mine." Use the phrase, "The name is _____, the sound is _____."
- Make the sound an additional time and ask the child to touch your throat. (**Voiced sounds** make a vibration in the throat. Vowels and most consonants create voiced sounds. Unvoiced consonants include: /p/, /t/, /sh/, /ch/, /k/, /ck/, /qu/, /s/.)

- Ask the child to repeat each sound and feel his or her own throat.

Any time you choose to emphasize a particular sound, use touch, movement, taste and smell. Olfactory (sense of smell) and gustatory (taste) provide your strongest senses. Use these extreme measures when the need justifies the additional work on your part. In the early grades, work with magnetic letters and games that require physical manipulation of letters or syllables.

Bibliography

Anderson, David, and S. O'Neal, C. David, P. Oruonyehu. *Dyslexia and Related Disorders* (Texas Education Agency, Sept, 1998).

Beauvois, M.F., and J. Derouesne. *Phonological Alexia: Three Dissociations*. Journal of Neurology, Neurosurgery and Psychiatry, 42, 1115-1124, 1979. **http://www.maccs.mq.edu.au/~max/AcqDys/PD.html**

Besner, D. "Deep Dyslexia and Right Hemiesphere Hypothesis." Can J Psychol 1983; Vol. 34, No. 4, pp. 565-571.

Carlson. "Types of Dyslexia." *Welcome to the Dyslexia Homepage*. Macalester College, 1998. <http://www.macalester.edu/psychology/whathap/UBNRP/Dyslexia/index.html>

Cox, Aylett R. *Structures and Techniques*. Cambridge, MA: Educators Publishing Service, Inc., 1984.

Cunningham, Patricia. *Systematic Sequential Phonics They Use*. Greensboro, NC: Carson-Dellosa Publishing Co., 2000.

Doyle, Dennis. "What is Phonics?" *K Smarties*. 2000-2010. <http://www.preksmarties.com/>

Ekwall, E. and J. Shanker. *Teaching Reading in Elementary School*. Columbus OH: Merrill Publishing Co., 1989.

Fox, Barbara. *Phonics and Structural Analysis for the Teacher of Reading*. Boston, MA: Allyn & Bacon, 2010.

Frandsen, B and S. Smith. *Dyslexia Analysis*. Austin, TX: Family School, 1998.

—*Yes! I Can Teach Literacy*. Austin, TX: Family School, 2006.

Gambrell, L. L. Morrow, S. Neuman, and M. Pressley. *Best Practices in Literacy Instruction*. New York, NY: Guilford Press, 1999.

Greene, V. and M.L. Enfield. *Project Read Phonology*. Language Bloomington, MN: Circle Enterprise.

Gunning, T. *Creating Reading Instruction for All Children*. Boston, MA: Allyn and Bacon, 2000.

Guszak, Frank. *Reading for Students with Special Needs*. Obique, Iowa: Kendall Hunt Publishing, 1997.

Heilman, Arthur. *Phonics in Proper Perspective*. Columbus, Ohio: Merrill Publishing Co., 1989.

Hittlemann, D. *Developmental Reading, K-8*. Columbus, OH: Merrill Publishing,1983.

Hull, Marion. Columbus, Ohio: *Phonics for the Teacher of Reading*. Merrill Publishing Co., 1989.

NCTE National Council of Teachers of English, International Reading Association, Newark, Delaware. <http://www.ncte.org/>

Norton, D. The Effective Teaching of Language Arts. Columbus, OH: Merrill Publishing Co., 1980

Smith, M. and E. Hogen. Multisensory Teaching Approach Linkages, EDMAR: Forney, TX 1987.

"Spelling Rules," *Reading from Scratch,* 2002. *<http://www.dyslexia>*

"Ultimate Phonics Scope and Sequence" *Spencer Learning.* 2010 *<http://spencerlearning.com/_downloads/phonics-scope-and-sequence. pdf>*

"What Is Phonics, Anyway?" *PBS Parents.* *<http://www.pbs.org/parents/readinglanguage/articles/phonics/main. html>*

Slaying the Fluency Dragon

"Fluency dragons" occur for many reasons: poor visual acuity, lack of interest, inadequate education, or even shyness. Two dragons, of particular interest, are described below.

Even when a child over uses phonics, oral fluency usually sounds good in kindergarten and first grade. As more irregular words lace the pages, fluency begins to falter. This type of problem is called **Surface Dyslexia**. Since many words in English are irregular and cannot be decoded with phonics, the over dependence on phonics becomes a barrier.

A second type of disability, **Deep Dyslexia**, manifests with omissions, insertions, repetitions and reversals. Oral reading is halting and painful. Amazingly, the child gains average to excellent comprehension.

Scotopic Sensitivity Syndrome (SSS) and **eye tracking** problems also contribute to poor oral fluency. SSS is caused when light rays create a sensation of letter movement for some children. Other children, with good visual acuity are unable to follow a line of print smoothly across a page.

Fluency

What Is Fluency?

Fluency includes rate (speed), accuracy, and intonation or expression. Fluency involves reading "connected" printed text (such as a sentence or paragraph) rather than reading words in isolation. Flow of words becomes important when reading text for understanding. "After it is fully developed, reading fluency refers to a level of accuracy and rate, where decoding is relatively effortless; where oral reading is smooth and accurate with correct prosody; and where attention can be allocated to comprehension." (Wolf & Katzir-Cohen, 2001, p. 219). **Word recognition**, the ability to decode print, influences fluency. When fluency and word recognition flow smoothly, the child's comprehension improves.

What Does Research Indicate?

In "New Research on an Old Problem," Marianne Wolf suggests that reading "automaticity" requires multiple skills including letter-sound rules, letter combinations, and vocabulary meanings. Wolf believes one way to bring new readers to the automaticity level involves multiple readings. Repeated reading of short passages is currently considered the best way to improve fluency. A second method, called assisted reading, is also believed to help. In assisted reading, the child reads along with an expert reader. Improvement happens due to the repetition as well as to the process of listening to a good model.

In 2005, the National Assessment of Educational Progress found that 44% of our 4th grade children demonstrated poor fluency. As students move into middle and senior high schools, their fluency continues to falter. According to one of the members, if a student struggles over more than 10% of the vocabulary words, fluency speed will be impaired.

Dyslexia Modification
According to research, schools and books often present print disabilities (term from congress). New research suggests changing text formation instead of focusing on "what's wrong with children."

Determining Reading Rates

In order to obtain an oral **reading rate** (or speed), mark a beginning place in the text, time the student's reading for one minute and mark the final word. Count the number of words read in one minute. You can speed up the process by timing for 30 seconds and multiplying by 2 or by timing for 15 seconds and multiplying by four.

To determine the rate for silent reading, ask a student to begin reading when you turn on your stopwatch. As you finish timing, indicate for the student to stop and point to the last word read silently.

See Dr. Guszak's expectations for instructional and independent reading below. **Independent reading** is material a child can read alone. **Instructional reading** material is appropriate for instruction, when you are there to scaffold.

Grade Level	Instructional	Independent
first	60 words per minute	80 words per minute
second	70 words per minute	90 words per minute
third	80 words per minute	100 words per minute
fourth	90 words per minute	110 words per minute
fifth and above	100 words per minute	120 words per minute

A Word About Scaffolding

Just as construction of a new building requires support beams and a foundation, emerging readers benefit from initial guidance, which is called **scaffolding**. When teachers provide significant help with little child involvement, one might consider the assistance as Scaffolding 3 (meaning significant assistance from the teacher). As children become more confident, the teacher reduces the amount of help to Scaffolding 2. The final level provides very little assistance. We can consider this Scaffolding 1.

The "What is This Word?" Question

When a child is reading orally, the emphasis should remain on fluency and comprehension. Save phonics, vocabulary, and spelling for separate times. The important question is, "What do I do in the middle of reading if a child doesn't know a word or if the child asks for help?" Below are suggestions for encouraging the child to use context and thinking skills.

- Encourage the child to start at the beginning of the sentence and insert an "uh" sound for the unknown word. Then ask, "What would be a logical word that would fit in that place?" Your purpose is to get the child to think about the context of the story and sentence (Guszak).

- If the child inserts an incorrect word that makes sense and does not change the meaning, let it go. Jot down the word said by the child as well as the printed word.
- On the other hand, if the child says a word that does not make sense, ask questions such as, "Did that make sense?" "Do we talk that way?"
- Later, analyze why the word was missed. Plan separate skill lessons to teach the skills needed to decode unknown words correctly.

> For example, if the child ignored a sound-to-symbol cue, teach or review the missed skill.

> If the word was missed due to incorrect grammar, teach a lesson on sentence structure.

> If the substituted word did not make sense, call attention to the fact and encourage thinking about the text.

A more typical, and less helpful response is to ask the child to sound out the unknown word. Whether to ask the child to sound out the word or not depends on the lesson objective. During skill lessons, your objective is about the skill being taught—not about fluency. If smooth fluency is the objective, maintain focus on supporting fluid reading with an appropriate rate. When comprehension is the major objective, ask questions to direct thinking about text. You may ask the child to look at the initial letter of the unknown word and plan to get the mouth ready to make the first sound when the child re-reads the sentence.

Importance of Large Print

Eye movements depend on typographic features such as letter size, font, and the length of each line. **Visual acuity** is the physical ability to see. Even when visual acuity is good, children may exhibit problems with the ability to focus on small print. Larger letters and shorter print lines help some children who experience difficulty with reading.

Chronological age or grade does not ensure that the eyes are ready for small print reading. Expecting a child to read small print before eyes are ready may arrest developmental processes, creating lasting damage. According to Barbara Vitale, a national expert on learning disabilities, most children need large print (like the print size used in early primary grades) through grade four.

One of the first things to do with a child who is experiencing reading problems (regardless of age) is to enlarge the size of the print.

If a reading problem is related to print size, you will notice that, in time, the developmental need will be satisfied and the child will make a transition to reading regular type. Regardless of age, the student with problems will probably benefit from:

- large print on the overhead screen, the whiteboard, or a chart,
- large print books with ¼ inch font such as those provided to children with limited vision,
- books from NIMAS (National Instructional Materials Accessibility Standard) at: *http://www.afb.org/Section. asp?SectionID=58&TopicID=255,*
- modified digital print from CAST (Center for Applied Special Technology) at: http://www.cast.org/,
- handheld reading material at a 30 to 45 degree angle.

Sometimes changing the angle supports the eyes. Taking the time and effort to experiment with different types of print or angles will never damage a child and may help.

Eye Tracking

In considering the importance of eye characteristics beyond visual acuity, counselors report good results using a controversial process called "eye movement desensitization reprocessing" (EMDR) to assist trauma victims. The treatment has been used successfully on Vietnam veterans suffering from post-traumatic stress syndrome. One theory states that a traumatic visual memory can become stored in the brain and that erratic eye movements indicate links to the frozen memory. For some children, learning to read becomes a traumatic experience.

No matter what the cause of jerky eye movements, the lack of smoothness when tracking print across a page interferes with reading fluency. Eye tracking movements suggested to correct jerkiness have the potential of releasing a child from memories of traumatic experiences. When the movements described below are practiced five minutes a day for 21 days, the eyes should begin to move smoothly across the page. See Eye Tracking in Assessment and Problems.

Visual Tracking Assessment

Directions: All activities are done approximately at arm's length from the student's face. During all eye movements, the student's head should not move. Watch for jerky eye movements, shallow breath, or blinking. If the student is unable to move his or her eyes smoothly, slow down and repeat movement over the jerky area.

Indicate level of mastery by using the following checkmarks: √+ = very good, √ = adequate, and √—= needs improvement.

- Hold a pencil or object at eye level and move it up and down. The student's head should not move. Watch for a smooth eye movement. Slowly repeat areas that are not smooth.
- Horizontally, move the object from side to side.
- Move the object diagonally.
- Move the object in circular motions.

If a child has difficulty with any of the movements above, the child may benefit from short tracking exercises for one to three minutes a day. Check with an eye specialist.

Use of Overlays

When a child suffers during oral reading from miscues, omissions, insertions and repetitions, it is not helpful to advise the child to "sound it out" or "pay attention." If the child has dyslexia or Scotopic Sensitivity Syndrome (SSS), the child is definitely trying very hard and is certainly paying attention to the print. SSS is sometimes referred to as "perceptual dyslexia." The condition occurs when the vibrations from fluorescent lights create a sensation of movement on the page. Glare may also create eye stress and discomfort. It is possible to bring relief with different colored paper, by creating a dimmer computer screen, or by laying colored transparencies over the page. See additional information on SSS in Assessing and Problems.

Assessing Overlays

Some children benefit from placing a colored transparency over the text being read. To determine the usefulness of this practice, follow these steps.

- Cover half of a page with one transparency color and ask, "Which side is sharper, clearer, easier for your eyes to see?"
- If the child chooses the side with the transparency, move it to the opposite side of the page.
- Place a different transparency color where the first one had been.
- Ask, "Which side is sharper, clearer, easier for your eyes to see?"
- Continue to show different transparency colors to the child.
- Continue to alternate sides of the page. With each comparison, ask, "Which side is sharper, clearer, easier for your eyes to see?"

Provide a variety of transparency colors and encourage children to experiment. Those who benefit will continue to use them.

Preparing for Fluency (LAMP)

Teaching Language Arts Mastery Program

For ELL students lacking adequate vocabulary, spend time each day in oral preparation for a new story or section to be read. This concept is from a program called LAMP (Language Arts Mastery Process), developed by Dr. George Gonzalez. The goal of LAMP is to develop competency at the oral level before asking students to attempt decoding print. In addition to ELL students, others will benefit from the oral preparation prior to reading.

Build an auditory base of oral vocabulary development and schema before presenting the written text to the students. For elementary children, use drama and acting as much as possible in order to help them understand and identify with the story plot and vocabulary.

Build Vocabulary Day #1

- Orally present new vocabulary words in a personal way that the students will understand.
- To assist the students in understanding the meaning of the words, use pictures and concrete objects.
- Dramatize the words and invite the students to participate in acting them out.

Read Aloud to Children on Day #1

Build background by reading the story aloud. Children will not see the story print. During this time, they are listening and building oral/aural understanding.

- Ask students to listen without seeing the text and to copy your facial expressions and actions.
- Read with as much expression and as many actions as possible.

Comprehension on Day #1

Main idea focuses on the most important character, tells the most important event in the story and tells when, where, and why it happened. Develop the main idea by writing the following words across the entire board with large spaces between words.

who—what—when—where—why

- Ask the students, "Who is the most important character in the story?" Write the most important character under "who."
- Continue guiding children to build the main idea by asking about the most important event, which will contain the verb. Add when, where, and why to complete one main idea sentence.
- When finished, explain to the students that they have pulled together the significant details to identify the main idea of the story.
- To the tune of "He's Got the Whole World in His Hands," sing, "We've Got the Main Idea in Our Hands."

Expanding Vocabulary Day #2

- Review the vocabulary from Day # 1. Use **realia** by providing concrete objects and dramatization. Realia uses real objects to make vocabulary more meaningful to ELL students. Continue to develop background by writing approximately ten important sentences on separate sentence strips. As on day one, students will not see the text.
- Read one sentence at a time to students. Ask students to "echo" each sentence as they mimic your expressions and actions.
- Some sentences can be repeated by "rapping." Other sentences can be sung, chanted, or whispered.

Comprehension on Day #2

To develop comprehension, ask the students whether the story is a fantasy or a factual account. Assist them in understanding why the story is fact or fantasy.

Mastering Vocabulary and Comprehension Day #3

On day #3, review vocabulary and reread the story using oral close. Students still do not have a copy of the text and will do this activity orally. In oral close, you occasionally leave out a word while reading aloud. Silently point to or touch one student or a group of students who will supply the missing word. Continue reading aloud. Follow oral close by giving one important sentence to each pair of students.

- Pass out sentences to pairs or groups of three. For the first time, children see printed words.
- Ask students to memorize their special sentences (with assistance from you).

- Encourage children to read and re-read sentences until they know them from memory. In addition, children will add motions to use as they recite sentences.
- Each pair or group of three will say its sentence with appropriate actions.

After listening to all sentences, the children will focus on comprehension by arranging sentences into the correct sequence.

Strategies for Oral Fluency

Teaching Echo Reading with Text

Echo Reading (with the text) is a modeling strategy that offers young children an opportunity to hear, see, and read print before reading alone.

- Read one sentence, using expression and phrasing.
- Immediately ask children to read the same sentence.
- Continue one sentence at a time.

Use Echo with primary children and English Language Learners (ELL). Do not use with 3rd grade or above.

Teaching Oral Close

After reading the story aloud to children, tell them you will repeat the story, but this time you will stop occasionally so one or more of the children can read the next word. Steps of Oral Close follow.

- Read orally, then stop and touch a child.
- The child who is touched will read the next word (only one word).
- Continue by reading and choosing different children to read single words.

If used for too long a time, Echo Reading and Oral Close become very boring. Alternate these strategies and add others to maintain interest.

Teaching Musical Reading

When working with emerging readers (and those with strong musical preferences), Musical Reading can open the door to decoding. Usually, teachers rehearse the words to a song and then put them to

Modifications
During Echo Reading and Oral Close, the teacher carries responsibility for reading. In addition, use:
- Enlarged print
- Overlays
- Dim lights
- Colored paper

Encourage the child to use fingers to keep his place.

Modifications
If you initially activate the part of the brain that involves music, you open another avenue for learning. You will be surprised at the benefit music offers to some children.

music. *The key is to sing words first, then ask children to read them.* Singing before teaching words of the song will feel incorrect to you. Trust the strategy.

For very young children, use familiar nursery rhymes or use familiar tunes to teach new words. Print the words of the song in a large font or use chart paper.

- Sing the words to the children. Then ask the children to sing along with you as your hand flows under the line of print. Repeat until children can sing the words.
- Once children can sing the words, ask them to read the lyrics without the melody.

You can use Musical Reading with all ages (including teens) if you adjust the music to meet interests.

Teaching Neurological Impress—NI

Any time you call on a child or even a small group of children to read aloud and discover that fluency and confidence are lacking, immediately join them. Reading slightly faster and louder is known as Neurological Impress (NI). Children have the benefit of hearing the text, seeing the words, and if they use their fingers as guides, touching the page.

Neurological Impress is especially appropriate when working with an individual child who is struggling with the words. When working with an individual child, use your own hand to guide the child's eyes to the correct words.

Dyslexia Modification
In NI, the child uses a multi-sensory approach with seeing print, hearing the words, and either touching the page or watching the teacher run fingers under the line of print.

Teaching Buddy Reading

Buddy Reading is done with partners. Children take turns reading consecutive passages aloud to one another. With very young children, give one a picture of lips and the second, a picture of an ear. The one with lips is the reader. It is helpful if one reader has slightly stronger skills than the other, although you want to avoid pairing readers with very strong skills with children lacking skills.

Modification
Don't give up until you have tried large, larger, and largest print.

Teaching I Read, You Read

The difference in Buddy Reading and I Read, You Read is that in Buddy Reading partners read different paragraphs. In I Read, You Read, the first partner reads a paragraph and the second child re-reads the same material. The emphasis shifts to reading with expression as well as smooth fluency.

Teaching Mumble Reading

Most first graders and many in second grade seem incapable of reading silently. Instead, they read in soft, mumbling voices. Mumble Reading is appropriate for early readers who need auditory input. It is also appropriate for Buddy Reading (see above). One of the best ways to improve fluency is for children to reread favorite passages using Mumble Reading.

Teaching Reader's Theater

Because research indicates that the best way to improve oral fluency is to read a short, favorite piece repeatedly, it is important to plan reasons for students to re-read passages. Most children with fluency challenges do not want to re-read material. One of the easiest ways to convince reluctant children to read a selection repeatedly is to create a dramatization (Reader's Theater). Children get to practice the same basic parts, by reading and re-rereading character scripts as in a play.

Gifted and talented children may choose to convert story text to a Reader's Theater by typing into a computer. Children can also become involved in creating props, costumes, and musical accompaniments. A Reader's Theater can be as simple or as involved as you choose to make it.

Although older students will resist, they enjoy a reader's theater as much as the younger children. The only requirement is to choose reading that is socially and developmentally appropriate for older students. Shakespeare's plays work beautifully.

Creating a Reader's Theater

Your first step is to locate a narrative story with appropriate content and vocabulary for the ages of your children. Choose a book that falls into the "independent" reading level for most of your group. Be sure to choose a story and section with both action and dialogue. Stories with several characters work best. When creating a Reader's Theater, keep all parts short.

Depending on the font size and the ages of the children, a typical Reader's Theater will be four to eight pages in length. Retype the story to include a narrator (who will read all background descriptions). In addition, type the scripts of all characters. Do not use quotation marks.

- Use a large print for easy reading. For primary children, use Times 22 as a guide. Older elementary children can read Times 20. For middle school and senior high children, drop to Times 18 or 16. It is better to err on the side of using a font that is too

GT Modification

Encourage better readers, who do not struggle with words, to embellish on the drama of a story.

Modification for Scatopic Sensitivity Syndrome

Try placing overlays on top of print.

The eyes of children with SSS do not work well in bright, fluorescent lighting.

SSS Modification

If a child crawls under a table to read, the child may be attempting to get away from the fluorescent light. You will quickly know if the dimmer light helps the child or if the child is trying to avoid work.

large than one that is too small for the reader's eyes to decode easily.

- Leave spaces between character parts. Type names of characters on the left and dialogue on the right. Keeping lines short helps children stay on track.

	Title
Child. 1	Script. Script
Child 2	Script. Script
Child 3	Script. Script

You may take liberty when converting a narrative story into a dramatization. Possibilities for changes include the list below:

- Change some of the narrator's words into a new character.
- Create Narrator 1 and Narrator 2.
- Substitute easier vocabulary.
- Reduce length of sentences.

Organization

Assign a part to each child. If you have more children than you do parts, set up two or three Reader's Theater groups. Although different groups may be practicing the same script, each group will have a very different interpretation. An alternative is to create a series of scripts that cover the entire story.

Give each child a copy of the entire script with the part assigned to that child highlighted.

Teaching Reader's Theater

- Initially, ask children to read through their parts several times, emphasizing only the words. Ask children to use Mumble Reading to practice individually. Model Mumble Reading and indicate places for children to practice parts alone.
- During the second practice session, ask children to read the script together and to read with expression. Model monotone reading and contrast by modeling expressive oral reading.

Dyslexia Modification
   If you have a child who needs larger print, use the larger font for the entire class. Some children with learning differences read more easily from lightly colored paper such as beige, light blue, or lavender.

- Finally, ask children to practice the entire drama with expression, action, and drama. Model expressive reading with the addition of actions. Be dramatic so your children will follow your example.

Teaching Assisted Reading

Assisted Reading provides another method of modeling the way good readers sound. Unlike Echo and Oral Close, children share an equal responsibility for decoding print using Assisted Reading. For this reason, Assisted Reading is more appropriate for guided reading than for shared reading. The strategy can be used with an individual or with a group of children. Assisted reading is also appropriate for middle school and high school students.

When using Assisted Reading with an individual, simply alternate reading orally. When using with a group or class, add variety to maintain interest. For example, after you read, you can call on one student, a pair, a small group, all boys, or everyone wearing red.

- Read one paragraph aloud as children follow the text with their eyes and fingers.
- Ask a group to read the next paragraph in unison.
- Resume by reading the third paragraph aloud.
- For the fourth paragraph, ask a pair to read.

Occasionally, ask an individual child to read a paragraph. Do *not* go from child to child. This practice is called Round Robin Reading and is boring for all and humiliating for some. Before and after asking a child or children to read, you must read orally to maintain the flow and model fluency.

DEAR—Listening to Recorded Reading

Drop Everything And Read (DEAR), which is sometimes called Sustained Silent Reading (SSR), benefits students in two ways: it enables them to bond reading with pleasure, and it stresses the importance of reading. DEAR requires everyone in the classroom (or better yet, everyone in the school) to stop all activity and read at the same time each day for approximately 15 minutes. The only requirement is that the reading material must be chosen by the reader and must be pleasurable. Questions and reports should not be included.

The program works well for all students except for nonreaders. For nonreaders, the time spent silently *pretending* to read is frustrating and stressful. Encourage children with poor fluency to listen to commercial or teacher-made CDs or tapes as their eyes and fingers follow the line of

ELL Modification
When you read a paragraph or section before asking students to read, you model good reading.

Modeling helps students with learning differences and ELL students.

Dyslexia Modification
IF a student visually follows words, while sliding a finger under the line of print, the listening process results in a strong modification.

Even if the child only listens without looking at the print, the child will gain comprehension.

print. If you choose to use DEAR in your classroom, take care of your nonreaders and be certain that they read using auditory assistance.

During DEAR, you should read also. Avoid using the quiet time to grade papers or write lesson plans. Marie Carbo developed a plan for creating and using recordings.

Creating Tapes

Marie Carbo originally designed Carbo recorded reading after discovering the benefits of allowing a child with weak skills to listen repeatedly to a short passage that had been recorded for her. After noting the student's rapid progress, Carbo began recording short selections for her student every day. From this beginning with an elementary student, the Carbo reading strategy developed and is now used with first graders through adults.

For repeated home and school practice, record short sections and ask students to *listen a minimum of three times* before reading to the teacher. When creating recordings, remember to do the following:

- Record only one section for approximately five minutes. Often shorter sections result in better results.
- Label the CD carefully so that your students will be able to locate each recording.
- State the name of the story and the exact page numbers included on the recording.
- In a whispered voice, tell the students, "Turn to page _____."
- At the end of the recording, tell the students that the selection is finished and it is time to rewind the tape and listen again.
- Ask the students how to improve the recordings.

Teaching Join-In

Join-in reading works best with poems and can be used with small groups or with whole class lessons. Join-in requires significant coaching and modeling at first, but it's worth the initial effort. Demonstrate a slow, steady pace so all can participate. Don't give up if this strategy does not work the first time! Explain the strategy in the following manner, using students' names.

- "I will read the first line to model pace and expression."
- "Student #1 will read the next line aloud with me." (Touch and name the student.)
- "Student #2 will join us on the third line." Say, "Now there will be three of us reading together." (Touch and name both students.)

ELL Modification
Read slowly, in phrases, to help children with learning differences and ELL students.

- "Student #3 will join the first two on the next line." Say, "Now there will be four of us reading together." (Touch and name each student.)
- Students continue to join the group one at a time until the end of the poem is reached.
- As you explain where to read, ask each student to put a finger or marker on the line where he or she will join the reading.

Throughout the reading, continue to read along with each child or group in order to maintain an appropriate pace. Lead with your voice and gesture for each child to begin reading. You will set the pace and tone by always reading with the children.

Whole Class Cooperative Learning

When using this strategy with the whole class, groups will replace individual students. Say, "I will read first. Group #1 will join me on line 2. Group #2 will join us on line 3." As with individual reading, you will model volume and speed for each step by leading with your voice. Gesture when the time comes for each group to join the reading.

Technology and Fluency

Technology and Modifications

According to Dr. David Rose, a major problem with reading lies with **print disability (PD)** rather than with learning disabilities in children. With the use of digital print, you can expand on recorded books. Explore *The Tortoise and Hare* on CAST UDL Book Builder at <*http://bookbuilder.cast.org/*>. (The book is listed as the Spotlight Book.) In addition, locate a list of books under "Model Books" and "Public Library Books" on the same site. As you examine the various books, you will discover the following features.

Dyslexia Modification
The ability to modify print materials will be one of the finest possible modifications for students with dyslexia. Take advantage of this opportunity to order and/or create digital textbooks.

Benefits to Readers

Features in Digital Print	Benefits
Books are printed with large, easy to read fonts.	Large print helps students with dyslexia.
The story can be read orally to the students.	Oral presentations provide another avenue for children who are hearing impaired, ELL students as well as for those with dyslexia.
The original version of the story is available for comparison.	GT students can compare and contrast the two versions.

92

An area is available for a student to type a prediction.	Making predictions is a good practice for all readers.
The student can listen as the page is read aloud.	The option to listen will benefit students with dyslexia as well as ELL students.
Clicking on one of the underlined words brings up the glossary.	The glossary is especially helpful to ELL students.
Words in the text are available in an alphabetical glossary. Each word in the glossary includes a real-life picture and explanation.	A glossary benefits all students and is especially helpful to ELL students.
The glossary sometimes includes advanced information about vocabulary.	The advanced definition serves GT students.
Three characters are available to help and make suggestions.	Suggestions are available to help all students.
Words in the text can be read in a variety of languages.	Translations are helpful for ELL students.
Books can be made available in Braille and in Spanish.	Braille provides a way for blind children to access books.

Book Building with Differentiation

On the <CAST.org/bookbuilder> site, you have the option to create your own digital books with modifications. According to Rose, by modifying digitally, you remove the PD (print disability) for many children. By using digital media, you can get every student in the proximal learning zone (Vygosky).

Rose states that congress created the term "print disabilities" and established NIMAS (National Instructional Materials Accessibility Standards), a source of digital textbooks. If you order digital textbooks for a child in your classroom, the publishers will be charged.

Frequent Fluency Miscues

The word "miscue" indicates that a reading mistake has been made because one of three "cues" was missed. Cues come from: 1) attention to phonetic sound-to-symbol connections, 2) grammar and word order, and 3) meaning. Below are some specific miscues (mistakes) commonly made when reading orally. Following each type of miscue, you will find suggestions for guiding the student.

Miscue (Reading Error)	Guidelines for Responding
Omits a word	**Omitted** words are left out. Unless the omitted word changes the meaning of the text, allow the child to continue reading. Write down the word that was omitted and at a later time, determine whether or not to teach the word.
Inserts non-meaningful words	**Insertions** add words. If the insertion does not work grammatically, ask, "Does that sound right? Is that the way we talk?" If the insertion changes the meaning, ask, "Does that make sense?"
Substitutes a wrong word.	**Substitutions** are incorrect words. If the word makes sense and works grammatically, allow the child to continue reading. If not, use the questions suggested for insertions.
Repeats words or phrases	**Repetitions**, rereading the same phrase or sentence, sometimes indicates lack of confidence. Try an easier book. Model phrasing and ask the student to echo you. To discourage **regressions** (re-reading a line of print), teach the child to push the eyes down the page by placing two fingers just above the line of print.
Word-by-word, slow reading	Ask, "How would you say that?" Encourage the child to re-read a favorite part, using good phrasing. Rereading short sections is more beneficial than repeating longer sections.
Very slow reading	Marie Carbo suggests using teacher-made or commercial recordings for students who read very slowly. Recorded reading must be slow enough for the student to follow easily. A student should re-read each short section multiple times until reaching the appropriate rate for the student's age.

Ignores punctuation	Teach movements to emphasize question marks, periods and explanation marks. • Ask child to shrug to dramatize a question mark. • Encourage the child to clap for an explanation mark. • Tell the child to hold up a hand to indicate, "Halt" for a period. Highlight ending punctuation. If you cannot highlight a book, use removable colored tape to highlight punctuation marks. In addition, model reading without punctuation first and then model correctly.
Reverses words or parts of words	Place a green dot on the left side of the page or at the left of a word that is frequently reversed. Ask, "How will your mouth look when you say the first sound of this word?"
Poor sight vocabulary	Encourage the child to study 3 words at a time. Add dramatic memory aids to each of the three words (color code word parts that are hard to recall, add movement, and/or attach an object to each word). After each set of three, review the set. If the child shows uncertainty, spend more time on that set before adding additional words.
Student loses place	Encourage the student to use one or two fingers to track words. Guszak warns against using paper markers, which block important information above and below the line of print being read.

Dr. Guszak, reading professor at the University of Texas, Austin, recommends using repeated reading and taped books for students with very poor fluency. If a student fails to improve after rereading taped materials, use easier reading materials or **predictable** books, which are books that repeat key phrases or words. Guszak also suggests that if a student continues to exhibit halting oral reading, test the silent reading rate. There are some students who will never read well orally but who can maintain good fluency and comprehension when allowed to read silently.

Dyslexia Modification
Allowing a child to read silently instead of orally is a form of modification.

Predictable books help hesitant readers.

Summarizing the Fluency Dragon

Surface Dyslexia and Fluency

Children with Surface Dyslexia are so proficient with phonics that they use this skill exclusively for all areas of decoding. When confronted with irregular words that do not follow phonemic rules, the emphasis on sounding out words falls apart. In the process, fluency is also damaged.

Treatment for Outlaws

In order to help the child who over-uses phonics, circle irregular words or cover them with colored, reusable tape. Say, "These are outlaw words (Open Court® term). Stop, look and listen when you see a circled (or covered) word. This word will NOT allow you to sound it out." The purpose of this activity is to encourage the child to take an educated guess and continue reading.

Grounding

Another important way to help children with Surface Dyslexia is to use Grounding. During the "point to . . ." step, choose irregular words for the child to locate. As you examine an irregular word with the child, point out the impossibility of sounding it out.

Think Aloud

Due to auditory strengths, children with Surface Dyslexia also benefit from a teacher's Think Aloud and will strive to copy the thinking modeled by the teacher.

Deep Dyslexia and Fluency

Although a child with Deep Dyslexia will gain good comprehension, the child will stammer and struggle to read orally. You may choose to adopt the attitude that as long as the child has good comprehension, you will not make an issue out of fluency. How many professions require oral reading? Not many.

On the other hand, you may believe you owe it to the child to do everything possible to improve oral fluency. Children with Deep Dyslexia are eligible for textbooks with large print as well as the talking books that are recorded for blind students. The alternative electronic modifications from CAST (Center for Applied Special Technology) will be more useful than materials from the Library of Congress for the Blind.

Fluency Help Surface *and* Deep Fluency

Additional ideas that benefit both types of dyslexia in the area of fluency include the suggestions below:

- Arrange Buddy Reading with peers.
- You can also use personally made or commercial recordings for the child to listen to and follow along with eyes and fingers.
- When using Reader's Theater, give the child a short part and encourage the child to repeat the section until it is almost memorized.

Word Blindness (Surface and Deep)

A more dramatic procedure compares the characteristics of students with Deep Dyslexia with behaviors of children with weak vision. Both groups experience "word blindness," which is a term coined by Dr. Samuel Orton in the 1800's. Children with Deep and Surface Dyslexia may benefit from the following ideas.

- Enlarge the print (to approximately Times 22).
- Experiment with various colored overlays.
- Encourage the child to touch the line of print.
- Copy text on a vertical surface.
- Provide a surface slanted approximately 30 degrees to prop reading material.
- Ask children to read and reread short passages using fingers to guide the eyes.

DEAR

If you use Drop Everything and Read (DEAR) in your room, provide recorded books for children with fluency problems. Otherwise, these children will be tempted to fake reading by turning pages when children in their area turn theirs. Encourage each child to follow the print with fingers while listening to recorded passages. If a child is unable or unwilling to follow the print while listening, you do not need to make this an issue.

Scotopic Sensitivity Syndrome

Another cause of fluency problems is **Scotopic Sensitivity Syndrome** (SSS). Although SSS is not the same as dyslexia, it often occurs in children with learning differences. SSS is not a visual acuity problem or even a challenge with **visual discrimination**, which is an inability to notice subtle differences in letters that look similar. Light rays from fluorescent lights (found in most classrooms) cause print to appear to vibrate or move. Children who display the symptoms below probably suffer from SSS.

If the child's eyes become red and irritated when reading or if the child complains about the letters moving, the child may be struggling with the light rays and print. You may also notice a child whose eyes tear when reading. Other signals come from the child who dims the light on the computer screen or who crawls under a table to read.

Children with these characteristics may benefit from colored overlays placed over the print or from printing text on colored paper. Overlays can be ordered from the Irlen Institute found in the bibliography. Allow the child to experiment each day to identify the color that helps the most. Initially, every child in your classroom will want a colored overlay. Eventually, the interest will pass and only the one or two children who need overlays will continue to choose them. Although many experts claim there is one perfect color for each child with SSS, experience suggests that the rays from natural light, amount of sleep and even allergies may alter color preferences. Always enlarge the print for children with Deep or Surface Dyslexia or with SSS.

Bibliography

Anderson, David, S. O'Neal, C. David, and P. Oruonyehu. *Dyslexia and Related Disorders*. Austin, Texas: Texas Education Agency, 1998.

Besner, D. "Deep Dyslexia and Right Hemiesphere Hypothesis." Can J Psychol 1983; Vol. 34, No. 4, pp. 565-571.

Boushey, G. and J. Moser "the sisters." *The Daily 5*. Portland MA: Stenhouse, 2006.

Carbo, Marie. *Reading Styles Inventory Manual*. Roslyn Heights, NY: National Reading Styles Institute, 1991.

Carlson. "Types of Dyslexia." *Welcome to the Dyslexia Homepage*. Macalester College, 1998.
<http://www.macalester.edu/psychology/whathap/UBNRP/Dyslexia/index.html>

CAST UDL Book Builder. Massachusetts Department of Elementary and Secondary Education, 2006-2011.
<http://bookbuilder.cast.org/>

Castles, A. and M. Coltheart. *Varieties of Developmental Dyslexia*. Cognition, 47, 149-180, 1993.
<http://www.maccs.mq.edu.au/~max/AcqDys/SD.htm>

Danger, C. "Assessment, Training and Tutoring Services" *Better Living Through Technology*. England: Brighton University, 2000.

Ekwall, E. and J. Shanker. *Teaching Reading in the Elementary School*. Columbus, OH: Merrill Publishing Co., 1989.

Frandsen, B. and S. Smith. *Dyslexia Analysis*. Austin, TX: Family School, 1990.
<http://www.teachersalley.com> (choose Dyslexia Analysis)

—. *Diversified Teaching: An Anthology of Teaching Strategies*. Austin, TX: Family School, 1993

—*Yes! I Can Teach Literacy*. Austin, Texas: Family School, 2006.

Fountas, Irene and G. Su Pinnell. *Guided Reading*. Portsmouth, NH: Heinemann, 1996.

Funnell, Elaine. "Surface Dyslexia." *Dictionary of Biological Psychology*. 1985.

Gambrell, Linda, L. Morrow, S. Neuman, and M. Pressley. *Best Practices in Literacy Instruction*. New York, NY: The Guilford Press, 1999.

Gonzalez, George. *Language Arts Mastery Process*. McAllen, TX: Scott, Foresman, 1993.

Gunning, Thomas G. *Creating Reading Instruction for All Children*. Boston, MA: Allyn & Bacon, 2003.

Guszak, Frank. *Reading for Students with Special Needs*. Dubuque, Iowa: Kendall/Hunt Publishing Company, 1997.

Hayes, John A. *Right Dyslexia Glasses* (different from Irlen lenses). Atlantic Beach, FL32233. <http://www.dyslexiaglasses.com>

Hittlemann, Daniel R. *Developmental Reading, K-8*. Columbus, OH: Merrill Publishing, 1983.

Hynd, Cynthia R. *Instruction of Reading Disabled/Dyslexic Students* (Teacher Education and Practice, Fall/Winter 1986-87).

Irlen, Helen. *Reading By the Colors*. Garden City Park, NY: Avery Publishing Group, 1991.

Johns, J. and Berglund, R. *Fluency Strategies and Assessments*. Dubuque, IA: Kendall/Hunt Publishers, 2006.

Lytton, W.W. and J.C.M. Brust. *Direct Dyslexia: Preserved Oral Reading of Real Words in Wernicke's Aphasia,* New York: Colunbia University College, 1988. *<http://brain.oxfordjournals.org>*

Marzano, R. and J. Pickering, and J. Pollock. *Classroom Instruction that Works: Research-based Strategies for Increasing Student Achievement*. Upper Saddle, NJ: Pearson, 2005.

NCTE *National Council of Teachers of English*. Newark, Delaware #151: International Reading Association.

Pytel, Barbara. "Scotopic Sensitivity Syndrome." Educational Issues: 2006. http://www.suite101.com/content/scotopics ensitivitysyndrome-a1537

Rose, David. "AIM Center at a Glance." National Center on *Accessible Instructional Materials:* Wakefield, MA. 2011.

—"Universal Design for Learning (UDL)." *Center for Applied Special Technology (CAST):* Wakefield, Massachusetts, 2009. http://www. youtube.com/watch?v=EAKSvBkjC-o

Webb, T. and D. Webb. *Accelerated Learning with Music*. Norcross, GA: Accelerated Learning Systems,1990.

Wilson, Stephen, S. Brambati, H. Roland. "The Neural Basis of Surface Dyslexia in Semantic Dementia." *Brain a Journal of Neurology*. Oxford Journals. 2009. <http://brain.oxfordjournals.org/content/132/1/71.abstract>

Wolf, M. & Katzir-Cohen, T. "Reading fluency and its intervention." *Scientific Studies of Reading*. (Special Issue on Fluency. Editors: E. Kameenui & D. Simmons). 5: 211-238. 2001.

Zintz, M. and M. Zelda. *The Reading Process: The Teacher and the Learner*. Dubuque, IA: Brown Publishers, 1970.

Slaying the Comprehension Dragon

Children lacking prior knowledge often face comprehension problems. Lack of motivation, inadequate intelligence and language differences also become obstacles to perception. In addition, children must come to school well fed and with adequate sleep to succeed.

An additional barrier, **Direct Dyslexia,** presents a greater challenge. Imagine a child who decodes any word that fits the rules of the language, recognizes irregular words, and reads well orally. The illusion of good reading ends once the child is unable to answer questions about the reading material or to retell events from the text.

Surface Dyslexia is another type of dyslexia that creates problems with comprehension. **Surface Dyslexia** puzzles teachers because, although the child has good phonics skills, comprehension declines when more irregular words are included in texts.

Comprehension and Dyslexia

What is Comprehension?

Comprehension always involves thinking and is synonymous with understanding. Whether comprehending a single word, a paragraph, a story, or an entire book, comprehension always focuses on gaining the message intended by the author. True reading requires the brain to decode the squiggles we call letters and to bring meaning to the task.

There are children who read the words beautifully but are unable to recall what was read or answer questions about the topic. These children sound proficient but they are not readers. Other children find that it is very difficult to break the code and read the words but gain understanding if you read to them. Both decoding the letters and understanding the meaning are required for reading to take place.

Teaching comprehension is much more than asking questions at the end of the passage. Although some children seem to automatically engage in the kind of thinking required for comprehension, others do not. Comprehending is not always intuitive; however, it can be modeled and taught.

What Does Research Indicate?

According to the National Reading Panel, students benefit when instruction focuses on reading as a problem-solving task. The panel suggests that students can be taught how to think when solving various reading challenges such as finding a main idea. Strategies, (which are not skills), can be used as plans to acquire understanding. Although strategies (plans) present guidance, you must avoid using them rigidly. Teaching thinking overrides teaching strategies.

Prior Schema and Comprehension

Never have teachers had access to as many video recordings as today. Include videos to fill in some of the gaps left by lack of real-life experiences. If you have children who have not had the bedtime reading experience, seat them as close to you as possible as you read aloud. You want to copy an experience that bonds reading and pleasure.

Prior schema, the background information a child brings to learning, contributes to reading comprehension. Schema involves making connections between what a child knows and new information. When reading a story about a park, a child who has never been to the park lacks a knowledge base on which to connect new information. In order to help fill in missing information, early childhood teachers provide many real and vicarious experiences through field trips, films, guest speakers, and by reading to children.

One way to teach children how to comprehend involves asking **predicting** questions before beginning reading as well as throughout the passage or story. Asking for predictions helps activate schema, sets a purpose for reading, and encourages thinking. A closely related activity involves teaching children how to create their own questions before and during reading.

In the section below, you will read several comprehension strategies. Keep in mind three powerful concepts: visualization, metacognition (thinking about and sharing your own thoughts), and using questions to promote thinking.

Comprehension Strategies

Visualization

When you read a novel, do you imagine how the hero looks? Can you mentally see the action that takes place as you read the words? Children who do not "run movies" as they read generally do not understand and will not recall ideas from the text. **Visualization** creates a powerful way to improve comprehension.

What Does the Research Indicate?

The National Reading Panel claims that you must teach cognitive processes, including visualization, that lead to understanding. Research further indicates that when students begin to imagine what they are reading, comprehension improves.

The National Reading Panel recommends strengthening the visualization process by teaching students to connect a key word or phrase to the vision being internalized.

One Way to Explain Visualizing

Several methods can be used to explain visualization to children. One method begins by sharing colorful objects that can be handled as well as seen. After allowing children to see, touch and describe the items, ask children to close their eyes and "see" items on the "magic screens behind their eyes." Most children will be able to recall and describe what they "see" with eyes closed. If more clarity is needed, ask children, "Do you remember what you saw? Can you remember how it looked?" When teaching visualization, use words related to vision and seeing.

Graduate from solid objects that can be handled to objects at a distance such as pets, their mothers, or their favorite toys. Point out that the children are describing items that cannot be seen at this time because of the distance. Their descriptions come from mental pictures—visions that exist in their heads.

ELL Modification

A common practice when teaching ELL students is to bring real objects and experiences into the classroom. This practice, called **"realia,"** benefits ELL students and also others who struggle with comprehension. Realia strengthens visualization by ensuring understanding.

Second Way to Explain Visualization

There is no need to cover pictures in a story when teaching visualization. In fact, the pictures will add clarity to students who rely on visual clues as well as for ELL students. The challenge is to see the characters or ideas in motion.

Another powerful method of explaining visualization involves asking children to describe favorite movie or television characters. After a child describes a favorite character, point out that it was not necessary to go to the theater to describe the character. Say, "It's like there is a magic screen behind your eyes."

Teaching With TV Recall

A psychologist created a method to help his 14-year old son improve comprehension. Knowing his son loved to play baseball, he seated the teenager in front of a blank television set and began to read a baseball story to him. The father instructed his son to pretend he was watching the story on television. After a brief time, he announced a commercial break and asked his son to tell him what he had seen on his imaginary television. The son recalled everything he had pretended to see as his father read to him. Gradually, the father increased the amount read between commercial breaks. Ultimately, his son was able to use the television analogy when he read the words for himself. Read the steps below.

Steps to TV Recall

Children who prefer visual input usually respond well to visualization in TV Recall. Children who need auditory input can focus on listening. Ask children to pretend to view television as you read to them. In doing so, you place all of their energy on listening and comprehending.

- Set a Purpose. "The purpose is to create pictures and visual movies in your head as you listen."
- Read a short passage to children and announce a commercial break.
- Ask children what they saw on their imaginary televisions. Suggest that children connect a key word or phrase to the mental images such as "first inning, homerun, pitching curve ball." The word or phrase will strengthen long-term recall.
- As you continue teaching the process, gradually lengthen the time between commercial breaks.
- After practicing several times, tell children that they can use the imaginary television even when they read the words for themselves.

Print Modification
Many students with reading disabilities need a copy of each text to highlight and annotate. The physical act of highlighting often assists students with disabilities. If you cannot guide the highlighting process, prepare a copy in advance. Ask yourself, "What essential points must every student understand?" Highlight the most basic concepts for students with reading disabilities. Limit assessment to the areas highlighted.

Think Aloud

Another way to teach how to comprehend involves sharing your own thought processes with children. Good readers systematically notice if their minds wander while decoding words. When you notice that you are not paying attention while reading, you know to re-read the passage and direct your thoughts. If you come to a word you do not know, you notice that you do not recognize the word. You may look the word up in a dictionary. Most of the time, you take an educated guess and continue reading, hoping that the content will indicate whether your guess was correct. Sharing your own cognitive processes—thoughts, questions, and feelings with children provides an example or model that they can adopt.

What Does Research Indicate?

Children who prefer to learn through auditory channels usually respond well to Think Aloud lessons. Modify for visual learners by providing pictures. The National Reading Panel suggests strongly that teachers provide specific, personal examples of thinking processes. The goal is for students to begin to copy and use the teacher's examples. **Metacomprehension** means that a reader engages in "self-monitoring" and realizes whether or not understanding is taking place during reading. With this realization comes the ability to deliberately shift strategies in order to facilitate comprehension. This strategy called Think Aloud (or Reading Think Aloud) models five types of reflection: predicting, describing visualization, making analogies, verbalizing confusion, and modeling strategies to help with confusion.

Teaching Think Aloud

The act of thinking aloud is a form of modification. You literally demonstrate how to think when reading. Most students intuitively know this. For those who do not know how to think when reading, your model provides an example. A Think Aloud focuses on what you say and do as you model the kind of thinking done by good readers. As you teach, you share your own thoughts. It is your intention that students will gradually begin to copy the type of thinking you are sharing. Ideally, students will develop their own metacognition. Below, you will find five examples to use. Tell students, "Good readers engage in this kind of thinking."

- *Predict* by using the title, pictures, and opening sentences. "From the title, I believe this part will be about . . ."

GT Modification
Encourage GT students to challenge themselves by asking the following questions.

"Am I bored?"

"What part do I already know?"

"What else do I want to know about this topic?"

"I'll ask the teacher if I can skip the part I know and study something new about this topic."

- *Describe* the picture that is forming internally. "In my mind, I see . . ."
- *Make analogies* by linking prior knowledge to new information. "This word is like . . ." (Compare the new word to another easily recognized word.)
- *Verbalize confusion* by pretending lack of understanding. "This doesn't make sense to me. I'm not certain what the author is suggesting."
- *Model strategies* to assist with decoding or comprehension. "I'd better read this part again," or "Perhaps if I read this section aloud, I will understand it better," or "If I think about the way we talk, I may be able to read this sentence better."

Although you have freedom to "think aloud" in other ways, the bulleted examples above provide strong examples for you to follow.

Question Generation Strategies

When you ask students to make up their own questions for the purpose of stumping you or their peers, they also need to locate the correct answers. The process of creating questions and finding their own answers strengthens one type of thinking needed for comprehension.

What Does Research Indicate?

According to the National Reading Panel, research indicates a correlation between **question generation** during reading and good comprehension and memory. Teaching students to create their own questions and identify their own answers promotes independent and active readers. "There is strong empirical and scientific evidence that instruction of question generation during reading benefits reading comprehension in terms of memory and answering questions based upon text as well as integrating and identifying main ideas" (National Reading Panel).

Teaching Self-Monitoring Strategies

Until a child can self-monitor, the child must depend on outside feedback to correct mistakes. Teaching self-monitoring encourages metacognition. To initiate and encourage self-monitoring, model the following questions.

- "Did that sound right?"
- After a word is missed ask, "Where is the tricky word?"
- "Why did you stop? Did something sound wrong to you?"

ELL Modification

Teach ELL students to ask themselves the following questions.

"Are there words I do not understand?"

"Should I take an educated guess or ask for help?"

"The word I said begins with the sound /m/. The word begins with the letter (n). Something must be wrong."

As a teacher, say:
- "Try again and think about what would make sense or sound right."
- "What could you try?"
- "What do you know that might help?"

- "Can you find out what the problem is?"
- "Did you look at the picture?"
- "Do we talk that way?"

Students' In-the-Head Questions

As children become good readers, they consciously or unconsciously engage in interactions with print and meaning. Teach students to ask themselves a few in-the-head thinking strategies such as the ones listed below.

- Good readers expect and check for meaning. Teach the children to ask, "Does this make sense?"
- Good readers notice whether the language structure matches expectations. "Is this the way we talk?"
- Facts from the text are compared with other sources of information. "Does the information match what I already know about this subject?"

Good readers make self-corrections by monitoring themselves. "If I say a different word, will the passage sound better or make more sense?"

Teaching With Reciprocal Teaching

Reciprocal teaching, which the National Reading Panel recommends, builds on Question Generation. Initially, you will demonstrate appropriate questions. Model and identify types of questions many times, before expecting students to complete questions from prompts or ask their own questions.

Types of Questions	Examples Modeled by Teachers
Predicting	"Based on the title, subtitles and pictures, what do you think this story will be about?" Ask students to continue asking predicting questions throughout the reading.
Questioning	During reading, good readers ask questions about what they are reading. "What is important?" "I wonder where this is leading?"

Clarifying	Readers often come across words that are confusing. Tell students to note confusing words, make educated guesses and continue reading. Thoughtful guesses can often clarify meaning.
Summarizing	"What are the most important parts of this text?" Summarizing guides concentration and organization.

Immediately after modeling each type of question, ask a student to provide another example. Discuss positive attributes of the question with the class.

Model Inappropriate Questions

Indicate inappropriate requests such as, "What is the fifth word on page ten?" In addition, advise students to only ask questions that can be answered by reading the passage. After modeling appropriate and inappropriate questions, follow the steps below.

- Ask a child who tends to want attention to think of another example of an inappropriate question.
- Hopefully, the student and the class will notice humor in the incorrect question. Point out reasons why the question represents what *not* to do when asking questions.
- Ask the same child who modeled incorrectly, to think of an appropriate question. Review and prompt if necessary.
- Discuss the quality of questions and guide children to discuss ways to improve questions.

Providing Prompts

Types of Questions	Prompts for Student Completion
Predicting	"When you look at the pictures, titles and subtitles, what thoughts run through your head? Can you complete the following, "Based on the title, what . . . ?"
Questioning	During reading, ask students to complete the following question. "Does anyone feel confused? Can you make up a question about your confusion?"
Clarifying	"List words that you are not certain you know. Can you form a question about one of the words?"

Summarizing	"Think about the main character and what is happening. Can you make up a summarizing question?"

Allow students to complete or develop questions by responding to your prompts. Eventually, expect students to create their own questions without your guidance. Below is another strategy that expects children to generate questions.

Teaching With ReQuest

After teaching students to ask good questions through Reciprocal Teaching, teach students to use ReQuest, a similar strategy. ReQuest encourages children to "stump the teacher" by creating and asking their own questions. The goal is for students to exhibit the same thinking processes and questions that you modeled in Think Aloud and Reciprocal Reading. When using ReQuest, follow the same guidelines that were suggested in Reciprocal Reading. Challenge children to "think like teachers" as they create and ask questions.

Usually, ReQuest works better with small groups than with individuals. Ask each group to create three questions. Before a group is allowed to ask the first question, the group members must know the answer to the question and the location in the text. Follow the steps below.

- The first group asks its first question. If you can answer correctly, the second group gets a chance to ask a question and attempt to stump you.
- If any group stumps you, the group asks a second question. Once again, if you do not know the answer, the group will ask its third and final question. If you are unable to answer any of the three questions, the group has truly "stumped the teacher."
- After each question that you do not answer, ask the group to guide you and the class to the correct information in the text.

Teaching Question the Author

Teachers are expected to teach students how to question the author. Research by McKeown, Beck and Sandora indicate that when students think in terms of questioning the author, their comprehension improves (Crawley, 198). Begin by confessing that sometimes authors do not clarify or explain exactly what they intend. Encourage students to notice when they are confused and consider a question for the writer. Below are a few examples of questions for authors.

- What is the author trying to tell us?
- Does this information make sense compared to a text read earlier?

Dysgraphia Modification
In order to make the questions for the author more meaningful, use a few with students when individual writing pieces are shared. Show novice writers how the same questions can be used for experts and beginners.

113

- Why did the author tell us this information?
- Did the author explain this part clearly?
- How might the author word this part for better understanding?

If you could advise the author, what would you suggest? (Allington, 149)

Sequence for Questioning the Author

Teach students to question the author by following the steps below.

- Divide the text into short sections. Consider one part at a time.
- Model appropriate questions. "If the author could join us, I would ask . . ."
- Initially, ask students to read each short section at least one or two times for the purpose of identifying confusion and possible questions.
- After considering questions and discussing the author's intentions, lead students to summarize each part.

Story Structure & Strategies

Fiction stories rely on four areas of development: characters, setting, problem and solution. By using the same basic structure, students grasp the concept that this is the way fiction stories operate. Understanding the concept helps with comprehending and later with writing fiction stories.

What Does the Research Indicate?

The National Reading Panel suggests teaching story structure as a way to help students understand text. The goal is broader than checking to see if children can remember details from a reading selection. The goal becomes teaching a structure, which will guide thinking during current and future reading experiences. Narrative Comprehension suggests a structure for fiction stories.

Teaching Narrative Comprehension

Although Narrative Comprehension appears similar to finding the main idea, the difference lies in identifying all of the characters, everything about setting, all related problems, and the steps toward solving the problems. Main idea focuses on the most important aspect in the story such as the most important character.

GT Modification
Use the basic NC strategy with GT and older students as a pre-writing activity rather than the complete assignment.

114

Variations for Younger Age Groups

In order for younger children to benefit from Narrative Comprehension, use the following explanations of characters, settings, problems, and solutions.

- Characters are the people or animals in the story.
- The setting is where the story takes place and what time events happen in the story.
- Problems sometimes make people feel unhappy. Unhappiness can come from anger, fights, or fears.
- Solutions are good ideas about ways to fix unhappiness.

With young children teach one part of Narrative Comprehension at a time. For example, begin with characters and spend as much as a week exploring different characters. While reading to children, use Think Aloud to make comments about the characters. After reading aloud, help children list all of the characters in the story. Once children understand characters, introduce and explain setting.

Some stories may involve several aspects of setting. If so, include them all. During reading, repeat the same process by using Think Aloud to verbalize information about settings. Following reading, help children list all the aspects of setting that apply.

Repeat the process for problems and again for solutions. In some cases, there may be more than one challenge and several steps toward solving problems. Many options exist for written responses to Narrative Comprehension including the examples listed below.

- *Lists:* Make lists of all of the characters, all aspects of the setting, and ideas concerning problems and solutions in the appropriate areas. For younger children, the lists will be the entire writing lesson. In addition, children can dictate ideas to you, write individually, or work in pairs. Older students can create individual lists or work with partners.
- *Sentences*: Another option is to write complete sentences about all four components.
- *Pre-Writing*: Older students can use the format for Narrative Comprehension as a pre-writing activity and later compose complete paragraphs. Older students can assimilate information about two, three, or all four parts of Narrative Comprehension during one lesson.

Booklet Format

Although the booklet format is less desirable than forms that build sentences, a booklet can be used to list ideas under each of the four

Dysgraphia Modification
For students with weak writing skills, allow lists or single sentences to count for the entire assignment.

Dyslexia Modification
Use removable colored tape to highlight key words for comprehension. Use a different color for characters, settings, problems and solutions.

Dyslexia Modification
Buy a second copy of the story and highlight important words to help with comprehension challenges.

categories. A simple format uses a fold and cut booklet. Create a booklet by folding paper vertically (hot dog style). Fold the form in half two additional times to create four sections. Cut the folds on the top half of the original page to create four flaps. On the outside of the top section, draw a picture to represent a character. On the inside list all of the characters. On the outside of the second flap, draw a representation of a setting. Inside the second flap, list everything about the settings. The third and fourth flaps will continue the process with drawings on the outside and words inside to expose problems and all ideas about solutions. (Dotted lines represent folds.)

A slightly different format folds a paper into four quartiles.

Characters A rabbit	*Setting* ran in the forest
Problem because a dog chased him	*Solution* until he hid in a hole.

Chart Paper Model

According to Dr. Guszak from the University of Texas, the best way to write ideas is to connect them into complete sentences. See the examples below.

Characters	Setting	Conflict	Solution
Mother cried	at home	because she missed her children	until they came home.
Sally drove	her new car	over the speed limit	to help her mother.
Dad left	work	worried about mother	and gave her a hug.

Teaching Mapping and Graphic Organizers

Story mapping, character maps and **graphic organizers** all provide visual images to recall and record information from a story. A story map demonstrates major aspects and details from the entire passage. A character map indicates aspects of a character analysis. Mapping integrates visual images and recall.

Summarizing Strategies

A **summary** is a brief statement that tells the most important aspects of the paragraph or reading piece. In order to be able to summarize, the reader must grasp the main idea and differentiate between relevant and irrelevant details.

What Research Indicates

Research indicates that learning to summarize improves ability to recall and to answer questions. Summarizing requires use of prior knowledge and grammar.

Teaching One Word Summary

One way to introduce summarizing is to read through a poem or short story for the purpose of choosing the single most important word to capture each of the following: the character, what the character desires, the barrier to the desire, and the solution to getting what is desired. For example, in the fabled story of Cinderella, one-word summaries might include the following words.

Character	Cinderella
Wanted	Love
Barrier/Problem	Stepmother
Solution	Prince

Teaching Extended Summary

An extended summary provides additional words within a structure of sentences.

Dysgraphia Modification
Summarizing provides an easy way to diversify. You will have students who struggle to get one word for each category on paper. Others will write pages about each area. Be willing to accept differences.

Dysgraphia Modification
Less proficient writers will fill in blanks. Students with greater needs can use a word bank.

117

*Somebody*_____ *wanted* _____ .
But _____ , *so then,* _____ .

Using the same Cinderella story, the structure might resemble the following example.

> *Cinderella* wanted *to be loved by the prince.*
>
> But *her stepmother said she couldn't go to the ball.*
>
> Then, *the fairy godmother helped her and the prince married her.*

Teaching Summary Writing With Choices

Before asking students to write their own summaries, teach the thinking process by modeling three versions of a summary (based on extended summary). Initially, guide students to choose which is the best summary. See choices below.

Sample Choices for Summaries

After reading the story, guide students to choose the best of three choices.

Choice #1. Cinderella's stepmother would not let her go to the ball. Cinderella was very sad. (This choice tells what Cinderella wanted as well as the problem. Critical parts are missing.)

Choice #2. Cinderella's Fairy God Mother turned a pumpkin into a coach and mice into horses. She gave Cinderella a beautiful dress so the prince would notice her. (This choice shares interesting details but does not state what Cinderella wanted, describe the problem, or state the outcome.)

Choice #3. Cinderella wanted to go to the ball but her stepmother did not allow her to go. The Fairy Godmother made it possible for Cinderella to go to the ball where she met the prince. Finally, Cinderella and the prince were married. (This choice tells what Cinderella wanted and named the problem. This summary tells how the problem was solved and states the final outcome.)

GT Modification
Your GT students may not ever need formulas or examples. If a student is capable, allow the student to skip choosing the best and write an original summary.

Dysgraphia Modification
Students who continue to struggle with writing their own summaries can continue to choose the best of three examples, provided by the teacher.

Choosing is an easier task than creating. After providing three sample summaries over several reading passages and modeling ways to choose the best, most students will be able to write their own.

Teaching Main Idea

Although identifying the main idea seems similar to Narrative Comprehension and summaries, the guiding words for main idea include: who, what, when, where, and why. Like Narrative Comprehension, when written across the page, a sentence can be formed. Main ideas only include the most important of each.

Who	What	When	Where	Why
Cinderella	found love	one night	at the ball	when she met the prince.

When a student can tell who, what, when (or where) and why, the student has gained the main idea.

Expository Comprehension

Unlike a narrative text that entertains by telling a story, an expository text provides factual information and requires a more concentrated approach. Reciprocal Teaching and ReQuest can be used with expository reading. The steps below list a different process for expository comprehension.

- The **subject** of the expository text is the idea that runs throughout the piece.
- Each paragraph explains a different aspect of the subject. For example, an expository text about dogs might include separate paragraphs about the following: differences in puppies and adult dogs, what dogs eat, how they play, and ways dogs can be useful to humans.
- Within each of the paragraphs, you will find a **topic sentence**, which would be called a main idea in a narrative text. The topic sentence will include a **key word** to let you know what that paragraph is about.
- In addition to the topic sentence and the key word, the paragraph will include some details to explain the key idea in the paragraph.
- Each paragraph focuses on the subject while providing very different information.

Dyslexia Modifications
As with narrative reading, experiment with the following ideas to make text more accessible:

- Larger print
- Overlays
- Dimmer lighting
- Fingers to guide.

Dyslexia Modifications
Indicate most important parts with colored removable tape or highlight a separate book.

Teaching Expository Comprehension

The following method of teaching expository comprehension comes from *Project Read Expository Comprehension®*. First model and then guide practice with questions as students follow the steps below:

Dyslexia Modification
Ask your school about digital textbooks. Ideally, you will be able to get a digital textbook for every subject and for every child with reading needs. Check out NIMAS (National Center on Accessible Instructional Materials).

- Notice the title of the passage. Decide if the title is unique and tricky or if the title names the subject.
- If the title does not name the subject, skim the entire passage to determine the subject.
- State what you believe the subject is.
- To prove you are right, skim a second time and circle all words that either name or are synonyms for the subject (such as he, his, puppy). Words can be pronouns as well as nouns.
- Draw an outline around the left side of the passage. Number each indentation with a Roman numeral.
- If there is an introduction begin the process with the second paragraph.
- Next, look for details about the key word. Label each detail with a lower case letter beginning with "a."
- Repeat the process with each of the remaining paragraphs.

I

II

Using Questions Effectively

In *Remediating Reading Difficulties* by Sharon Crawley, the author suggests the following guidelines for using questioning strategies with students.

- Ask questions to prompt thinking. Never use questions to punish or embarrass students.
- Increase your wait time to allow time for students who need to think longer before responding. The Texas Education Agency (TEA) recommends a five to seven second wait time before prompting or telling the answer.
- Say, "It's okay not to know but it's not okay not to think."
- Pose your question, pause, and then call on a student. As soon as you name a student, others will believe they are "off the hook" and will stop thinking. Keep them wondering as long as possible.

- Require students to answer in complete sentences using the question as a stem.
- If a student responds well to a question, tell the student why the answer was strong. For example, "Jose, your answer was based on clues from the text."
- When a student suggests a correct answer, probe to extend the thinking by saying, "Yes, that is correct. Can you explain more about why you chose this answer?"
- Ask other students to extend by adding to the answer.
- If you wait five to seven seconds and no one answers, you have probably lost your students. You may even notice a glazed expression. Restate the question and ask everyone in the room to talk to a neighbor about a possible answer. Once students confer with one another, ask the question again. Giving students a chance to talk to one another increases confidence. In addition, the activity will help students wake up!
- If you have a student who never answers, provide the student with a written question before class. Make certain the student knows the answer or is capable of locating the answer. Say, "Be ready."
- If you use graphic organizers or maps as students answer questions, create an example and expect the students to either copy your map or create their own.

Bloom's Taxonomy

One way to avoid getting in the common rut of only asking factual recall questions is to refer to Bloom's Taxonomy and make certain you create at least one question from each area.

Knowledge questions basically ask who, what, when, where, and how. Usually knowledge level questions can be answered in one or two words (unless you insist on a complete sentence). It is conceivable that a student can answer correctly without truly understanding. Select words from the list below when forming knowledge-level questions.

who	what	when
where	how	select
list	omit	match
how much	choose an answer	quote

Comprehension questions require more advanced thinking. Students must go beyond memorization of facts and be able to demonstrate understanding. Answers will require more than one or two words.

state the main idea	condense the paragraph	paraphrase
give an example	translate the graph	indicate what is meant by . . .
convert into your own words	reword	rephrase
summarize	explain	state in your own words

Application goes beyond merely memorizing and understanding and requires the student to use information in a new way. Attach responses to real-life when possible.

predict (requires a new application of prior knowledge)	what questions will you ask?	construct (by following directions—not a creative idea)
apply information	discover (from doing an experiment)	demonstrate (your ability to use new information)
show evidence that you understand by doing something	solve a problem using new facts	how can you make use of new information?
prepare (for an experiment or demonstration)	tell why something happened/worked the way it did	what approach will you use?

Analysis requires enough knowledge and understanding to be able to "take an idea apart" and to draw conclusions. Notice that at each level of Bloom's Taxonomy, the students must have basic information in order to move into higher order thinking.

infer . . .	diagnose	distinguish
diagram	divide	differentiate
compare/contrast	what is the relationship?	what evidence can you find?
what category?	analyze	examine

Synthesis moves thinking into the area of creativity. Creativity comes from within the learner and brings originality to a task.

create	compose an original	how else could this be done?
design a new way	combine to form a new model	originate
synthesize	conceive	write (creatively)
invent	propose an alternative	integrate

Evaluative thinking involves making judgments about the intrinsic value of an event or issue. Answering evaluative questions requires examination of integrity and is associated with critical thinking.

defend (a character's choice)	judge which action is (ethical, honest, more helpful)	criticize
which is more important?	critique	recommend
evaluate	justify	do you agree?
what is your opinion?	what choice would you make?	prioritize

Technology and Comprehension

Use of technology in education has greatly expanded from the early days of computer drills for remediation. The following information comes from *Learning to Read in the Digital Age* by David Rose and Bridget Dalton. Rose and Dalton make a strong case for using digital technology to individualize material and methods for reading instruction.

What Does the Research Indicate?

According to Rose and Dalton, readers face three challenges when learning to read. The first challenge involves applying the alphabetic principle. In order to read, the student must first grasp the idea that letters—words—represent speech. The second challenge involves relating comprehension from spoken language to the world of print. Lastly, the reader must be motivated to learn to read. Each of these activities takes place in a different part of the brain. Digital adaptations can assist in all three areas.

Dyslexia Modification
Prompts and definitions will aid students with dyslexia and allow them to read the same text as their peers.

Teaching With Digital Modifications

When students fail to comprehend reading material, digital text can provide prompts. For example, key words can be highlighted or spoken. Students can choose to hear word definitions while viewing graphics. ELL students have options for translations in their primary languages. Summaries can be provided. Digital adaptations also assist with motivation by offering choices and interaction with media. Although the prompts can be made available for all students, they can be used on an "as needed" basis.

Universal Design and CAST

Universal Design requires inclusion of ramps, knocked out curbs, and special facilities in order for individuals with disabilities to have access to services. Teachers can refer to the Universal Design for Learning (UDL) at CAST (Center for Applied Special Technology) *<http://www.cast.org>* for ways to make print available for all students. UDL provides modifications that take the disability out of print. Check out the Resource Library to view clarifying videos.

According to a video in the CAST Resource Library, it is the classrooms, curriculum and print that are disabled—not the students. Rose claims that we have a problem with **print disability (PD)** instead of students with disabilities. His goal is remove all "stigma" from students. Universal Design Learning (UDL) emphasizes modification of goals, materials, methods of teaching and assessment.

- *Make Print Available*: UDL suggests offering many ways to present print information. Print size and font can be altered and classroom, manipulative materials can be added.
- *Support Demonstration of Comprehension*: Another suggestion is to present various ways for children to express what they are learning.
- *Motivate*: New learning must be valuable and important to learners. Often, technology provides its own motivation.

According to Rose and Dalton, the U.S. Department of Education passed a standard supporting digital forms of all textbooks in 2004. This standard is called the National Instructional Materials Accessibility Standard (NIMAS). NIMAS was created as part of IDEA (Individuals with Disabilities Education Act) for the purpose of assisting elementary and secondary students with reading challenges.

Semantic Features

The word, "**semantic**," refers to meaning. Semantic features include the definition of words, the coherence of the words within a

ELL Modification
Oral definitions (in both languages) plus the advantage of reading in one's primary language will help ELL students.

Dysgraphia Modification
UDL benefits children who know answers but are not able to put pen to paper and express that they have learned.

sentence, and the context of the communication. Coherence means figuratively sticking together. Three basic approaches can help with semantic meanings.

- **Definitions**: Dictionaries offer word meanings.
- **Coherence**: A coherent message is a message that connects words logically. More simply, the words come together in ways that create meaningful sentences.
- **Context**: Even if you understand the meaning of each word in a sentence, and the words form a coherent statement, the communication may change according to the context of the message.

English, a language with rich vocabulary that comes from a wide variety of sources, abounds with idiomatic and slang expressions. Part of teaching semantics includes:

- **Antonyms** are words that mean opposites such as black and white
- **Synonyms** are words with the same meaning, such as happy and glad.
- **Homonyms** are words that are spelled the same and pronounced the same but have different meanings, as a coat to wear and a coat of paint.
- **Homophones** are words that sound the same but are spelled differently such as bare and bear.
- **Homographs** are words that are spelled the same but pronounced differently and have different meanings such as a tear to cry and to tear a dress.

Additional examples of homonyms, homographs, and homophones are found below.

Homophones	Homographs	Homonyms
bare and bear	tear to cry and tear a dress,	saw a person and saw a log
sea and see	read (today) and read (yesterday)	bowl to eat from and to bowl a game
capital (city) and capitol (building)	present (a gift) and to present a person	dress a turkey and wear a dress
principal (of the school) and a principle	bow (in hair) and to bow to the king	slip and fall and to wear a slip

stationary (unmoving) and stationery (paper)	polish the silver Polish language	mole (on her nose) and a mole in the yard
write and right	refuse (to say no) and refuse (trash)	draw the drapes and to draw art
rain and reign	resume (to start) and resume (a document)	bills on birds and bills you owe

Act out metaphors and similes such as "She's a witch." After acting out, discuss possible reasons the metaphor or simile came into existence.

Metaphors

Metaphors compare unlike objects. For native English speakers, metaphors are fun and engaging. For students who are learning English as a second language, metaphors make no sense. Consider the examples below.

I'm all ears	I have a green thumb	she's a witch	he's a pig
tongue tied	keep your head above water	cried my eyes out	fell flat on her face
give him a hand	it's a dog's life	gone to the dogs	a mountain man

Similes

A simile closely resembles a metaphor with one exception. Similes always include the words, "like" or "as" in the sentence.

sharp as a tack	crazy as a loon	sly as a fox	tough as nails
pretty as a picture	crazy as a bed bug	proud as a peacock	quiet as a mouse
roared like a lion	jumps like a rabbit	sings like a bird	climbs like a monkey

Syntactic Features

Syntax refers to the grammar of a language and includes the rules for combining words to create sentences. *Framing Your Thoughts by*

Project Read® offers an excellent approach to teaching syntactic transformation features.

One aspect of syntax involves **word order**. For example, in English, one says, "I have a pocket watch," rather than, "I have a watch pocket."

Syntax involves **parts of speech** such as nouns, verbs, adjectives, adverbs, and prepositional phrases.

Sentence transformation makes up a third aspect of syntax. Notice the following ways to transform sentences.

- **Positive to Negative**: Sentences can change from positive to negative. *"I can go home,"* changes to, *"I cannot go home."*
- **Statement to Question**: A statement can be transformed to become a question. *"I can go,"* can change to, *"Can I go?"*
- **Active to Passive**: When transforming an active sentence into a passive one, take the direct object and turn it into the subject of the transformed sentence. The verb becomes: is, are, was, were, be, being, been, will be, or should. *"The man planted the garden." "The garden was planted by the man."*
- **Verb to Noun**: Verb-to-noun transformations are demonstrated by changing, *"John works,"* to *"John is a worker."* The verb "works" becomes a noun—worker.
- **Because, When, Until**: Transformations are created by using, because, when, and until.
  — *"I came home early,"* changes to *"I came home early because the library closed."*
  — *Another example includes, "I came home early until I got a second job."*
  — *Yet another sentence transformation occurs with, "I came home early when I lost the job."*
- **Compound Sentences**: Compound sentences create transformations by combining two independent clauses with words such as *and, but, or, so,* or *yet.* For example, *"The man was honest. The man was helpful,"* changes to *"The man was honest and the man was helpful."* A **compound sentence** has two subjects and two verbs.
- **Adjectives and Adverbs**: Adjectives and adverbs create transformations in sentences. *"Cars race,"* changes to, *"Small cars race madly."*

Cues for Reading

Children must be taught that during reading they are problem-solving by using the following specific "**cues**" for reading: **pragmatics** (social context), **semantics** (meaning), **syntax** (structure, grammar and word

ELL Modification
Compare and contrast the word order in the student's primary language and in English.

Repeat the comparison until the student can read the sentence in English easily.

order) and **graphophonics** (alphabetic, orthographic, sound to symbol process).

Teach reading strategies in the context of authentic reading tasks. **Authentic reading** includes real books and materials instead of phonics drills and workbook pages.

Providing Graphophonic Cues

Graphophonic cues involve sound-to-symbol or **grapheme-to-phoneme cues**. Using graphophonic cues results in decoding (breaking the symbolic code). Encourage children to apply their **decoding** (phonics) skills within the context of the text by asking themselves the following questions.

- "Does it look right for what I said?"
- "Did it sound right for that letter?"
- "Did I match the number of words I said with the words on the page?"
- "I need to take a closer look at that word."
- "Is that right? How do I know?"

Providing Semantic (Meaning) Cues

Since reading includes more than breaking the code, you must also teach children to think as they read. **Semantics** involves using cues to gain meaning. In order to encourage children to connect meaning with decoding, teach them to ask themselves the following questions.

- "Did that make sense?"
- "Look at the pictures. What is happening?"
- "What happened when?"
- "What will probably happen next?"

Providing Syntax (Sentence Structure) Cues

Good reading also must consider the way **syntax**, the sentence structure comes together in a specific language. For example, English speakers say, "I see the beautiful house." In Spanish, a speaker with the same message will state, "I see the house beautiful." The questions below guide children to ask themselves questions about the role of language in reading.

- "Can we say it that way in English?"
- "Can I say it another way?"
- "What word might sound right?"

Benefit of Cues

If you make a note of the types of miscues a student makes while reading orally, you can determine whether the mistakes are made because sound-to-symbol (grapheme to phoneme) cues are being ignored. If so, you will plan a skill lesson based on information from your assessment.

On the other hand, if the student's miscues indicate lack of thinking during reading, you will re-emphasize the importance of focusing on the content while decoding the words. This assessment information might lead to additional lessons on metacognition or visualization.

Miscues due to incorrect language structure or grammar indicate a need for instruction in parts of speech, grammar, and the general structure of the English language. Refer to the Syntax modification for suggestions to support ELL students.

Summarizing Comprehension Dragons

The comprehension module began with descriptions of two types of dyslexia: Surface and Direct Dyslexia. Both types damage comprehension. Before reading suggestions for Surface and Direct Dyslexia, re-read the introductory dragon page at the beginning of this module.

Help for Surface Dyslexia

In kindergarten and early first grade, a child with **Surface Dyslexia** demonstrates adequate comprehension. Once irregular words become common, comprehension usually suffers because the child exerts too much thought and energy attempting to sound out irregular words. Because a child with Surface Dyslexia benefits from auditory input, working with reading partners will help. Before reading, children can discuss possible predictions. After a brief time, the children will stop reading and talk about the accuracy of their predictions. More ideas are suggested under *Comprehension Help for Surface and Direct*.

Help for Direct Dyslexia

Another type of dyslexia occurs when children who apply phonics, memorize sight vocabulary and read well orally, fail to grasp the meaning of a text. Teach children with **Direct Dyslexia**, who have strong visual and auditory skills, to visualize each short section. Encourage them to use pictures in the book as comprehension clues. TV Recall provides a beneficial strategy for comprehension. There are some children who do not realize the importance of thinking while reading. Explaining the purpose for forming visual pictures and running movies sometimes improves comprehension for children with Direct Dyslexia.

Comprehension Help for Surface *and* Direct

Children with Surface Dyslexia and Direct Dyslexia will benefit from the following activities.

- Break reading assignments into very short sections. After each section, stop and ask children to physically do something with new information such as discuss, take notes, create graphic organizers, or draw pictures.
- Set a purpose for reading. For example, read questions first. The purpose then becomes reading to locate answers.
- Ask children to make predictions over each short part, read and then check the accuracy of the predictions.
- Knowing that the children with Surface and Direct Dyslexia respond well to auditory input, you can provide help for comprehension by using Think Aloud. Ideally, the children will begin to copy your thinking patterns to develop improved understanding while reading.
- Allow children to listen to recorded texts. Both types of dyslexia will benefit from the auditory input.
- Class discussions over reading selections will benefit both Surface and Direct with comprehension.

Bibliography

Anderson, David, and S. O'Neal, C. David, P. Oruonyehu. *Dyslexia and Related Disorders* (Texas Education Agency, Sept, 1998). Allington, R. *What Really Matters for Struggling Readers*. Boston, MA: Pearson, 2012.

Bacon Educational Group. "Reciprocal Questioning (ReQuest)." *Just Read Now!* Panama City, Florida; Beacon Learning Center. 1997.

Besner, D. "Deep Dyslexia and Right Hemiesphere Hypothesis." Can J Psychol 1983; Vol. 34, No. 4, pp. 565-571.

Carlson. "Types of Dyslexia." *Welcome to the Dyslexia Homepage.* Macalester College, 1998. <http://www.macalester.edu/psychology/ whathap/UBNRP/Dyslexia/index.html>

Crawley, S. *Remediating Reading Difficulties*. New York, NY:McGraw Hill, 2012.

Frandsen, B. *Yes! I Can Teach Literacy*. Austin, TX: Family School, 2006.

Frandsen, B. *Making a Difference for Students with Differences*. Austin, TX: Family School. 2001.

Greene, V. and M. Enfield. *Project Read—Narrative Comprehension.* Bloomington, MN: Language Circle Enterprise, 1973.

Gunning, Thomas G. *Creating Reading Instruction for All Children.* Boston, MA: Allyn and Bacon, 1992.

Guszak, Frank. *Diagnostic Reading Instruction in the Elementary School.* New York, NY: Harper and Row, 1978.

—*Reading for Students with Special Needs*. Kendall/Hunt Publishing: Dubuque, Iowa. 1997.

Gunning, T. *Creating Literacy Instruction for All Children*. Boston, MA: Allyn and Bacon, 2003.

Hayes, John A. *Right Dyslexia Glasses* (different from Irlen lenses). Atlantic Beach, FL32233. <http://www.dyslexiaglasses.com>

Irlen, Helen. *Reading By the Colors*. Garden City Park, NY: Avery Publishing Group, 1991.

Lytton, W.W. and J.C.M. Brust. *Direct Dyslexia: Preserved Oral Reading of Real Words in Wernicke's Aphasia,* New York: Columbia University College, 1988.*<http://brain.oxfordjournals.org>*

Manzo, A. "The ReQuest procedure." *Journal of Reading*, 13, 123-127, 1969.

Marzano, R. J., Pickering, D. J., & Pollock, J. E. *Classroom instruction that works: Research-based strategies for increasing student achievement*. Upper Saddle, NJ: Pearson, 2005.

Rose, D. and B. Dalton. *Learning to Read in the Digital Age*. Wakefield, MA: CAST, Inc., 2009.

Singer, H. "Active comprehension: From answering to asking questions." *The Reading Teacher*, 31, 901-908, 1978.

Slaying the Vocabulary & Spelling Dragon

Children with **Deep Dyslexia** face challenges when learning new vocabulary. Often, substitutions occur with words that look similar and words with similar meanings. Not only is the child challenged with sight vocabulary but also when spelling words with similar sounds.

Children with **Surface Dyslexia** also have problems with sight word recognition and when spelling words with irregular patterns. Phonetically regular words do not cause problems with reading or spelling.

Other causes of poor vocabulary include poor visual or auditory acuity, lack of life-experiences, fatigue from inadequate diet or sleep and lack of motivation. Children who are learning English as a second language also face challenges.

Watch for modifications throughout this module and summaries of the two types of dyslexia at the end.

Vocabulary Instruction

What Is Vocabulary?

The "science of reading" includes vocabulary instruction as one of the five components of reading. **Vocabulary**—learning meanings and uses of words includes speaking, listening, reading and writing. Without vocabulary, we have no language.

Shared conversations and reading aloud to children provide two ways to incidentally teach vocabulary. Studies indicate that connections exist between vocabulary and intelligence and between vocabulary and income potential. Knowing the importance of vocabulary leads teachers to use a variety of methods.

One older method involves teaching vocabulary through definitions. In this method, children usually look up words, write definitions and memorize meanings. A major problem with this method includes the fact that a dictionary usually provides multiple definitions. Which one relates to the reading material? In addition, dictionary definitions often provide ambiguous information.

A second method relies on **context clues**, which are clues about unknown words from surrounding information. Although context clues provide assistance with reading comprehension, the clues often lack enough clarity to define a specific word. Another challenge with depending on context clues to master vocabulary occurs when children make incorrect decisions about word meanings.

Research supports use of games and authorities often recommend games and word-sorts to teach vocabulary. Correlating commercial word games with specific reading material may prove difficult. Ideally, teachers construct their own games related to material being read. However, creating games requires tremendous energy and time from the teacher.

What Does Research Indicate?

Experts generally agree that using a variety of approaches works best. The National Reading Panel concludes that there is no one best

Barbara Frandsen

way to teach vocabulary. In *Classroom Instruction That Works: Research Based Strategies*, Marzano encourages the following ideas:

- Teach words that relate to the material being read.
- Never teach more than 10 to 15 words at one time.
- Include pictures when possible.
- Give children an oral definition that clearly relates to reading material.
- Ask children to write the teacher's definition in their own words and add a picture.

The United States Department of Education suggests teaching word-study methods such as the dictionary, context clues, and **morphology** (study of word parts). Multiple exposures support long-term memory. Finally, experts conclude that there is no replacement for **"voluminous" reading** to build vocabulary. Voluminous reading is defined as extensive reading from a wide variety of sources.

Research also indicates that students benefit from **generative methods** of vocabulary instruction, which require students to make their own connections between prior knowledge and new words. Instead of defining a word such as "opulent" for students, provide them with pictures of money and luxurious houses and encourage them to make their own connections. Making connections benefits students much more than **additive methods**, which use definitions provided by the teacher along with memorization. In order for generative learning to take place, students also engage in selecting words and determine personal ways to remember word meanings.

Types of Vocabulary Words

Two distinct types of vocabulary lists exist. The first list is made up of **basic words**, which are the most commonly used words in English and are also referred to as **high frequency** words. The second type of list is made up of **personal** words, which are words of interest to individual children. Ideally, children will be able to recognize high frequency and personal words instantly. Words that are instantly recognized without sounding out, using a dictionary, or asking for help are called **sight words**. Some sight words can be decoded phonetically and others rely on memorization of letter sequence. Either way, sight vocabulary requires instant recognition.

High Frequency Sight Words

As a teacher, you will experience a variety of high frequency lists written by different authors. The first 100 words in the Dolch list are below.

the	at	do	big	from
to	him	can	went	good
and	with	could	are	any
he	up	when	come	about
a	all	did	if	around
I	look	what	now	want
you	is	so	long	don't
it	her	see	no	how
of	there	not	came	know
in	some	were	ask	right
was	out	get	very	put
said	as	them	an	too
his	be	like	over	got
that	have	one	yours	take
she	go	this	its	where
for	we	my	ride	every
on	am	would	into	pretty
they	then	me	just	jump
but	little	will	blue	green
had	down	yes	red	four

Personal Sight Words

Before starting school, a young child may begin to read the **environment** by recognizing restaurant and store signs and logos such as, "Taco Bell®," "Toys-R-Us®," and many more familiar signs. Environmental reading is also known as **logographics**. The child may also read his or her own name or the name of a pet. Words such as these make up each child's personal sight vocabulary.

Strategies and Modifications

Teaching Grounding for Vocabulary

Modification
Grounding amounts to a modification since you will not use the strategy with all children. The process adds extra steps toward mastering vocabulary.

Grounding is a three-step process of preparing the children to read by identifying challenging vocabulary before beginning a passage. In effect, grounding lays a foundation by sequencing the level of difficulty for new vocabulary. Asking a child to locate a specific word is not as challenging as asking, "What is this word?" Begin with the easier level.

Step One = Point To . . .

As you look at the first paragraph or page, hold an index card under one line of print and ask the student to identify a specific word by saying, "Find the word . . ." Continue by selecting lines with challenging words.

- Use words that may stump the student.
- Check difficult words one line at a time.
- Stop at the end of the first paragraph or page and begin the step two.

Step Two = Silent Reading

In step two, ask the student to read the same paragraph or page silently for the purpose of identifying any unknown words. If a child asks for help during this step, provide lessons, and as much support as needed for mastery.

Step Three = Oral Reading

After giving the child time to read silently and assisting with unknown words, ask the child to read orally. As you listen, note miscues, fluency and confidence. Ideally, the child will read accurately and smoothly.

If the child continues to struggle, offer reading material of comparable difficulty, written in large print on chart paper or on the chalkboard. Often, unsuccessful readers can succeed when offered large print on a vertical surface. If the child reads well after using grounding or with large print, the child is demonstrating a problem other than a reading problem. In these cases, reading difficulties probably stem from erratic eye movements, poor fixation, or even lack of confidence.

If the student continues to experience frustration, drop to easier reading material. In addition, ask for visual and auditory assessments, check the home environment, and hold parent conferences in an effort to gain insight and understanding.

Teaching Memory Strategy for Vocabulary

Although you want to stress higher-level thinking, you must also make certain children have a vocabulary foundation. Memorization helps develop the background needed before expecting more in depth comprehension. The Memory Strategy is excellent for any task involving memorization. **Sight words**—words that should be instantly recognized by children—work well with the Memory Strategy.

Limit the number of items to be memorized to approximately 9 to 12. Divide your list into sets of three. Choose your first three words and think of a memory aid (reminder) for each one.

Modification
When helping readers who struggle, reduce the number of words to be mastered. Choose most important words.

Dyslexia Modification
Large print might be ¼ to ½ inch tall. Experiment to determine the best size.

Often, a vertical or slanted surface helps.

In addition, try using paper with various colors. Colored overlays may be helpful.

Memory Aid	Type of Intelligence
Story	Auditory
Song or rhythm	Musical, rhythmic
Action or movement	Kinesthetic
Object to touch or feel	Tactile
Computation	Mathematical, logical
Picture	Visual
Food	Taste and smell

Although taste and smell are not considered types of intelligence, these two sensory experiences tend to provide powerful links for long-term memory. If your children are not succeeding at learning a skill or objective, connect food in a logical way to reinforce learning. (This is not a suggestion to reward performance with food, however.)

Once you have introduced three words with appropriate memory associations, stop and review. This is a formative check for the purpose of assessing understanding and mastery. If children are successful in recalling the first three words, introduce three additional ones with their own memory aids. If the children do not recall the first three, review and re-teach them using different forms of memory aids. If the first three words are not mastered, introducing additional words will only overload the brain's "computer" system.

Dyslexia Modification
Keep in mind that taste and smell are our strongest sensory modalities. When all else fails, be creative and link the needed vocabulary word to a smell or a taste.

Teaching ELL Students by Combining Strategies

In order to get maximum benefit from Grounding and the Memory Strategy, combine the two in the following ways. Begin with Grounding:

- Choose a reading selection for Grounding. Within a short passage, locate three to five vocabulary words you think may be challenging.
- Ask the child (or children) to point to one word at a time. Take time to teach words that cannot be easily located.
- Complete Grounding over the paragraph or page by asking the child to read for the purpose of locating any difficult words. Next, ask the child to read orally to check accuracy and fluency.

Visual Strategy

Immediately, create flash cards with memory aids for the three to five words chosen during Grounding. Limit the number of words to no more than five.

Dyslexia Modification
Additional differentiation can be added by providing clay, bags of sealed, hair-styling gel to feel, or pans of cornmeal for tracing.

Explain and then model how to create a visual flash card that is color-coded or decorated in a way to help with memory. Large index cards usually work best. Indicate how large the letters need to be (approximately one half to one fourth inch tall) and where to place words on an index card. Warn children to avoid adding so many decorations that the letters are impossible to discern. Write words on the front of cards and definitions on the back.

Once each child has created a minimum of three color-coded cards, explain and model visualizing one word. Hold your own card above your head, stare at the word, shut your eyes and "see" the word printed on your card. When you become very good at visualizing, you will be able to read the letters of the word backward. For vocabulary development, focus on seeing and then defining the word. When definitions cannot be remembered, check the back of the card.

Add Auditory

Students work in pairs to review one another. Partner one gives cards to partner two. Partner two reads one new vocabulary word and asks for a definition. If the owner of the card is successful, the partner will continue with the next word. If not, the child will be encouraged to read the word and definition again. After each set of 3 words, partners will trade roles.

Kinesthetic Movement

In order to promote mastery, encourage children to separate words that were hard to define and to spend additional time on them. Ask partners to study with one another by taking turns saying each word and acting out the definition. Make certain each child moves, sings, or touches something to demonstrate the meaning of each challenging word. Once both partners finish practicing together, the pairs will repeat the auditory step as a formative assessment.

Grounding a Second Time for ELL

- If time permits, return to the text and use the Grounding Strategy to locate and learn three to five additional words.
- Following the second use of Grounding, create flash cards and memory aids for the second set of words.
- Complete the process by reviewing all words learned.
- The values gained from combining the two strategies include the following ideas.
- If you immediately create flash cards and include memory aids, you "lock in" long term memory. It is better to master a few words than to gain surface understanding of many.

- Acting out, moving, or touching helps ELL children gain in-depth understanding of vocabulary. Movement also helps children with dyslexia.
- Integrating steps of Grounding and Memory Strategy reinforces both strategies.

Context Clues

One of the most important skills to teach young readers involves the use of picture and word clues provided by the author or artist. Encourage readers to make "educated" guesses or inferences about the meaning of an unknown word based on surrounding context. Within a few paragraphs, the reader generally realizes whether the inferred meaning is accurate or not. Using these clues requires thinking on the part of the reader. If a child makes a miscue that totally changes the meaning ask, "Is that logical? Does it make sense?"

What Does Research Indicate?

According to the National Reading Panel, a variety of methods are encouraged, including the following ideas:

- Teach students to use context clues when reading and to include clues within their own writing.
- Teach vocabulary within context rather than in isolation.
- While identifying vocabulary in context, ask students to think about possible meanings.
- Encourage use of morphology to study word parts to gain meaning.
- Use games and word sorts.
- Frequent and **spaced repetitions** (repetitions with time in between) and multiple exposures help develop long-term memory.
- Extensive reading builds vocabulary.

Types of Context Clues

There are several types of context clues. Use Think Aloud to point out context clues when reading to students. Teach context clues as a means to help comprehension. Later, ask students to add clues to writing.

GT Modification
Once you are certain students with stronger vocabulary skills have mastered the basic vocabulary words, allow them to substitute more challenging (and more interesting words).

One way to challenge within the context of material being studied is to ask students to create their own context clues using the various methods such as synonyms, antonyms, comparisons, or function indicators.

Definition

A definition is often included in the sentence or passage. Look for words such as: *means, refers to, is, are.* An example might be, "A morpheme is the smallest part of a word."

Appositive

An appositive is the same as a definition but is separated with a dash or comma. For example, "A morpheme-the smallest part of a word-helps understand the meaning of the word."

Synonym

A synonym clue uses a different word with the same meaning to explain the target word. Tip-off words include: *also, too, same, identical, as, similar.* A sample sentence might read, "Like structural analysis, morphology also studies parts of words."

Antonym or Comparison

Opposite words or phrases show meaning through a contrast. You may see words such as: *however, unlike, instead of, but, differs from.* An example might be, "Unlike individual sounds called phonemes, morphemes study small parts of words."

Examples

Examples sometimes provide clues to the meaning of a word. Tip-offs may include: *for example, including.* Consider the sample sentence, *Morphemes include prefixes, suffixes, compound words, possessives and contractions.*

Function Indicators

Function indicators always refer to machinery or types of equipment. See the example of a function indicator, *The derrick lifted the glider into the sky.*

Pictures and Background

Prior schema provides help with context clues. Pictures also give clues and should be encouraged during early reading.

Modification

Highlight context clues or cover clues with removable tape.

Teach the target words using the Memory Strategy. When modifying, use more dramatic memory aids such as movement, taste, or smell.

Teaching Context Clues

Good readers think as they read. Good readers use metacognition by asking, *Does it look right?* Looking at the word builds visual discrimination. *Does it sound right?* Asking if it sounds right stresses grammar and real usage as well as auditory discrimination. *Does it make sense?* Making sense out of text develops the type of thinking good readers must master.

A major part of your job as a reading teacher must include asking the question, "What do you do when you're stuck on a word?" Teach children to use context clues by applying the following ideas.

- Suggest, *Back up and read the sentence again.* Contrast trying to jump a hurdle flat-footed with jumping a hurdle from a running start.
- Ask, *What makes sense in this sentence? What is the story about?* This question involves **semantic cues** or meaning.
- In addition to asking what makes sense, ask children, *What sounds the way we talk?* You are encouraging attention to the structure and grammar of language. When you ask about how we talk, you are encouraging use of **syntax cues**. Syntax deals with grammar and word order.
- Use pictures as clues. Pictures build on **prior knowledge**, or background information.
- Look at the first letter. Ask, *What letter begins that word? What sound does that letter usually make? How will your mouth look if you say this word?* Comparing **graphophonic cues** teaches children to match sounds to the symbols (**graphemes to phonemes**).
- Examine the word, the line and the story for other clues, such as small words inside large words, endings, suffixes, or prefixes.

GT Modification
Challenge gifted learners by asking them to apply context clues to their own writing pieces.

Expect the child to put clues together and make educated attempts at unknown words.

- Tell children, "*Skip the word and continue reading.*"
- Encourage, "*After trying all of the ideas* (suggested above), *ask two neighbors for help.*"
- Finally, "*After trying all resources, ask me.*"

Teaching an Introductory Clues Lesson

Collect examples of context clues by locating passages or sentences with words that will challenge your students. When introducing context clues, follow the steps below, which come from *The Vocabulary Enriched Classroom.*

- Use a sticky note to cover an unknown word in a single sentence. Ask students to take educated guesses about the covered word based on the other information in the sentence.
- Share the next sentence and ask students whether additional information changes their guesses.
- Move the sticky note to show the first letter of the covered word.
- Compare the first letter of the covered word to guesses previously made by students. Rule out guesses with different beginnings.
- Continue to reveal additional letters in the covered word and encourage students to think about information from the text.

Once the covered word has been identified, remind students that the type of thinking they exhibited and the clues they used provided a strategy they can use any time they are confronted by an unknown word.

Teaching Self-Generative Process

In order to bolster motivation for learning vocabulary, allow students to self-select words to study. The *Vocabulary Enriched Classroom* suggests the following steps.

- Initially, students read for the purpose of identifying at least two interesting and challenging words.
- Each student writes the words on separate index cards to share with others.
- The class compiles all words and chooses eight to ten to master. (You might choose to vary this step and allow each student to self-select five to eight words to develop individual lists.)
- Record words on charts along with definitions.

Web sites for Creating Words Sets: <*http://www.wordless.com*>, <http://scrabble.com>, <*http://www.wordsmith.org/anagram*>,

Word Sorts

A different way to master vocabulary and spelling requires students to examine and **sort** or arrange words according to various categories. Frequently, in *Words Their Way*, the authors use the phrase, *teaching is not telling*. The authors want to communicate that children learn through manipulating word parts. They also claim that the most beneficial word lists come from students' reading material.

What Are Word Sorts?

Word sorts categorize words according to three principles for spelling: alphabetic, pattern and meaning. The alphabet system utilizes the sound to symbol relationships of letters. Patterns make use of word families or **phonograms**. Meaning uses groups that represent meanings such as the Greek root, *photo* in *photograph*. **Morphology**, a study of word parts, falls in the category of meaning.

Sound Sorts

Pictures are used for sound sorts and can be organized by initial sounds, rhymes, number of syllables, or the stressed syllable. Sound sorts can also include consonant blends, digraphs, or vowel sounds.

Pattern Sorts

Word sorts examine patterns in words. For example, when should you double the consonant in the middle of a word? Examine the words below to arrive at a pattern.

human	rabbit
hotel	dinner
silent	kitten
baby	summer

What is the difference in the vowel before one consonant and the vowel preceding two consonants? When possible, allow children to discover the differences.

Meaning Sorts

Concepts or meanings can also provide a way to sort words. Meaning sorts work well for content areas such as math or science. The following lists are from *Vocabulary Their Way*.

Math	Science	History
fraction	atom	Allied Powers
negative number	ecosystem	depression
polygon	gene	diplomacy
logarithm	DNA	women's suffrage

ELL Modification
Even students who are unable to read English words can begin with picture sorts. As students repeat names on cards and sort them into categories, their English vocabulary is strengthened.

GT Modification
Students who have a gift for words and language enjoy sorting lists of words according to content or word origin. This activity should be done instead of (not in addition to) the assignment for the class.

Open and Closed Sorts

When teachers indicate the categories and model a procedure, the activity is a **closed sort**. When teachers tell students to sort words in ways that are beneficial to them, the students are engaging in **open sorts**. Open sorts indicate areas of strength and areas where students are insecure. Sorts can also be oral or written.

The teacher can model a sort and ask students to guess what sort the teacher is using. Brainstorming can be used to develop examples of sorts. Repeating sorts until words are recognized automatically benefits students. Cut and paste sorts can be designed using pictures from magazines. A sample form below suggests one possible method to organize a picture sort.

1 Syllable Words	2 Syllable Words	3 Syllable Words

Etymology

Studies also include **etymology**, which is the study of word origins. Greek and Latin influences produced many words that we use today in English. Notice the number of words derived from the Latin root *vis*, meaning to see.

Invisible   vision   revision   visit   visibility   visor   supervise

From the Latin *dict*, meaning to say, we have these words.

Predict   dictate   contradict   dictionary   predictable

Greek roots also influence English vocabulary. Consider the Greek influence of the root words, *micro* meaning small, *peri* meaning around, *tele* meaning distant, *phon* meaning sound, *scop* meaning to look at, and *photo* meaning light. Locate the Greek roots in the words below.

microscope	periscope	telecommunication
microscopic	periphery	telemetry
microphone	perimeter	television

GT Modification

Allow GT students to trade the regular assignment for a study of etymology. If you require the regular work in addition to a special study, the brighter students will feel punished.

Origins and Meanings of Roots

A word from which other words grow is considered a root. **Roots** usually require other word parts to be complete. By teaching root words inductively, through asking questions and guiding children to discover patterns, you take advantage of every opportunity to expand vocabulary. Teaching origins creates additional understanding of morphemic elements. Examine the following list of commonly used roots and their origins.

Root	Meaning	Example	Origin
graph	writing	autograph	Greek
tele	distance	telescope	Greek
port	carry	import	Latin
saur	lizard	dinosaur	Greek
phon	sound	telephone	Greek
vid, vis	see	visible	Latin
astro	star	astronaut	Greek
cred	believe	incredible	Latin
duct	lead	conductor	Latin
tri	three	triangle	Greek
aud	hearing	auditory	Latin
auto	self	autograph	Greek
bi	two	bicycle	Latin
scrib, scrip	writing	inscription	Latin
therm	heat	thermometer	Greek
mid	middle	midday	Latin
ped	foot	pedestrian	Latin
chrono	time	chronological	Greek
dict	say	dictate	Latin
hemi	half	hemisphere	Greek
manu	hand	manuscript	Latin
bio	life	biology	Greek
geo	earth	geology	Greek
micro	small	microscope	Greek
mono	one	monotone	Greek
semi	half, part	semisweet	Latin

GT Modification
Studies of the meanings and origins of roots can be stimulating for GT students. Allow them to skip the regular assignment and create stories or games and activities based on root words.

Morphology

If **phonology** is the study of the smallest unit of sound, **morphology** is the study of each meaningful word part. The study of morphemes examines the way word parts fit together.

Bound and Free

A **base word** is a word that generally needs no help from affixes to be an adequate word. Because base words make sense by themselves, they are considered **free morphemes**.

For instance, in the word *unhappy, un* is bound; it cannot stand alone. The base, *happy*, is a complete word and is a free morpheme. Language experts refer to this type of morpheme as a **derivational prefix**, because a new word has been derived.

Roots usually come from Greek, Latin, or other languages. Roots are usually **bound morphemes** because they generally need additional word parts to make sense. For example, the root, *saur* makes no sense by itself. Add *dino* and you create a complete word: *dinosaur*.

Inflectional suffixes do not affect the bases to which they are attached (*Words Their Way*, p. 212). Morphemes that do not change words by adding (s), (es), or (ed), fall into the category of **inflectional suffixes**. For example, the (s) in *coats* is a bound morpheme while *coat* has meaning on its own.

Morphology also examines ways actual words are compounded or combined to create new words. A few examples of compound words include the following;

backyard   baseball   grandmother   football   lifetime

Structural Analysis

Closely related to morphology, structural analysis also considers ways words are put together. Items that frequently fall under structural analysis (and also under morphology), include the following examples.

- Inflectional endings such as (-s), (-es), (-ed), (-ing), (-ly),
- Contractions such as *isn't, can't, don't, won't, haven't,*
- Possessives including *John's, the students', a student's,*
- Compound words such as *superman, overthrow, mandate,*
- Syllables including: open, closed, vowel digraph, silent e. r-controlled, diphthongs, final stable,
- Base words such as *fold, run, penny, decorate, tie, great, hard,*
- Words with prefixes such as *unfold, rerun, advance, expand,*
- Words with suffixes such as *penniless, greatest, harder, hardest,*
- Roots such as *ambi* meaning both sides as in *ambidextrous, luc* meaning light as in *translucent, semi* meaning partial as in *semiannual*, or *zoo* meaning animal life as in *zoology* also fit the category of structural analysis.

Stages of Spelling

Stage I Emerging Spelling

Emerging literacy unfolds in individual children as they encounter sources of language and experiment with various forms of literacy. The initial marks that small children make may not seem important, but early scribbling lays the foundation for future writing and even spelling.

Initial scribbling appears sometime between ages two and four. The child begins with **disordered scribbling**, which lacks hand control or direction. Once a child experiences an "aha" moment, he realizes that certain movements of the pen result in predictable marks. With this realization, the child moves into **controlled scribbling**. During early stages of scribbling, the child is not drawing or writing. Marks are made for the joy of the activity.

Disordered Scribbling, Dalton

Supply the child with large, plain pieces of paper and markers or crayons. Always avoid asking, "What is it?" At this stage, shun the question because the child is not attempting to draw a picture or write a story. Later, avoid the question because it may be insulting.

However, encourage language by saying, "Tell me about your work." It is probably wise to call the project "work" rather than either

151

art or writing. Below, you will notice similarities and differences between controlled and disordered scribbling. Although similarities exist, you see distinct vertical and horizontal lines in controlled efforts below.

Controlled Scribbling, Lane

Naming Art—Beginning of Storytelling

As oral language improves, the child begins naming objects or telling a story about the scribbles. Although the story may change from one telling to the next, there is cause to celebrate because the child has connected marks on paper with communication of ideas. At this stage of writing and drawing, color is not important to the child. A child might tell a story about a cow. Shortly after, the same piece may become a story about planting a garden. At this stage, avoid all attempts to teach correct colors or forms.

Art	Writing	Spelling
Disordered scribbles are made randomly.	No way to tell the difference in art or writing	
Controlled scribbles begin when the child realizes that movements produce marks.	Initial sequence includes: • Vertical • Horizontal • Diagonal • Circular	
Naming scribbling often looks the same as controlled but includes an oral story.	Scribble drawing and writing look the same.	**Scribbles** are a child's first attempts at written communication.

Stage II Pre-Schematic

As children observe the writing of peers and adults, they begin to produce random letters and scribbles that resemble script. In the beginning, children rely on the names of letters rather than phonemes. Strings of letters often represent a word. Words are also formed with letter names that sound like words such as (U) for *you*, (C) for *see*, (ft) for *float*, (B) for *bee*.

Preschematic, Dalton

Art has also evolved from scribbling to head-leg figures, which represent the child. All drawings are about "self" and often include items floating around the head-legs figure. Color remains unimportant to the child. If the child's picture of self is purple, your job is to be totally accepting. Continue to avoid lessons in proper colors or realistic shapes. Supply the child with plain paper, markers, or crayons.

Art	Writing	Spelling
Pre-schematic drawings are usually self-representations with a head and legs.	Random strings of letters represent writing.	Random letters represent the first attempts at spelling in the **pre-communicative** stage of spelling.

Alphabetic Spelling and Schematic Art

As children learn more about writing and spelling patterns, they implement these generalizations into their fledgling writing experiences. No longer will a letter suffice for an entire word. Matching sounds to symbols now rules the day! For example, the word *said* sounds like /s/, /e/, /d/. Invented spelling enters the picture based on the phonetic rules being learned. It is now possible for you and the child to read what has been scribed on paper.

Around the same time, art takes on a new significance. Just as the child has developed a "schema" or plan for spelling words, pictures also have a schema. All trees look alike, all flowers, and all people will bear a genetic resemblance. Previously color was not important; now correct color is non-negotiable. Grass must be green, the sky is blue, and every object is drawn according to a set plan. Often a blue skyline is included along with a brown or green base line. Motivation moves from a focus on self to an interest in peers and group activities such as going to the park or visiting the zoo with friends.

Schematic Flowers, Dalton

Art	Writing	Spelling—Phonetic
Schematic drawings appear with repetition and rigid use of color.	Spaces appear between words. Words look more like real print.	With the **phonetic** stage comes **invented spelling**, based on phonetic generalizations.

Stage III Word Patterns

As children move into independent reading and writing, they learn to recognize different types of syllables such as open, closed, vowel team, silent e, and r-controlled. Children also recognize consonant blends and digraphs. Instead of matching each individual letter name and sound, children see patterns in words. The appropriate question to ask is, "Do you see the word pattern?" Below, read the lists of words, which show a few examples of common patterns.

-dge	-ge	-g
edge	cage	bag
ridge	huge	twig
badge	stage	slug
judge	page	flag

Word Patterns and Art

As spelling becomes more sophisticated, art development also changes. This art stage is sometimes referred to as the Gang Stage because peers have taken on new importance. Art now becomes more complex and mature with variations of colors, attempts at horizons and endeavors to draw correct proportions. Although peers now provide the greatest interest, social issues are also becoming important motivators.

Stage IV Syllables and Affixes

As students move from primary to intermediate grades, they read multisyllabic words and base words with inflectional endings such as the word sorts listed below (Bear, 208).

CVVC/ CVCC	CVC	CVCe	end with y
resting	jogging	raking	crying
reading	running	making	playing
feeding	shopping	hiking	drying
walking	winning	joking	shying

GT Modification
Advanced meaning sorts can be used with GT students instead (not in addition to) regular assignments.

Suffixes such as (-s), (-ed), and (-ing) change the number and tense of base words without changing the basic meaning (Bear, 208).

Stage V Derivational Relations

Students learn about derivational endings beginning in upper elementary grades and extending through high school and college. Often the second vowel is treated like a schwa (an unaccented vowel that sounds like a short /u/.) At this higher level, spelling is derived from base or root words by adding prefixes and suffixes. Notice sets of words below that are connected by common meanings.

GT Motivation
Derivational relations and word meanings provide challenging sorts for children who are gifted with words and language.

155

define definition definitive	sign signage signature	muscle muscular
finish final finite infinite	punish punitive impunity	courage courageous courageously encourage discourage discouraging discouragingly
elect election	extinct extinction	possess possession
confess confession	oppress oppression	predict prediction

The broad stages of development in spelling, coupled loosely with art and writing, are seen in the chart below.

Levels of Orthography (Spelling)

Emerging	Letter Name and Alphabetic	Within word Pattern	Syllables & Affixes	Derivational
disordered and controlled scribbles, letter strings	letter names (*bd* for *bad*) alphabetic principles such as short vowels (cvc), blends, digraphs	short/long vowels, r-controlled, silent e, v teams, diphthongs content area concepts such as water, plants, animals, states,	inflectional endings such as (-ed), (-s) and (-es), plurals with (y), syllables, compound words	suffixes, final stable syllables such as (-ion), prefixes, roots such as Latin, Greek, science

(pp. 320-331 in *Words Their Way*)

Discovery Teaching Sequence

For both art and spelling, avoid telling and encourage discovery through word sorts and experimentation. The suggested pattern is for students to 1) study words, 2) discover patterns, 3) at the end of the study, determine a rule. When you encourage students to discover a pattern and create their own generalization, you are using a constructivist approach.

GT Modification
Although all students benefit from being allowed to discover and create their own learning experience, this is especially true for GT students. Discovery strengthens long-term recall.

A Weekly Plan for Spelling

Spelling builds on phonological awareness and alphabetic understanding. Without these background skills, **phonetic spelling** will be difficult, since many words are spelled according to letter sounds. Other words rely on remembering the sequence of letters, which is called **orthographic spelling**. Both types of spelling are required for successful writing in English.

Knowing how to study makes a difference in the success or failure of spellers. One of your goals in teaching spelling is to help each child discover which method of studying is the most beneficial. Once children understand how they learn, they will have gained information that will enhance all future learning. Sensory Spelling provides a series of steps that can be used to determine what works best for each individual. The plan, which begins with assessment, is designed to first provide sensory steps and then to combine all senses for a multisensory approach. The initial assessment, which is a type of pretest, is called Check and Correct.

Check and Correct

The name Check and Correct is suggested instead of pretest because many children resist any kind of test. The purpose of Check and Correct is to discover which words need to be studied and which ones have already been mastered.

Steps to Get Ready

Model each step the first few times you use Check and Correct.

- Ask children to fold their papers hot dog style in order to create a second margin down the middle of the paper.
- Children will number from one to ten against the left margin. Using the same lines, children repeat the numbers by writing them against the fold.
- Instruct children to leave a blank line between each numbered line.

GT Modification
A way to modify for the Gifted and Talented children (and all children with outstanding skills in spelling) is to provide "bonus" words for children who can spell the regular list on Check and Correct. Instead of re-writing the regular word along the fold, ask the child to choose a bonus word from a previously prepared list.

Giving Check and Correct

The steps for giving any spelling test are listed below.

- Say the word once.
- Use the word in a sentence.
- Say the word a final time. Stop. (Avoid additional repetition or children will decide it is not important to listen.)

Check and Correct adds a forth step by immediately showing the correct spelling of each word. Use the pattern above for the first word. Immediately show the correct spelling by sharing a large copy of the word or by writing the word on the board. Ask children to rewrite the word on the same line against the middle fold. Those children who miss the word have an immediate opportunity to see and write the word correctly. Children who originally spell the word correctly get verification and a chance to lock in the spelling with the repetition. Continue with the entire list by immediately correcting each mistake. Immediate feedback is the key.

Tuesday through Thursday

Even though students made immediate corrections during Check and Correct on Monday, you cannot count on total accuracy by students. To make certain students study correct spellings, recheck all words written against the centerfold. If necessary, re-write words so that correct letters can easily be read. The need to rewrite a word for a student forms the rationale for leaving a blank line between numbered lines. On Tuesdays, return spelling papers and instruct students to only use the corrected list written down the middle.

Individuals choose from one to five words to master. After studying, partnerships form to assess one another's accuracy. If a student correctly spells all words, add three to five new ones.

- Children with weak spelling skills will choose the most important words but will not be expected to master the entire list.
- Students who learn slowly will continue until mastery is gained over the most important five words.
- Children who begin the week knowing all spelling words choose bonus words that are relevant to their reading or writing.

Summative Assessment on Friday

On Friday, give a **summative test** for a weekly grade. Spelling is one of the best ways to accommodate diverse needs because there are

Dysgraphia Modification
Give a copy of the word to any child who has difficulty reading from a distance and then copying onto paper.

Modification
After teaching children to study with an emphasis on visual, then auditory, and finally using all senses, encourage them to notice which method works best. By doing so, you are emphasizing learning preferences.

many ways to modify for exceptional students. When testing children who are challenged in spelling, reduce the number of required words. Struggling spellers benefit more when allowed to master as few as five words a week than when forced to stumble through 15 or 20 and never truly learn any of them. Allow children with special challenges to choose words from the standard list that are the most important for them to master. On the weekly test, instruct students who master fewer words to place small stars next to the words they studied. These are the words you hold the students accountable for on the test.

It is equally important to challenge students who are strong spellers. A student who scores 90% or above on Check and Correct does not need to study words already learned and can substitute more challenging ones. You may prefer to choose the bonus words or you may give individuals this task. Either way, the words chosen should be valuable to gifted spellers. Before giving the spelling test, ask students with bonus words to turn in their lists with their names.

Students with stronger skills are usually tested over the original list plus bonus words. You may decide to only test gifted spellers over the words missed from the original list plus any bonus words studied. If other students want to try to spell bonus words, allow them to do so.

Another option is to help each student create individualized spelling lists based on their writing and reading. The number of words as well as the words chosen will vary. This option eliminates Check and Correct although Sensory Spelling remains useful. If you individualize to this extent, allow children to take individual tests during writing conferences.

Determining Spelling Grades

When determining a grade, you have at least three distinct groups to consider. You have gifted spellers who are easily accountable for all words on the regular list in addition to many bonus words. You have students for whom the basic list is appropriate along with a few bonus words. There are students who find the regular list so challenging that you will need to reduce the required number. Consider assessment of each of the three groups described below.

Gifted Speller

On Check and Correct, Aidan correctly spelled 8 out of the 10 words on the basic list. Aidan will spend time mastering the 2 words missed on Check and Correct first. He will also study the eight bonus words that replaced the words he already knew on Monday. Aidan's summative test will include: 10 words from the basic list + 8 bonus words = 18 words. All words carry equal value so if Aidan correctly spells 17 of the 18 words on his summative test, divide 17 by 18 for a grade of 94.

Grade Level Speller

On Monday, Emma missed 5 out of 10 words from the basic spelling list. You are confident that Emma will be able to master the 5 words missed by Friday's test. On the summative test, Emma writes all words from the basic list. When you call out the bonus words, Emma decides to try 5 bonus words, which she did not study. Her summative test includes: 10 words from the regular list plus 5 bonus words.

Emma correctly spelled 9 of the 10 basic words and 1 of the 5 bonus words for a total of 10 correctly spelled words. Since Emma didn't study bonus words, you will only count the one bonus word she spelled correctly for a total of 11 words. To determine the grade, divide the 10 correctly spelled words by the 11 words counted for a grade of 90.

Remedial Speller

Marty only spelled 2 words correctly on Monday's Check and Correct. You also know that mastering new words takes more time for Marty than for most students in your class. In addition to the two words Marty spelled correctly on Monday, ask him to choose 3 to 5 additional words to study by asking, "Which of these words will be the most useful to you?" During the week, Marty commits to five words from the basic list including the two he initially spelled correctly. This suggestion is made because children who struggle are often inconsistent from one day to the next. The question is, "Will the two words spelled correctly on Monday be spelled the same way the rest of the week?"

On Friday, Marty attempts all 10 of the words from the original list. Each time he hears a word he studied, he draws a small star beside the word to remind you to grade that word. You assure Marty that if he misses words that do not have stars, you will not count them against him. However, if he spells a word without a star word correctly, you will count it toward his total correct and his number of attempted words.

Marty spells 4 of his 5 starred words correctly as well as one additional word that he did not study for a total of 5 correct words. The one word that was not studied but was spelled correctly is added to Marty's number of words for a total of 6 attempted words. Divide the 5 correct words by the 6 attempted for a grade of 83.

Steps of Sensory Spelling

Sensory Spelling makes use of all senses. Initially, one **sensory modality** (visual, auditory, tactile, or kinesthetic) at a time is emphasized. The final step integrates all senses into a multisensory process. Steps to Sensory Spelling are suggested below. When teaching Sensory Spelling for the first few times, you will explain and model each step before asking children to begin work.

Modification
In order for each spelling test to look similar, ask students who are responsible for fewer words to attempt to spell all words. The star beside the words studied will remind you which words to grade.

Modification
After teaching children to study with an emphasis on visual, then auditory, and finally using all senses, encourage children to notice which method works best. By so doing, you are emphasizing learning preferences or intelligences.

Visual Learning

The first step in Sensory Spelling is for children to create flash cards with strong visual memory clues. Children who tend to think visually will enthusiastically decorate cards. Make certain they do not decorate to the point of losing sight of the letters. Those lacking visual imagination can use a different color to write tricky parts of the word in order to make those letters more noticeable.

Once three to five cards have been decorated or color-coded, teach children to hold one card at a time above eye level and look closely at the word. Then ask children to close their eyes and see the word on the imaginary screens behind their eyes.

Auditory Learning

The auditory step involves working in pairs. One child gives his or her one to five flash cards to a partner who calls out one word at a time. The child being quizzed uses visual memory to mentally see each word while spelling it orally. When a word is spelled correctly, the partner goes to the next word. Each misspelled word is returned with instructions to "Look at the word again." Children take turns calling out words and spelling them. After orally spelling words correctly, you may want to ask students to write the words.

Modification
A teacher discovered a child with good hearing who had learned sign language. When the child signed letters before writing them, her spelling improved.

Multisensory

During the final stage, all senses are simultaneously integrated. Simultaneous use of senses is sometimes referred to as a **Visual-Auditory-Kinesthetic-Tactile (VAKT)** experience. Integrating all senses includes coordinating the following activities.

- Look at one card at a time.
  While looking at the card, orally spell the letter names in the word.
- Simultaneously, pretend to trace each letter of the word on a large textured surface such as a wall or carpet.

Backward Spelling and Dashes

Once a child has mastered visual memory, the child will be able to internally see a word so well that the word can be spelled backwards. Test visual mastery by using the following procedure.

Modifications
When you encourage children to experiment with different ways to learn, such as backwards or dashes, you are modifying and adapting for diversity. Be open to new ways for children to learn.

- Create a flashcard. Under each letter of the word, draw a dash.

<u>D a s h</u>

- On the back of the card, write only the dashes to represent letters.

- Point to the dashes out of sequence and ask, "What letter goes here?"
- Ask the child to visualize the word and spell it backwards. End by asking the child to spell words in correct sequence.

Vertical Spelling

Since fine motor skills initially develop vertically, some students find it easier to spell vertically than horizontally. For many, vertical spelling will eliminate **transposals** (writing letters correctly but in the wrong sequence).

- Use circles or ovals (because circles are developmentally conceptualized before other shapes), write spelling words vertically.
- On the reverse side of the circle, write the word horizontally.

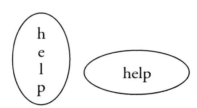

Modification
After repeated failures, a student may respond well to a different way to study. As long as the method results in correct spelling, be willing to experiment.

Teach children to close their eyes and visualize the words vertically or horizontally.

Dividing Words into Parts

If a child cannot spell a particular word, tell the student to divide the word in different ways. For example, for the purpose of creating a spelling aid, "considerate" can be written:

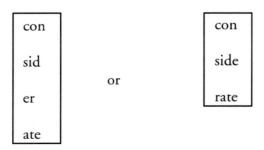

Either way, write each part in a different color. After experimenting, let each student choose a pattern of word division that facilitates spelling recall.

An Alternative Weekly Spelling Plan

When working with children in third grade or above, create a horizontal form similar to the one below. Include a section for children to write the week's spelling words, another section for a pretest, and a third column for a post-test.

Insert the form horizontally inside a folder. Cut the top of the folder to create three flaps; one for each column. In this way, students can cover the list while taking the pretest. When the time comes for the final test, students will cover the first two columns.

Words	Pretest	Post Test
———	———	———
———	———	———
———	———	———
———	———	———
———	———	———
Challenge Words		
———	———	———
———	———	———
———	———	———

Use the same idea for younger children with the following exception. Instead of asking children to write the original list, write the words for the children. Use the second column for children to copy the words and the third for their weekly test.

Dysgraphia Modifications

Even older children with **dysgraphia** may copy the original list incorrectly. If you decide to provide the original list, do so for everyone in the class.

If students copy words, check lists before asking students to study.

Summarizing the Vocabulary Dragons

The module on Vocabulary and Spelling includes multisensory strategies, which are designed to accommodate many different learning needs. Within dyslexia, two types stand out as needing additional help with vocabulary.

Surface Dyslexia and Vocabulary

Because students with Surface Dyslexia have good auditory processing, additional auditory input such as stories, chants or songs will strengthen the flash cards and support the visual memory. This is especially important for irregular words that can never be sounded out.

In spite of the challenge, children with Surface Dyslexia must master the most frequently used irregular words. In order to make this task more accessible to them, use the Memory Strategy along with stories, songs, chants and rhymes. It is your job to combine strong auditory aids to the words that must be memorized. For a child with Surface Dyslexia, simply looking at a word will not work well. Ask yourself, "What would I do to help a child with poor vision?" The answer is that you would add as many auditory prompts as possible.

Deep Dyslexia and Vocabulary

Because learning vocabulary words visually is extremely difficult for students with Deep Dyslexia, only choose the most important words. Words that are less important should be eliminated or delayed until a later time. Adding auditory clues provides only minimal support.

Context Clues

Context clues provide important glimpses into new vocabulary words for children with Deep Dyslexia. Teach types of context clues and ways to use them to discern meanings of new vocabulary words. Children with Deep Dyslexia have good understanding as well as the ability to think deeply. Teaching vocabulary within context and through context clues will be much more resourceful than with other methods such as memorization.

Vocabulary Help Surface *and* Deep

Both Surface and Deep Dyslexia lack the visual discrimination or visual memory skills needed to learn vocabulary using traditional flash cards. **Visual discrimination** relates to the ability to see small differences in the way letters and words look. **Visual memory** enables a learner to recall how a letter or word appears. Although children with Surface Dyslexia have the advantage of strong auditory skills, children with Deep Dyslexia lack both visual and auditory strengths. In order to create lasting memory for vocabulary words, add movement, touch, taste and smell.

- Integrate taste and smell into the meaning of a word.
- Add exaggerated physical movements and drama to strengthen weak visual processes.
- Trace words with 1) two fingers, 2) a colored marker, and finally 3) with a pen or pencil.
- Teach steps of Sensory Spelling and modify for vocabulary meaning.
- Enlarge print to support visual skills, which are weak for both types of dyslexia.
- Experiment with colored overlays or with words written on different colored index cards. Colored paper or overlays may support weak visual skills.

Word Blindness (Surface and Deep)

Although visual acuity is usually good, children with Surface and Deep dyslexia almost seem to have "word blindness," which is a term coined by Dr. Samuel Orton in the 1800's. How would you teach a child with limited vision? You would do everything possible to help the child grasp the word or concept by utilizing all other senses. Consider the following ideas:

- Tell stories using movements, drama, taste and smell.
- Encourage the child to touch the print; trace the letters of a word.
- Listen to teacher-made and commercial materials using the targeted vocabulary words.

Bibliography

Anderson, David, and S. O'Neal, C. David, P. Oruonyehu. *Dyslexia and Related Disorders* (Texas Education Agency, Sept, 1998).

Besner, D. "Deep Dyslexia and Right Hemiesphere Hypothesis." *Can J Psychol* 1983; Vol. 34, No. 4, pp. 565-571.

Bear, R, M.Invernizzi, S. Templeton, F. Johnson. *Words Their Way.* Upper Saddle River, New Jersey: Pearson, 2008.

Block, Cathy, and J. Mangieri. *The Vocabulary Enriched Classroom.* New York, NY: Scholastic, 2006.

Butler, Linda. "Lessons We Learned in Washington, D.C. Schools" *Reading Rockets*: U.S. Department of Education Washington, DC: Washington Educational Television Association (Weta), 2011. <http://www.readingrockets.org/article/361.L

Carlson. "Types of Dyslexia." *Welcome to the Dyslexia Homepage.* Macalester College, 1998. <http://www.macalester.edu/psychology/whathap/UBNRP/Dyslexia/index.html>

Cox, A. *Structures and Techniques.* Cambridge, MA: Educators Publishing Service, Inc.: 1984.

Fischer, B., M. Liaison, R. Warda. "Vocabulary and Spelling Coaching." *Learn That Word.* Sebastopol. CA. <http://www.learnthat.org/vocabulary/pages/view/about_us.html>

Fountas, I. And G. Pinnell. *Guided Reading.* Portsmouth, HN: Heinemann, 1996.

Frandsen, B. *Yes! I Can Teach Literacy.* Austin, TX: Family School, 2006.

"Guiding Visions" *National Council of Teachers of English*. Urbana, IL: International Reading Association, 2011. <http://www.ncte.org/standards>

Marzano. R. J., D. Pickering, J. Pollock. *Classroom Instruction that Works: Research-based Strategies for Increasing Student Achievement*. Upper Saddle, NJ: Pearson, 2005.

Read, J. "Research in Teaching Vocabulary" *Annual Review of Applied Linguistics,* 24, pp. 146-161. 2004. <http://journals.cambridge.org/action/displayAbstract?fromPage= online&aid=223399>

Templeton, S, D. Bear, M Invernizzi, F. Johnston. *Vocabulary Their Way*. Upper Saddle River, New Jersey: Pearson, 2010.

Slaying the Writing Dragon

Some children are reluctant to write because they have few ideas. Many students are unmotivated to write. Teachers can help with both of these challenges.

Other children face a much more serious issue with **dysgraphia**, a disability with writing letters. When this happens, children with great ideas feel blocked by an inability to write their ideas in ways others can read. Dysgraphia is usually related to eye-hand coordination in which the eyes tell the hand what to do. Many children with dysgraphia would benefit from work with an occupational therapist. However, generally the job becomes the work of a classroom teacher.

Watch for modifications and a summary of dysgraphia at the end of the module.

Learning to Write

Handwriting

Putting pen to paper to create graphic representations of ideas is an extremely complicated and skilled fine motor activity. Not all children are ready when we want them to write. Always follow the child's lead and comply with each child's developmental needs.

Writing Grips

Several grips are suitable for writing. Three efficient grips are shown below. Allow students to experiment and choose the one that feels best.

This is the adapted tripod grip.

This is the quadrupod grip.

This is the more traditional tripod grip.

Any time you ask children to write, watch for those who struggle putting pen to paper. Provide the following options to all children. Once the newness wears off, only the ones who benefit will continue to use modifications.

- Use large chart paper. Fold to create lines and dotted lines.
- Start with **gross motor** (large muscles) by asking children to write on a vertical surface such as a white board or chalkboard.
- Use paper with raised lines (Meade).

Quills, the original writing pens, established the handgrip used today. We actually should place the pencil between the first two fingers with the thumb underneath. Avoid large, fat pencils, even for young children.

What Does Research Indicate?

According to an October, 2010 issue of *The Wall Street Journal*, one's hand has a unique relationship with one's brain. According to a research expert, finger movements activate areas of the brain involved with thinking and language. Magnetic Resonance Imaging (MRI) tools show that writing goes beyond forming letters on paper. The activity actually enhances composition and expression as well as fine-motor development. Even though electronic communication appears to be replacing old-fashioned handwriting, schools still maintain handwriting lessons. Research indicates that children who receive penmanship lessons demonstrate more neural brain activity and out perform children who do not receive any handwriting instruction.

Teaching a Multisensory Teaching Approach

Children who lack fine motor skills can follow the procedures suggested below with large pieces of paper and markers. Other students will use traditional school paper.

Provide each student with a piece of paper on which several models of a letter are written in the top left section. Fold papers into four equal parts. Using one section for each step, guide students to complete the following sequence:

- upper left section—trace the model with a fingertip and then with a pencil or marker,
- upper right section—copy the model,
- bottom left section—position the pencil or marker on the paper and write the letter with eyes closed. Sometimes students with fine motor problems write better with eyes closed.
- bottom right section—write the letter from memory with eyes open.

1. Trace B b B b B b	2. Copy
3. Write eyes closed	4. Write best from memory

Dysgraphia Modifications

In addition to altered surfaces, offer the following tools to children:

- Pencil grips,
- Various writing tools such as markers, pencils, or grip-crayons.

Tracing Sequence
- Trace with two fingers,
- Trace with a marker,
- Trace with a pencil.

Dysgraphia Modification

Writing with eyes closed seems to help children with learning differences.

If a child has trouble remembering how to form the letter for step 4, modify the request to "Copy the letter as well as you possibly can."

Correct Letter Formation

In *Nurture Shock*, Bronson and Merryman recommend teaching emerging writers to use self-talk when learning to form new letters. "When the kids are learning the capital (C), they all say in unison, 'Start at the top and go around' as they start to print. No one ever stops the kids from saying it out loud, but after a few minutes most students cease the oral directions. A couple of minutes later, a few kids are still saying it out loud—but most of the kids are saying it in their heads."

Naming the letter strokes by chanting and repeating the steps may avoid the frequent problem of children learning to form letters incorrectly and from incorrect starting places.

Writing to Learn

Reading, Writing Connection

When you strengthen reading, you also build writing skills. When you improve writing, you enhance reading. You write for children by putting names on their desks, sending notes home to be signed, and writing assignments on the whiteboard. Any time you write daily schedules on the board, jot down page numbers, or offer written instructions, you demonstrate writing for children. Always model correct handwriting, grammar, and punctuation. If time is limited, tell children, "I'm going to use 'telegraph' writing, which allows short phrases that are not complete sentences. I'm doing this to save time."

To provide a smooth transition from reading comprehension into writing, encourage children to write about their reading experiences. In this way, you provide a fluid experience connecting the two disciplines. The following ideas suggest possible responses children can make to narrative reading.

- Write a comparison of yourself and one of the characters.
- Select a favorite passage and explain why the sentence or paragraph caught your interest.
- Create an imaginary dialogue between one of the characters and yourself.
- Change one part of the story to make it funny, scary, spooky, suspenseful, or magical.
- Which words in the story helped create a mood or feeling? List those words.
- Add yourself as a new character in the plot. How will you respond to events in the story?
- Analyze the book. What will you tell other children about the book? Will you recommend it? Tell why or why not.
- Compare one character in the story with a character in a different story.
- Write a new ending for the story.
- Pretend you are a newspaper reporter. Write a newspaper account of one exciting event.

Dysgraphia Modification
On some occasions, when the thinking process outweighs the physical task of writing, you can allow a student with dysgraphia alternative methods of expression.

- Allow students with disabilities to make oral reports rather than written ones.
- Allow students to record ideas on CD's.
- Provide a graphic organizer, which will serve as a template for writing.
- Allow art or music alternatives to writing.

- Did any part of the story bore you? Rewrite that part and make it more interesting.
- Which character in the story would you like to be? Why?
- Did any part of the story confuse you? What would you like to ask the author?

Guided Writing Instruction

Language Experience Approach

Language Experience Approach (LEA) is also found in *Begin at the Beginning*. The strategy is important enough to also include in the writing module. In this process, you are the scribe for children who provide the thoughts. Although the basic philosophy of LEA is to accept everything suggested by the child or children, consider altering spelling when words are mispronounced. Below, you will find the basic steps of LEA.

- Begin with an experience. The experience can be as simple as looking at clouds or as expansive as a field trip to the zoo.
- Engage the children in a conversation about the experience. As children talk, write a few key words on chart paper.
- Point to and read the key words to the children. Invite them to help you create a story.
- Guide children to develop a title and assist with an opening sentence.
- As children think of ideas, write them on the chart paper. Alternatives are to write on scratch paper or to type the story into a computer.
- The next day, bring a carefully printed or typed copy of the story to share with children.
- Initially, read the story to children. After modeling two to four times, invite children to "read" with you. Repeat the process until some of the children can read the story independently.
- Examine the story for examples of phonics generalizations you are teaching or for important sight vocabulary. For example, if you are teaching the H Brothers, look for words using (ch), (sh), (th), or (wh).

Shared Writing

Shared writing frequently involves the Language Experience Approach (LEA), which combines thinking, talking, writing and

176

reading. Children, as composers, create a class script. You, acting as a scribe, demonstrate that talk can be written down and read by others as you take dictation from children. In **shared writing**, you modify ideas from the children as you demonstrate correct writing structure. Another difference in shared writing is **sharing the pen**.

Interactive Writing and *Sharing the Pen*

Interactive writing begins as shared writing. Although the concept is based on the language experience approach, **interactive writing** evolves into a situation in which both you and your students act as scribes. At certain points while jointly composing a class story, a child takes the pen and adds letters or even a word to the text. This is a wonderful experience for the child doing the writing. However, if the child is allowed to be the scribe for more than a few minutes, your class will get bored and restless. Before boredom sets in, you must get the entire class involved.

One way to include all children (even when one child shares the pen) is to furnish lapboards or paper and clipboards for each student. As ideas are added to the group story, each individual also writes and remains physically engaged.

What About THE Spelling Question?

As soon as you invite children of any age to write independently, you begin to hear the question, "How do you spell . . . . ?" You are faced with many possibilities including the ideas listed below.

Response	Disadvantage	Advantage
You spell the word orally for the child.	Spelling is rarely an oral activity. Although the child may remember the word long enough to write it down, very little chance for learning is provided. You may be fostering dependence.	The flow of writing can continue as soon as the unknown word is written down. When writing expressively, it is important to keep ideas and words flowing.
You tell the child to "sound it out."	Many words do not follow phonics rules. Even with phonetically regular words, some children will feel frustrated.	You are promoting independence. (Children who find matching sounds to symbols difficult will lose the flow.)

"Spell the word the best you can."	Some children will feel frustrated by this suggestion.	You are promoting independence and keeping the flow of words going.
Say, "Write the word the best you can and circle it to show your uncertainty."	Unless the child is terribly uncomfortable not knowing, no harm is done.	The flow can continue and the child is learning to attempt the unknown.
Tell the child to write the first letter of the word and draw a line. At a later time, you will help complete the word.	There are children who are miserable until they absolutely know the word is correct. You may have to "give" a little for these children.	You are promoting independence. You also insisted that the child write at least one letter. That is a good start.
Write the word on a small piece of paper or on a sticky note.	A few educators might say you are helping too much.	Seeing and copying the unknown word is a good learning experience. For the child who cannot live peacefully without knowing the correct spelling, this is a good response.

The Writing Process

Marie Clay and Helen Depress from New Zealand encourage use of guided writing lessons for children in emergent literacy programs. The child's existing knowledge determines the starting point. You will guide and **scaffold** (provide support) with unknown elements. The term scaffolding suggests providing a framework much like the framing of a building before adding walls. For example, you might ask, "What sound do you hear? Yes, the word starts with the /m/ sound."

Sometimes, the best writing comes from other content areas such as math or science. Although children should write every day, they will not take every piece of writing through the entire writing process. Even first graders, whose early writing pieces are often one sentence long, can produce a minimum of one piece to analyze, revise, edit and recopy for presentation or publication each week. During a week's time, some students will have numerous examples that include all steps in process writing. Others struggle to complete the writing process over one piece.

At the end of the week, allow each child to choose one item for a summative evaluation in your grade book. In addition, you should maintain a folder for each child with a writing sample at the beginning of the year, another sample in January, and a third at the end of the year. These three writing samples will provide benchmarks for each child's teacher in following year as well as documentation for you and the child during the current year. The following steps outline a sequence of activities that define the writing process.

Dysgraphia Modification

You will have children who complete several writing pieces during a week. The possibility for each student to "choose" one to be graded provides a face-saving modification for the child who spent the entire week completing a single writing product.

Teaching How to Get Ideas for Writing

Some children produce prolific writing and even creative writing without a specific suggestion for a writing topic. When this is true, allow children the freedom to choose. Other students require help to get started. Class lists can be used for permanent bulletin boards to help students think of ideas for writing. Follow the steps below to create a class list of potential writing topics.

- Ask each student to write a list of ten ideas for writing.
- Groups of three or four students read one another's lists.

Modification

Instead of using the class list as a requirement for writing, offer it as an aid for children needing ideas from which to choose.

- Each group chooses three or four topics of interest and importance (determined by number of students in each group).
- Combine group lists to create a class list of interesting writing topics to post on a bulletin board or in a learning center.
- Encourage students to think creatively beyond the class list and to imagine additional interesting topics.

Prewriting Activities

Once a topic has been determined, each student will need to complete one of several activities for pre-writing in order to generate a flow of ideas. Teach a variety of prewriting methods and allow students to use the ones that are the most beneficial. For example: 1) Writing frames provide excellent tools for prewriting. 2) Both outlining and mind mapping provide visual forms for organizing ideas. 3) In addition, the act of brainstorming facilitates a flow of ideas. Keep in mind that brainstorming, often referred to as green light thinking, includes all ideas without any comments or evaluations. Since brainstorming is a group activity, children benefit from listening to one another. 4) Free writing amounts to silent, personal brainstorming in that each student writes any and all words that come to mind concerning a topic or idea. Below, you will find two specific prewriting strategies.

Teaching Blueprinting

Blueprinting connects art with writing by asking children to draw outlines of their homes or apartments on large pieces of paper. Within the outlines, students mark off specific rooms. Ask students to choose at least one major room on the blueprint to create a column of words, phrases, or activities that take place in that room. Lists of words might include the following possibilities.

- Activities that frequently take place in the room.
- People who share the room.
- Contents of the room.
- A special memory attached to the room.

Dysgraphia Modification

Prewriting is especially important for students who lack confidence with writing. You may have students who find it difficult to write more than a few words. In special cases, the prewriting activity can be used as the final product.

Visual Modification

Students who learn and express themselves well using visual graphics and visual words, will enjoy and benefit from using Blueprinting.

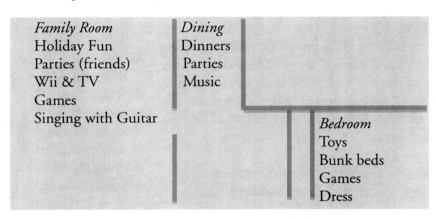

Family Room
Holiday Fun
Parties (friends)
Wii & TV
Games
Singing with Guitar

Dining
Dinners
Parties
Music

Bedroom
Toys
Bunk beds
Games
Dress

A single list or a combination of lists provides prompts for rough draft paragraphs.

Teaching Listing

Encourage students to commit to a general topic such as "Getting Ready for Christmas." Once the topic is determined, the strategy involves creating a series of lists. Steps are suggested below.

- List all the things needed for Christmas, such as paper, cards, ribbon, food, decorations, and gift ideas.
- Circle one idea from the first list. For example, choose *decorations*. Create a second list with decoration items such as inside or outside lights, balls, angels, stockings, holly, outside decorations and wreaths.
- Circle one item from the second list to begin a third list. For example, you might choose *outside decorations*. The third list might include: tree lights, outside lights, extension cords, blinking lights, traditional versus light emitting diode (LED) lights and timers.

Teaching with Warm-Up Activities

Sometimes writers need to warm up to get their mental juices flowing before beginning rough draft writing. Allow students to work in pairs or alone.

- Write as many feeling words as possible.
- Write **onomatopoeia** sound words such as giggle, whoosh, murmur, or buzz. Vary the activity with words for sight, touch, taste, and smell.
- Suggest various new ways to use common objects such as spoons, shoeboxes, napkins, clothespins, coat hangers, or paper plates.
- State six reasons for and against ideas such as school, fights, pets, eating vegetables, free time, cafeteria lunches, group work, homework, or chores.
- Begin with a simple sentence and make it more interesting.
- Select an object from a box of items and list ten words to describe it. Use the words to compose a paragraph.
- Name three wishes you want to make.

Allowing the writer to choose from a variety of prewriting methods suggests respect for various intelligences.

Modifications
Notice how many of the warm-up activities use touch, sounds, visuals and motions. Allow students to choose activities that appeal to their learning preferences.

Preference Modifications
Providing menus of ways to complete assignments appeals to students' learning preferences, which are sometimes called types of learning intelligence. Choices increase motivation and demonstrate your respect for students.

Visual Spatial	Auditory Verbal	Kinesthetic Tactile
Map ideas	Brainstorm orally	Map ideas on large pieces of paper
Draw	Use guided imagery	Draw large pictures
Visualize	Tell a story to a partner	Sort ideas on index cards
Write a list	Use cartoon balloons	Circle main ideas
Make a timeline, flowchart, or outline	Discuss ideas within small groups	Draw arrows to indicate a sequence of pictures
Use writing frames	Record your story on a CD	

Rough Drafts

The purpose of a rough draft is to transform pre-writing ideas into paragraph form. A piece that a child selects for the entire writing process may need as many as four different drafts. Rough drafts focus on the flow of ideas rather than mechanics and form. Ideally, you will have enough technology for each student to create rough drafts using word processors. Encourage students to use double spacing and to save all work. Remind students to consider the audience and purpose for writing.

When teaching children how to write rough drafts on paper, include the following suggestions.

- Leave spaces between lines so ideas can be added.
- Write with a pencil. Save all work.
- Address the following: your audience, your purpose, and the setting (place and time).
- Go for an exciting "grabber" in the introduction to gain attention.

Revising

Revising focuses on the sequence and logic of ideas rather than mechanics such as punctuation or spelling. Save all versions during the revising process. When teaching students to revise paragraphs for connections and coherence, include the following questions and suggestions.

- "How does your title fit your story?"
- "How does your story sound when you read it aloud? Do all the ideas focus on the same idea?"

Dysgraphia Modification
Students who struggle with pen to paper application may benefit from paper with raised lines. Pencil/pen grips also help students who grip pens incorrectly or who squeeze pens until knuckles are white. Try a variety.

Dysgraphia Modification
Technology affords a new method to write rough drafts, revise and edit. Ideally, you will have enough computers for all who prefer using technology.

- "Is there any idea that doesn't seem to fit?"
- "What do you mean by _____ ?"
- "Substitute six more interesting verbs."
- "Add an exciting adjective to six different nouns."
- "Add some elaboration."
- "Does your paragraph have a beginning, a middle section, and an ending?"

CAKES for Revising

Avoid marking on any student's paper for two reasons. First, a page full of red marks becomes devastating for many students. Second, your students will learn more if they have to figure out how to repair their own errors. Your job is to indicate that the author needs to make a change. Notes and marks on a checklist indicate areas for the student to address.

C = confusing—clear it up,

A = add ideas—not enough details,

K = kick it out—not needed,

E = examples—are needed,

S = sequence—needs changing

When teaching children to use CAKES, instruct them to put a checkmark under, "Great," if no problems are noted. Otherwise, children are to suggest ideas. Either way, ask students to sign their initials indicating responsibility for feedback to the writer.

CAKES Revising

	Great	Line Numbers	Initials
Clear it up			
Add ideas			
Kick it out			
Examples			
Sequence			

Encourage students who are revising to use a variety of methods in order to meet their individual preferences.

Visual Spatial	Auditory Verbal	Kinesthetic Tactile
Scan to check for flow	Read aloud to self	Cut and paste ideas by hand
Read written feedback from a teacher or peers	Read aloud to a partner	Use a computer to cut and paste

Editing

Once the writer has completed changes to large ideas, it is time to edit smaller aspects such as spelling and punctuation. The following questions are appropriate for the editing stage. Often, even after beginning to edit, revision ideas may emerge.

- "Check the first word of each sentence for capitals."
- "Check all cities, proper names, states, and streets for capitals."
- "Does each sentence end with a form of punctuation?"
- "Do you have commas between cities and states, dates and the year, after greetings and closing, within a series, and within quotations?"
- "Did you use quotation marks for each piece of dialogue?"

Note: Periods and commas go inside quotation marks. A question mark goes inside the quotation marks if the entire sentence is a question. If a single word is put inside quotations marks, the punctuation goes outside quotation marks. (Willard)

- "Did you use parentheses correctly?"

Note: Periods go inside the parentheses only if the entire sentence is in the parentheses. Periods go outside the parentheses if the word grouping is not a complete sentence. (Willard)

- "Are your sentences complete?"
- "Have you checked your spelling?"
- "Is your handwriting neat and easy to read?" When using a word processor, ask, "Is the font easy to read? Is the font too large or too small? Did you leave white spaces between paragraphs and in the margins?"

Caution
Always point out positive qualities about each child's written expression. Motivation builds on successes; not on failures.

Focus on one item at a time to edit.

CUPS for Editing

An editing form called CUPS can be used to provide feedback to the author. Ask editors to initial suggestions made to the writer. A CUPS form represents these items:

C = capitals,

U = usage of language (grammar, agreement of nouns and pronouns, agreement of nouns and verbs and tenses),

P = punctuation,

S = spelling.

CUPS Editing

	Great	Line #'s and Ideas	Initials
Capitals			
Usage			
Punctuation			
Spelling			

It is important to provide forms on which editors can make notes and suggestions since neither you nor the children should write on students' papers. The strategy below, Clocking, is designed to engage children in editing with and for one another.

Teaching Clocking

Divide the class into groups of eight students. Ask children to meet you at a designated location with: 1) a writing piece to be edited, 2) a CUPS Editing form, 3) a clipboard and 4) a pencil. Arrange four students in a circle. Once the circle is formed, ask each child to turn and face outward. Place the remaining four students in an outer circle with each child facing a partner.

Students facing one another trade papers (with editing forms attached). Remind students to only write on the editing forms. Instruct children to focus on one element at a time. For example, advise students to check for use of commas. After five minutes, writers retrieve papers and forms and explain suggestions to one another. Authors can decide to reject or accept suggestions.

Children on the inside circle move clockwise to form new partnerships. Students trade again and either 1) continue to edit the same skill where the first editor stopped, 2) repeat the previously edited section and skill, or 3) start at the beginning of the piece editing a

Caution

The purpose of using forms such as CUPS and CAKES is to avoid writing on a student's paper. A written piece covered with red corrections is devastating to a child who struggles to write.

Modification

Clocking provides the benefit of getting students out of their seats and moving. With clipboards, they can make notes while standing.

Feedback

Providing frequent feedback is one of the best ways to help students improve writing. Focus on one or two items at a time. Avoid overwhelming writers.

different skill. Use a 1 - 2 - 3 Chart as another way to provide feedback.

Teaching With a 1 - 2 - 3 Chart

A 1-2-3 Chart provides another way to provide feedback to one another.

1 = not ok, 2 = ok, 3 = good

Components	1	2	3	Initials
Title—Does the title catch your attention?				
Introduction—Does the introduction hook the reader?				
Purpose—Is the reason for writing clear?				
Interest—Is the piece interesting?				
Sequence—Do events happen in logical order?				
Ending—Does the ending tie all the ideas together?				
Grammar—Do subjects and verbs agree?				
Usage—Is the language used correctly?				
Spelling—Are words spelled correctly?				
Punctuation—Is ending punctuation correct?				
Commas—Are commas used correctly?				
Quotations—Are quotation marks used correctly?				

Build on personal strengths by encouraging student editors to experiment with various editing methods.

Visual Spatial	Auditory Verbal	Kinesthetic Tactile
Apply removable colored tape to point the author to problems.	While editing, ask someone to read the piece aloud	Circle errors

Use a highlight pen to show where editing is needed.	Read aloud to yourself	Color code mistakes with colored markers

Using Track Changes for Revising and Editing

Beginning in second grade, students can be taught to understand and use Track Changes within Microsoft Word software to indicate suggestions. Authors can either accept or reject suggestions. Once students become familiar with the Track Changes function, you can teach them to apply the system for peer revisions and editing.

On a Macintosh computer, Track Changes can be found under Tools. Indicate that you want to "Highlight Changes." You will also be asked to choose the option to "Track changes while editing."

On a PC computer, you can locate Track Changes under the Tools menu or you can press Control, Shift and E simultaneously. Changes will show up in the right-hand margin. Right click on any suggestion to accept or to reject the change.

Presenting in the Author's Chair

To create a product worthy of an audience remains the real goal of most writers. Real audiences give writing purpose and authenticity.

At the end of writing and conferencing, hold a sharing time each day. Another option is to have one day a week designated for sharing in the author's chair. One to three students may want to sit in the "Author's Chair" and read their finished pieces or their works-in-progress to the class. An author's chair should be decorated or labeled to make it special to children. Introduce sharing time with mini-lessons on appropriate ways to share as well as courteous audience responses. Sometimes, a writer may ask the class for revision ideas or suggestions for improvement. Students who are too shy to read personal work from the author's chair may pass or ask a friend to read with or for them.

Presentations create special interest when children employ a variety of methods. Both presenters and audience participants will enjoy suggestions listed below each preference.

Teach Audience Skills
Teach and rehearse appropriate behavior from an audience. Emphasize positives in each child's writing.

Visual Spatial	**Auditory Verbal**	**Kinesthetic Tactile**
Draw a picture depicting an event	Read favorite sections aloud	Create dialogue and involve others
Create a cartoon strip	Summarize orally	Pantomime characters
Draw a web of characters and events	Answer questions from the audience	Act out a scene

Publishing

In *A Nation of Writers*, R. Cramer states that publishing, the final and most formal way of sharing, promotes motivation, pride, and confidence. Publishing can be as simple as stapling pages together or as elaborate as covering and binding writing collections at a print shop. Class books, including poems, stories, and pieces selected by students, make wonderful additions to the reading center and final-draft articles contribute to individual portfolios. Provide a variety of publishing sources to meet individual needs and preferences.

Visual Spatial	Auditory Verbal	Kinesthetic
Publish in a class newspaper	Read the piece in author's chair	Dramatize the piece
Place the work on a bulletin board	Record or videotape the story	Publish a book

The writing process flows through and becomes part of a writing workshop as individual students apply the process according to their personal rates, abilities and interests.

Publishing Caution

It is tempting to display only products from the best writers in class. In addition, include less-than-perfect pieces from less skilled writers. "I gave 100%" can be reason enough to exhibit a piece of writing.

Writing Workshop

Although generally students follow a sequence in the Writing Process, the class is not locked together. The beauty of a writer's workshop is that every student works at the level and the speed that is most appropriate for that individual. With the exception of a mini-lesson, there is no need to keep the class together. This is diversification at its best and requires little effort on your part. The various parts of the writing process fit within the structure of a Writing Workshop.

"Just as students learn to read by reading, they learn to write by writing." (Gunning, p. 501) During a writer's workshop, the majority of the time is devoted to students engaging in writing. Below, read about the major components of a workshop.

Components of a Writing Workshop

A writer's workshop includes a mini-lesson, record keeping, writing, conferencing and sharing.

Writing Mini-Lessons

Usually, you will teach a mini-lesson to the whole class over a need demonstrated in students' work. Consider the sequence suggested below.

- Explain the skill and provide support for the value of that skill. For example, ending punctuation tells the reader where to stop.
- Demonstrate the correct way to use the skill.
- Follow your demonstration with examples and **non-examples** (incorrect samples to demonstrate common errors).
- Continue with samples for children to complete under your guidance. Keep the lesson brief (approximately five to seven minutes). Follow your mini-lesson by determining the writing status of each student.

Record Keeping (Class Status)

If your principal or a parent asks how or what a student is doing in writing, you want and need to be able to respond factually. Following your mini-lesson each day, ask each student to share a plan for the day, which you will record on your class status form. Although it is a challenge to keep track of each child in your classroom, you will be able to do so with a systematic plan. Record keeping will also help you keep track of students needing conferences with you. Some students will require many conference times with you. Set a goal to conference with each student at least one time each week. There are various methods for maintaining records, as you will see below.

A Class Record Form

In addition to writing notes, you may benefit from a single class record form on which to quickly jot down the anticipated actions of each child. In reality, each student may engage in several activities on a given day. On your record form, only indicate the initial activity for each student. You may find the following abbreviations useful.

- I = Getting Ideas,
- PW = Prewriting Activity,
- RD = Rough Draft,
- C = Conference with Teacher,
- CP = Conference with a Peer,
- R = Revising,
- E = Editing,
- PR = Presenting in the author's chair,
- PU = Publishing.

Name	Mon.	Tues.	Wed.	Thurs.	Fri.
Adam	C				
Bill	R				
Cheryl	E				
Edward	PR				
Jose	PU				

Index Cards

Another form of record keeping includes maintaining a large index card for each student. Each day, spend a few seconds with each student to record what the student will be working on. In addition to writing notes, you may benefit from using the code suggested above.

Binder With Labels

You may find it easier to maintain a binder with a page for each student. As you systematically go through your binder, you will jot down activities, strengths and needs. You may also use the abbreviated codes suggested above. Ideally, your binder will be alphabetized and you will collect information from each child in the correct sequence. In reality, you will often notice a random student engaging in interesting and relevant work. It takes time to flip through the binder to locate the student's name.

To save time, carry a clipboard with large self-sticking labels. If you notice a student doing exceptionally well or one who needs immediate assistance, you can quickly write the student's name and the date on the label. At a later time, transfer the label to that child's page in your binder.

Writing during Workshop Time

During a writer's workshop (approximately 30 minutes a day) children write and hold conferences. In pre-kindergarten, kindergarten and first grade, students draw and write by using **invented spelling**. Invented spelling is non-conventional spelling in which a child uses sounds and letter combinations known at that time. In older grades, students' writing may take many forms, including using writing frames (graphic organizers), outlines, or cartoon characters. English Language Learners (ELL) students may use a combination of their first language and English.

During a writer's workshop, students write individually and **independently**. Independent writing by children occurs when children write with minimal assistance from you or from peers. Initially, emerging writing may consist of scribbles. This practice, which amounts to "**pretend writing**" is usually called **approximation**. Some authors refer to pretend reading as **talking like a book**. This initial stage of independent writing marks an important beginning and should be applauded.

Making tools available, providing time, and motivating students become your primary tasks in creating independent writers. While students write independently, you will use your time to hold writing conferences. Many activities will be happening at the same time and the scene may appear confusing. However, out of confusion rises a community of writers.

Guidelines for Writers

Each student should maintain two folders. In one folder, a **storage folder,** the student will keep copies and drafts of all previous writing. A second folder, the **working folder**, will hold drafts of the current writing project (Guszak, p. 183). During the writing workshop, students engage in all parts of the writing process. In addition, instruct students to follow the guidelines below.

- "Avoid erasing (in order to keep a record of thinking)."
- "Only write on one side of a page (to make it easier to cut and paste)."
- "Leave a blank space between each line (to provide a place to write ideas)."
- "Save everything (to create a history of writing)."
- "Date and label everything (draft #1, #2, etc.)."
- "Talk quietly so that others can think."

Teaching Conferencing

During writing time, circulate around the room, pausing to talk to individuals as they write. Hold two-minute conversations with as many students as possible. Encourage students to use all steps of process writing (pre-writing, writing rough drafts, revising, editing, presenting and publishing). According to Guszak, some teachers require a minimum of four drafts in students' working folders. You encourage writing as you take the following actions:

- move to your students rather than asking them to come to you,
- make eye contact, sit or kneel close to each writer,
- avoid writing on a student's paper,
- build on what each writer knows and is writing,
- ask questions that truly interest you.

There are three types of questions to ask during conferencing. Initially, ask, "How is your writing coming along?" Your second question will depend on the student's answer to your first question. Finally, ask process questions such as, "What do you need to do next? Are you stuck? How can I help?"

At a student's request or in response to a need, longer conferences may be held. Offer information during individual conferences or during mini-lessons on a "needs to know" basis rather than looking for a chance to teach technique.

Sharing

Either at the end of each day or on one special day of the week, allow students to share their written pieces. This provides an opportunity for peers to ask questions and make suggestions.

Grading Written Work

Wouldn't it be wonderful if you never had to assign grades? Though exceptions exist, your district will probably expect you to indicate your students' academic progress either through letter or number grades. In addition to meeting state and local requirements, you benefit your students by providing frequent feedback to them.

As a teacher, you have a responsibility to offer feedback and grades in ways that promote positive self-esteem. Student self-assessments, status reports at the end of mini-lessons, notes from writing conferences, checklists, and your own pre-determined criteria will help make decisions about grades. When required to grade a written assignment, dignify individual writers by applying the following ideas.

- Respond to a student's writing with one positive comment and one suggestion for improvement.
- Instead of writing an example of a needed correction, simply check the sentence where the error is located (√) or indicate on a separate form. The student will benefit more from locating the error and determining how to remediate the situation.
- Avoid use of red pens that give a "bloody" look to the page.
- Allow each student to select one paper to be graded each week.

Self-Assessment and Peer Feedback

After experiencing your feedback and suggestions, students in grade two and above can be encouraged to self-assess and peer-assess. Initially, only ask peers to assess and give feedback on one item at a time, such as capital letters at the beginning of sentences. Not only will this save you a small amount of time and effort, it will strengthen the students' ability to think critically.

Do not try to grade every piece of writing every student does each week. Too much emphasis on grading will discourage you from assigning writing opportunities. Too much grading also discourages students from writing for pleasure. Not everything a student writes goes through the entire revision and editing process. Allow students to choose which selections to polish and refine for presentations, publication and assessment.

Journal Writing

Journals offer another way for students to write independently. Journals can be used during writer's workshops or at a separate time. Often, journal writing can also be used in a content area such as math or science. Art Scaffolding Journals are also found in *Begin at the Beginning*.

Teaching Beginning Journals

Even if all children can do is scribble, wean them from dictation and encourage them to write independently. If you accept scribbling, the child will soon progress to the next writing stage. In **Art Scaffolding Journals**, begin by asking the child to draw a picture. For some children, you will need to set a time limit on drawing.

- Allow the child to complete a picture.
- Say, "Tell me about your picture." Avoid asking, "What is it?" which seems insulting and fails to engage the child in extended use of language.
- As the child describes the picture, label people and objects in the picture by writing single words on Post-It® notes. Avoid writing on the child's page.
- Ask, "What would you like to write about your picture?" For most young children, a story consists of one sentence.

Dysgraphia Modification
When working with young children, get one complete sentence from each child (even if scribbling is used as a form of writing).

Children who are capable can be encouraged to write additional sentences.

Teaching Composition Sentences

One of the most powerful ways to enhance the reading/writing connection is through composition sentences. Connect the sentences to art scaffolding above.

- Encourage the child to repeat the sentence from the art—scaffolding journal several times before beginning to write.
- The child begins writing (or scribbling) the sentence on the same page as the picture. Encourage the child to rely on what

he or she already knows as well as the words on Post-It® notes (provided during art-scaffolding).

- In addition, ask questions such as, "Can you spell _____? If not, can you find that word on one of the notes? What letter do you hear at the beginning?" As you assist, you gain opportunities to teach and explain literacy concepts.
- As you listen and observe, write the child's exact words on a separate page or sentence strip. Say, "Another way to write what you said looks like this."
- Read the sentence (from your copy) several times.

Scramble Words

- Add, "I'm going to try to trick you." As the child watches, cut your sentence into separate words. Leave the ending punctuation with the last word in the sentence.
- Scramble the words and ask the child to put the words back into the order of the sentence. Scaffold by asking, "What kind of letter do you need at the beginning? What will come after the last word in the sentence?"
- Once the child has correctly sequenced the sentence, ask the child to read and re-read the sentence. Once the child can successfully read the composition sentence, the child has moved beyond **approximation** (pretend reading) into actual reading.

Save for Future Reading

On the outside of a small envelope, write the child's entire composition sentence. Place the individual words inside the envelope for future independent reading experiences.

- Follow up the next day by pointing to the sentence the child wrote in the journal and asking, "Can you read what you wrote in your journal yesterday?"
- Present the individual words from the envelope and ask the child to organize the words into the original sentence. When a child can put words in the correct sequence and read them correctly, the child is experiencing independent reading.
- Repeat the same composition sentences many times during independent reading times to build confidence and fluency.

Teaching Personal Response Journals

As students become more confident writers, they enjoy describing experiences, feelings, and reflections in their personal journals. Personal journals require and deserve respect and your students should control

Modification

Combining a child's journal sentence into a composition sentence is one of the most powerful ways to teach reading. There will be children who need to continue this activity. As long as the child can unscramble and read the words, the child is making progress.

whether to share writings or indicate privacy by vertically folding the page in half. When students choose to share personal thoughts with you, respond as quickly as possible. Avoid all temptations to correct spelling, punctuation, or handwriting. Benefits of sharing personal agendas through journal writing include:

- setting a purpose for writing—to share with you,
- creating a dialogue between you and the child,
- allowing a healthy expression of strong emotions, which may result in strong and generally inappropriate vocabulary (which you will accept in this context),
- giving you an opportunity to remind the student of strengths and accomplishments,
- providing a personal way for you to quietly suggest new ways to handle negative emotions by asking, "Have you considered _____?" Always phrase as a question and not as a demand. Remove all judgment from your thinking.
- opening a venue for problem solving by the student with assistance from you.

Several times each week, set aside time for personal journal writing. When you collect personal journals, instruct students to fold pages that they choose to keep totally private. You will only read unfolded pages and will never correct any personal writing. Only respond to content and feelings shared by the student. Sharing between students and teachers becomes particularly precious and bonding.

NOTE: If you read a journal entry depicting abuse, neglect, or threats to harm others, you are legally responsible to report the entries to the Department of Public Safety. Although you will share concerns with your principal and school counselor, you must be the one to make the report. Reports can be made anonymously and unless a case goes to trial, parents will not know who made the report. Other dangers and concerns exist, however. When cases of abuse are reported, the situation sometimes gets worse for the child. Very few children are removed from homes because there are so few foster homes available, which means a child may literally be stuck in the home situation.

Another concern is that the child may feel betrayed by you. Regardless of what parents do, children usually want to be loyal. The possibility of removal can be threatening to a child. Hopefully, your school counselor will be available to help the child as well as to advise you. Generally, but not always, it is preferable for the teacher to be honest with the child if a report is filed. Each situation comes with unique circumstances.

Teaching Response Journals

When students write in journals after reading their own selections, the activity is called a **reading response**. A few starters for both literature and response journals include the following instructions to students.

- "Describe three events or ideas from the reading selection that remind you of an experience you have had."
- "If you were the main character, what would you do in a similar situation?"
- "What values was the author attempting to suggest?"
- "What did you learn that you plan to use in your own life?"
- "Did the author express any ideas that you believe are incorrect?"

Your responses to your students' reactions provide insight and an opportunity to dialogue through writing.

When children write in response to a selection you read to them, refer to the activity as a **literature response**. You may use the same types of questions as for reading responses, or you may replace or add to specific comprehension questions by inviting students to share reactions to reading selections.

Slaying the Writing Dragon

There are children with wonderful ideas who feel like failures because they are unable to put their thoughts on paper. For example, a very intelligent and creative fourth grader shared that he cries privately because he writes like a first grader. Teachers, parents and the student feel discouraged and confused. Dysgraphia is the name of the "dragon" that hinders both legible handwriting and expressive writing.

Handwriting Challenges and Solutions

A child with dysgraphia may form unfinished letters with open gaps. In addition, letters may have uneven sizes, be off the line, and poorly spaced. To help with letter formation experiment with the following:

- Ask parents to purchase paper with raised lines.
- Offer a variety of pencil grips to the student.
- Encourage students who struggle to practice on a large vertical surface such as a whiteboard or chart.
- Fold chart paper on the lines to provide a tactual page.
- Take time to teach handwriting. If possible, teach one small group at a time so you can observe each child's grip and letter formation.
- Model and orally describe formative strokes for each letter.
- During lessons on handwriting, teach oral reminders such as the following for the letter (b), "Start at the top. Pull down. Stop at the bottom line. Halfway up the line, swing up and around to form the circular part of the letter."
- Encourage children to state descriptions of the strokes with you. Soon, most children will no longer need to hear themselves name the movements. A few children will continue to mumble the steps until mastery is complete.

Expressive Writing Suggestions

In order to unlock the wonderful thoughts trapped in a child's mind by lack of hand control, offer the following modifications:

- Teach the child correct key boarding and encourage use of a computer or word processor.
- Allow the student with dysgraphia to dictate ideas and responses to parents, another adult, or even a peer.
- Allow some of the writing assignments to be completed with partners. Pair one child with good ideas and another who writes easily and legibly.
- Encourage the student with dysgraphia to talk into a recorder. At a later time, the student will type or write what he or she recorded earlier.
- Allow alternatives such as oral reports, drama, or art to complete traditional writing assignments.

Bibliography

Bounds, G. "How Handwriting Trains the Brain." *The Wall Street Journal.* Princeton, MJ. Oct. 2010.

Bronson, P, A. Meryman. *NurtureShock.* New York, NY: Twelve Hachette Group, 2009.

Clay, Marie, S.A. Warner, E. Richardson, and D. Holdaway. *Dancing With the Pen: The Learner As a Writer.* New Zealand: Ministry of Education, 1992.

Deuel, Rosemary. "Dysgraphia and Motor Skills Disorders." *Journal of Child Neurology.* Vol.10.Supp 1. January 1995. Pp. S6 - S8.

Frandsen, B. *Yes! I Can Teach Literacy.* Austin, TX: Family School, 2006.

—*Making a Difference for Students with Differences.* Austin, TX: Family School, 2001.

Gambrell, L., L. Morrow, S. Neuman, and M. Pressley. *Best Practices in Literacy Instruction.* New York, NY:Guilford Press, 1999.

Graves, D. All Children Can Write (Learning Disabilities Focus), fall, 1995.

Guszak, F. *Reading for Students With Special Needs.* Dubuque, Iowa: Kendall Hunt Publishers, 1992.

Gunning, T. *Creating Literacy Instruction for All Children.* Boston, MA: Pearson, 2003.

Hambly, J. *How to Track Changes in Microsoft Word. Be Your Own IT.* Menomonee Falls, Wisconsin, 2010. *http://www.beyourownit.com/ how-to-track-changes-in-microsoft-word-2.html*

Logsdon, Ann. *Understanding Dysgraphia—Learn about Dysgrphia, a Writing Disorder.* Argosy University. The New York Times Co. 2011. <http://learningdisabilities.about.com/od/learningdisabilitybasics/p/dysgraphia.htm>

Roe, B,Smith, Burns. *Teaching Reading in Today's Elementary Classroom.* Boston, MA:Houghton Mifflin Company, 2005.

Smith, M. and E. Hogen. *Multisensory Teaching Approach Linkages.* Forney, TX: EDMAR Publishing, 1987.

More than One Way: Approaches to Reading Instruction

Guided Reading Approach

Read Aloud—Reading to Children

Even older children and adults enjoy listening to a good reader share a book with expression and good phrasing. When you read aloud to children, you effectively act as the author. As you represent the author, children get to enjoy the author's ideas without struggling with mechanics. Any time you read wonderful stories to children using obvious excitement, you help children create an attachment between reading and pleasure. From listening to you read, children become motivated to learn to read or to become better readers. Even older students benefit from listening to good readers share their reading and thinking processes. Choose a variety of genres and rich collections of literature that feature diverse societies and cultures.

What Does Research Indicate?

According to the 1985 Commission on Reading, "The single most important activity for building the knowledge required for eventual success in reading is reading aloud to children." One study described a child who had never had a story read to her when she entered school. Another child in her classroom had heard a minimum of four stories a day. Not surprisingly, the child who had been read to before coming to school experienced success when tested at age ten. The child who lacked the home experience of being read to was last in her group.

Conducting a Read Aloud

When reading to young children, do your best to copy the common bedtime routine of reading to children by creating a close, cozy and comfortable setting. This is a time to gather children on the carpet around your rocking chair. You may prefer to sit on the carpet with the children. Depending on your own personality, decide whether you want to assign seating, place children in a semi-circle around the edge of the carpet, or allow them to gather spontaneously and freely. Keep in mind that young children cannot sit comfortably for longer than ten minutes without moving.

It is not necessary that you hold the book sideways so children can see the pictures. Instead, model the correct way to hold a book, read a short selection and share the pictures. If you believe the picture will benefit understanding, you may choose to show the picture before reading a section.

Preparation to Read Aloud

Most of us read with more expression and better phrasing if we practice reading the selection ahead of time. In addition to rehearsing expressive reading, consider places to stop and think aloud. On Post Its®, remind yourself to ask for predictions and to stop and ask children to share how accurately their predictions matched the text. Include questions related to schema. In addition, consider ideas in the text that invite personal evaluations and critical thinking concerning choices made by characters or ethical concerns brought on by events in the reading. Ideas listed below work well for Reading Aloud, Shared Reading and Guided Reading lessons.

Modification for ELL
Before reading aloud to ELL students, explain and demonstrate vocabulary within context. When possible, use real objects.

Before Reading

Before reading, follow the steps below.

- Share the cover of the book as well as the title, author and illustrator.
- Allow children to discuss any prior knowledge or experiences with the topic.
- Tell children if the book will be a fantasy, folktale, fable, or book with predictable text.
- Introduce children to the main characters in the story.
- Always set a purpose for listening or reading.

During Reading

During reading, apply the following ideas.

- Ask children to make predictions. Make certain to notice whether predictions come to pass in the text.
- From time to time, reflect on events or characters. Conduct a Think Aloud, in which you share your own thoughts, concerns, questions and visual pictures.
- If possible, determine ways for children to participate by moving, clapping, swaying, or acting out appropriate parts of the story.

- Remember that children cannot sit long without **gross** (large) motor movements. Be sensitive enough to notice restlessness and allow children to move or stand and listen. When children send the message that they are finished, be gracious enough to cease. You can finish the story at another time.

After Reading

After the story, complete the process by reviewing the characters, setting, problem and solution. Guide children to connect the story to events in their lives. When possible, follow the story with a related activity such as art or writing.

Shared Reading

What Is Shared Reading?

During shared reading, you are the dominant reader and your entire class joins you in ways that are appropriate for the text and compatible with their abilities. Young children are usually seated on the carpet. An invitation to, "Read along with me," differentiates shared reading from simply reading aloud to children. Using a **big book**, which is a large version of a children's copy, you basically read the text in the large book to children while pointing out clues such as pictures, key words and ending punctuation. In addition, you look for passages that children can read with you. Make sure the font is large enough for children to see easily.

Shared reading works best with material that includes repetition. Chants, songs, and poems often work well. Texts with predictable passages invite children to participate. For example, in *The Little Red Hen*, an old fable that was passed down by word of mouth, each section ends with, "And so she did it herself." Children quickly grasp the phrase and with little prompting, join in each time you read the sentence. Other selections that work well for shared reading end with rhyming words or refrains. When conducting shared reading, follow the guidelines below.

- Point out the title, author and illustrator. Demonstrate front and back covers, turning pages, and directional reading from top to bottom and left to right.
- Indicate the sentence, phrase, or word that the children will read with you.
- Initially, read the story to children using good expression. As you read, let your fingers flow under the line of print.
- Read a second time and invite children to join you at appropriate times. When children read, you must continue to read with them to set the pace and to keep the group together.

Modification for ELL
If possible, use "realia" (real objects) to make vocabulary come alive. There is no value in repeating phrases that do not hold meaning. Never assume children understand.

207

Older & Second Language Learners

You can use shared reading with older students, second language learners and even with adults by using poetry with repeating phrases. Initially model the entire poem. During repeated readings, invite the students to join you when reading phrases that are either identical or predictable. When working with English language learners, take the time to explain and demonstrate vocabulary.

Guided Reading Instruction

Guided Reading at the Instructional Level

In many reading programs, guided reading is one of several components including reading to children, shared reading and independent reading. Guided reading should be delivered at the instructional reading level. **Instructional reading** requires a student to demonstrate a minimum of **75% comprehension**. In addition, the child should demonstrate **90% word recognition. Word recognition** is simply the ability to read the printed word. A simple way to determine 90% is to listen to a child read 10 words. Within 10 words, the child should not make more than one miscue. Based on reading ability, you will form **dynamic groups**, which means children can join and leave groups according to their needs. **Traditional groups** are considered those that usually remain permanent. When groups become long-term, a child in a low group has little chance of moving up. Likewise, a child in a higher group may begin to slip but will remain with the initial placement. If you are uncertain about which group is best for an individual child, allow the child to read with two groups for one or two weeks before making your decision. Ideally, you keep each child reading at the instructional level. Notice the scaffolding chart below. The major emphasis of guided reading is to nurture comprehension by guiding thinking processes with questions before, during and after reading.

What Does Research Indicate?

The National Reading Panel shared findings in reports called "Teaching Children to Read." Studies indicated that children in guided reading programs made significant gains in primary and intermediate grades.

What Happens During Guided Reading?

During guided reading, children read with assistance from you. This guidance is often referred to as **scaffolding**. Text should be at each child's instructional level. Reading material that is too easy will not provide adequate decoding practice. Material that is too difficult creates frustration and resistance to reading. A continuum of support includes the following parts of a total reading program.

Scaffolding Continuum

Highest Support	High Support	Moderate Support	Low Support
Read Aloud	Shared Reading	Guided Reading	Independent Reading
Teacher reads aloud to children who listen for enjoyment	Teacher models good reading and all read together (often chorally)	Children read and the teacher prompts	Children read as teacher observes and assesses

Assessments and Levels

Differentiated instruction occurs when text difficulty is matched to individual abilities. Usually, guided reading occurs within small homogeneous groups. Although, the teacher's role is critical, children read the majority of the text. Scholastic provides the following chart indicating levels of books for each grade from kindergarten through grade six. Levels include Scholastic books, *Developmental Reading Assessment (DRA)* levels and Lexile levels

In order to make appropriate assignments for each child's instructional reading level, teachers spend time at the beginning of the year completing one-on-one assessments called **benchmarks**. Although time consuming, the results indicate a starting point for each child's guided reading level. DRA books, which are leveled from A to Z, provide scores for reading rate, fluency and comprehension.

Each child also receives a *Lexile*® measure by taking a standardized test. Lexiles® combine numbers with the letter "L" (with a range from 200L to 1700L). In addition to giving each student a *Lexile*® *reader measure*, books are also assessed for a *Lexile*® *text measure* based on word frequency (repeated use of 15% of the words) and sentence length. When a student's level is matched to the corresponding text level, the result is a **target** reading experience.

<http://lexile.com/about-lexile/lexile-overview/>. Check out the Lexile® Overview Video at *<http://lexile.com/about-lexile/lexile-video/>*.

	Scholastic	DRA Levels	Lexie Level
Kindergarten	A	A-1	BR-100
	B	2	
	C	3-4	
	D	6	
First Grade	A	A-1	200-400
	B	2	
	C	3-4	
	D	6	
	E	8	
	F	10	
	G	12	
	H	14	
	I	16	
Second Grade	E	8	300-600
	F	10	
	G	12	
	H	14	
	I	16	
	J-K	16-18	
	L-M	20-24	
	N	28-30	
Third Grade	J-K	16-18	500-750
	L-M	20-24	
	N	28-30	
	O-P	34-38	
	Q	40	
Fourth Grade	M	20-24	600-900
	N	28-30	
	O-P	34-38	
	Q-R	40	
	S-T	40-50	
Fifth Grade	Q-R	40	700 - 1000
	S-V	40-50	
	W	60	
Sixth Grade	T-V	50	800-1050
	W-Y	60	
	Z	70	

For a complete list of book titles from A to Z, go to the following web site: <http://wces.ucps.k12.nc.us/php/DRA_list.htm>.

Steps of a Guided Reading Lesson

Unlike shared reading in which you do most of the reading and children participate as a whole class, **guided reading** requires children to read with assistance from you. Guided reading works best when you have three to four small groups of readers with **homogeneous** (similar) reading levels and processing skills. One sequence for a guided reading lesson includes the following ideas.

- Begin with an examination of the title, author's name, illustrator's name, and pictures on the cover. Ask for predictions about the story.
- Guide children as they take a "picture walk" through the story by discussing many of the pictures. Use this opportunity to connect ideas to **prior schema** or background information and to invite additional predictions.
- Go through the story again and lead children in a "word walk" through the story. Cover all but one line and say, "Point to the word . . ." (choose a challenging word). Take time to examine the word carefully and to teach any skills needed to decode the word. Examine a minimum of one to five pages. Differences depend on ages of children and number of words on each page.
- On each page, encourage children to locate any additional words that challenge them. Provide help and teach skills as needed.
- Model by reading page one of the story aloud.
- Set a purpose for reading the first part of the selection. Purpose can relate to checking predictions, noticing similarity to schema, or can be based on a question built from a picture title, or subtitle.
- Ask children to mumble read alone or in pairs. As children read, monitor one child at a time to make certain the child is reading at his or her instructional level. Ask the child you are monitoring to retell what has just been read. Note decoding errors, fluency (including rate), and understanding.
- After the children finish reading, ask if their predictions were accurate. Expect them to prove their responses by citing facts from the story. In addition, ask them to share new information learned from the story.
- Following the guided reading lesson, connect an art or writing experience to the story.

Although you may choose to alternate days when you conduct guided reading for groups with stronger skills, plan to provide guided reading lessons every day for your group with the lowest reading ability. Spend as much time as needed for each group to obtain mastery of word recognition and comprehension before starting a new story.

Please view the video on the link below. The teacher, Lori Jamison Rog does an excellent job answering questions about guided reading. *http://www.youtube.com/watch?v=txC-Qo_8GiU.*

Learning Centers for Use With Guided Reading

You will have between three and five groups of children for guided reading. Group sizes might range from a single child to a group of six or seven. While you work with small groups during guided reading, other children in the class will need to actively work on relevant tasks. Learning centers provide a resource for your classroom and one possible method of keeping children engaged with independent activities.

In the beginning of the school year, set up and rope off all learning centers. Introduce and teach expectations for one center at a time. Children should understand how to function in one center before you open a second one. Taking time to explain, model, practice and review expectations for centers will help avoid chaos and interruptions. Your goal is for children to function independently at centers so you can work with individuals and small groups. While teaching one group, seat yourself so you can continue to glance up and monitor the other children.

Teaching Pedagogy for a New Skill

Any time you teach a new skill or procedure to your class, follow the suggestions from the paragraph above, which are now listed as a series of steps. Ideas come from *Daily 5.*

- Explain the procedure and model the exact behavior you want children to exhibit.
- Involve children in writing all expectations on a poster board or chart paper.
- Ask two children to roll-play the desired behaviors. Refer to the chart to make certain all expectations were met.
- Ask two different children to dramatize inappropriate ways to behave. The authors of *Daily 5* recommend that you choose children who are likely to misbehave due to needs for attention.
- After referring to the expectations on the chart, ask the students to correct behaviors and model appropriate expectations.

(The children have now gotten the needed attention and have rehearsed correct behavior.)

- Review written expectations a final time.

The first day you open a center (or start any new procedure), observe and monitor. Do not attempt to teach any guided reading groups until behaviors in centers are mastered. At the first sign of any student getting off-task in the learning center, reconvene the entire class on the carpet and review expectations. Additional rehearsals may also be needed. If you have one or two children who continue to misbehave at a learning center, you will possibly become frustrated and feel like you are wasting time. Usually, the lost instructional time will pay off in the long run.

Worst Case Contingency Plan

However, there are children, who may never be capable of following expectations. In such cases, you can either reduce expectations for exceptional children or provide an alternative activity for those who are not able or willing to comply. If you modify assignments for a child with exceptional needs, you will need to explain to the class that _____ has different needs. Explain that "fair" does not mean everyone gets the same treatment. Fair means that you will do your best to provide the best learning possible for each child.

Physical Needs for a Learning Center

A learning center requires a physical space designated for appropriate materials and activities. Centers can be structured and highly organized with sequentially difficult activities or can be arranged for exploration and creative projects.

Develop a system for rotating through centers. If your guided reading lesson serves as one group center, all groups will rotate from center to center. With very young children, use icons along with a chart to guide groups to correct locations. Learning centers are usually permanent throughout the year. Update materials and learning activities as children's skills become stronger. Begin with: 1) a reading center filled with trade books, 2) a writing center with various types of paper and writing tools, and 3) an art center with supplies that can be handled independently. Other types of learning centers include the following:

- An alphabet center provides letters to manipulate. Materials include stamps, block letters, tactile letters, wooden letters, felt letters, flannel boards, alphabet charts, and alphabet puzzles.
- An art center will rotate materials such as thick tempera paint, crayons, colored chalk, pens, scissors, paper of various sizes and textures, and finger paint.

- A big book center provides opportunities to practice directionality and other book concepts. Include an easel and a collection of big books.
- A dramatic play center encourages young students to solve problems and experiment with real-world roles. Types of dramatic centers include home living, a doctor's office, a restaurant, or mom or dad's office.
- A listening center encourages listening to music as well as to literature. Hopefully, you will include a recorder, headphones, a variety of stories, poems, songs on tape, and phonics activities.
- A mathematics center provides a collection of math-related literature along with math items to manipulate. Math centers allow students to create patterns, create number and shape books, record and interpret graphs, create math story problems, and solve problems using items to manipulate.
- A poetry center allows children to listen to and read poetry. Children may create puppets to dramatize poems or songs. They may also create their own poems for the center.
- A recording center provides an opportunity for children to practice decoding print as they retell a story or record themselves reading.
- A science center allows children to explore materials and record data as well as explore literature related to science concepts. Provide exhibits such as fish, rocks, shells, or animals. Provide journals so children can write about their observations.
- A writing center encourages children to retell or write their own stories or to create new versions of stories previously read. Provide an assortment of writing tools and paper of all sizes and kinds, including recycled birthday cards, invitations, stationery, index cards, and envelopes.
- Another possibility is to create a spelling center. Each student chooses from 5 to 10 words selected either from the student's own writing or from a topic being studied. While at the spelling center, children create and decorate word cards and spelling aids.

Technology has opened the world of computers with a wealth of game and Internet possibilities. In addition, see centers shown on the link below. *http://www.youtube.com/watch?v=r6v9gC-q7oM&feature=fvwrel.*

Guided Reading at High School

The guided reading process can also be used with middle school and high school students. At all ages, students benefit from the background information and guidance from activities before, during and after reading. See the video on the following link *<http://www. ehow.com/list_6576211_guided-high-school-world-history.html>*.

Independent Reading

What Is Independent Reading?

Independent reading consists of material a child can read at the **independent reading level**, which is material the child can read with very little or no assistance. The child who reads independently knows how to choose appropriate reading material, decides to read, decodes appropriately, and gains meaning from print. When faced with challenges, the independent reader takes responsibility for overcoming obstacles. The independent reader also recognizes when to ask for assistance.

Word recognition for independent reading is approximately **99 percent** with **comprehension** no lower than **95 percent**. Begin independent reading with each child reading a book of his or her choice. Many teachers maintain tubs or boxes of leveled books. If you have collections of books organized according to reading difficulty, you can indicate an appropriate box and allow each child to choose from that level. Make no assignments during independent reading. The purpose is for each child to read and reread a book that is comfortable.

Independent reading differs from DEAR (drop everything and read) in that during independent reading you rove, monitor, assess, and assist. The philosophy of DEAR suggests that everyone—you, the administrators, custodians, and any visitors—must "drop everything and read" with children.

As you rove, take 15 second reading rates, make written notes of specific skills, write down miscues, and check comprehension broadly by asking each child to tell about the reading selection.

Values of Independent Reading

Initially, you will struggle to find reading material that is easy enough for emerging readers. Sources for independent reading are even more important for beginning readers than materials for instructional reading. It is through independent reading that children build confidence, independence and love of reading. Independent reading always benefits a child by providing success.

Some teachers in their sincere attempts to promote **rigor**, which is thoughtful challenge, actually inflict permanent damage by forcing children to struggle with frustration level reading day after day. Nothing destroys love of literature more than a daily dose of misery. If you worry about children getting stuck on easy books with little new vocabulary, set your concerns aside. Children who are succeeding want to read more books and seek books that are more challenging.

Materials for Independent Reading

You will find lengthy descriptions of appropriate materials for independent reading in the Beginning at the Beginning Module. At this time, consider the list suggested below.

- Sticker books are books made by teachers. A phrase is repeated on each of three to four pages along with an appropriate sticker.
- Environmental books are exactly like sticker books except that logos are used in place of stickers.
- Individual composition sentences are one of the surest ways to get beginning readers started. Sentences can be developed from material you read to children or from their own journal writing.
- Build-Up Readers are also created by teachers and are usually based on vocabulary from beginning basal readers.
- Word Ladders and Phonograms are charts demonstrating ways words can be built from one initial phonogram such as "at".
- Reading the Room occurs when teachers post signs on familiar objects in the classroom such as "door" "wall" or "desk".
- Word Walls can be found in many classrooms. Letters of the alphabet are spaced across the top of a large bulletin board. Beneath each letter, teachers add names of children and words from books that begin with that letter.

Basal Readers as Reading Material

Book publishers develop and sell sets of books that are carefully sequenced in levels of increasing difficulty. Usually, the beginning basal readers are decodable texts. **Decodable texts** repeat sight words and build on **phonograms**, which are word families such as it, bit, sit. Basal readers can be used for scientific based reading or for individualized reading programs. Vocabulary control and development of a scope and sequence characterize each text. The **scope** lists all skills included in the basal reading program. The **sequence** lists the order in which skills should be taught. This **scope and sequence** approach indicates sequential progression of each skill.

Books usually consist of: pre-primer 1, pre-primer 2, pre-primer 3, and primer (**prī-mər**). Each primer builds on similar vocabulary and each is slightly more difficult than the one before. Most children complete all primers by Christmas and read book 1 during the second semester of first grade. A teacher's edition includes pre-reading questions, statements and questions to use during reading, and follow-up activities after reading. Workbooks, charts, word cards, big books and supplementary materials also come with a basal reading program.

Children who proceed on schedule into second grade begin reading an easy second grade text (2.1) and continue with a more difficult book (2.2) in the spring. Each grade continues to build on the same format and same vocabulary.

Proponents of basal readers defend the fact that each text supposedly controls difficulty, thus making it easier for you to match a child with an appropriate book following assessment. In a basal reading series with carefully sequenced vocabulary and skill lessons, you will feel confident that all, or at least most, reading skills receive attention. Since experts create basal reading programs, they include many excellent ideas for teaching and assessing reading and writing. Not all of the ideas are useful to all of your students, however. It is your job to discern good ideas from those that will waste time.

Opponents of basal reading programs argue that texts often contain reading passages that are much more difficult than suggested by publishers. Particularly anthologies based on great literature often contain interesting but difficult vocabulary. In contrast, opponents contend that when vocabulary is too carefully controlled, stories tend to be boring and stifled.

Ability Grouping With Basal Readers

Ability groups are an important component of basal reading instruction as well as for guided reading. For many years, reading programs developed around formation of homogeneous (same skill level) reading groups. Most teachers created three groups: low, grade-level, and high.

Today, homogeneous groups, often referred to as **guided reading groups or clusters**, are used. Experts encourage teachers to group children with similar reading strategies. Although the wording differs from past years, the result, grouping children on the basis of reading abilities, remains the same. With this approach, teachers lead guided reading with one small group at a time while the remaining children work independently at centers.

Proponents insist that grouping children according to abilities avoids **frustration level reading**, which is always too difficult, and creates easy planning for teachers. Better readers will read challenging material; readers with weaker reading skills will be allowed to read easier material at a slower pace.

Those against ability groups claim that children reading in low groups understand grouping arrangements and resent the humiliation. Another concern is that not all children fit neatly into slow, average, or high ability groups. In order to meet individual needs, you may need to form as many as eight reading groups. However, keeping track of numerous groups and maintaining individual learning contracts may become overwhelming.

Balanced Literacy

One of the important movements, which is integrated into Guided Reading is called Balanced Literacy. After years of literacy wars between proponents of predominate skill lessons and whole language enthusiasts, most literacy experts determined that a balance of both philosophies is the best approach for most learners. In addition, **Balanced Literacy** focuses on a balance between reading and writing using authentic materials. The balance also includes acceptance of many approaches to teaching literacy. "Balanced Literacy incorporates all reading approaches realizing that students need to use numerous devices in order to become proficient readers. It provides and improves the skills of reading, writing, thinking, speaking and listening for all students. A Balanced Literacy program not only balances the reading philosophies, it also balances reading and writing instruction. In a balanced literacy program, students read in order to write and write in order to read." (What is Balanced Literacy? *http://mrscarosclass.com/balanced_literacy.htm.*)

View a YouTube video called *The Components of Balanced Literacy* to gain insight into many components of Guided Reading—Balanced Literacy at the following web site: *http://www.youtube.com/watch?v=8n hZ7g0955Q&feature=related.*

According to a Scholastic web site, Balanced Literacy includes the following ideas:

- Skill lessons should be taught to children. When possible, teach skills within the context of literature.
- Students should experience guided reading as well as independent reading each day. Use **flexible groups** (sometimes called **dynamic groups**). Flexible/dynamic groups are fluid enough for students to enter and leave as needed. Traditional groups tend to remain fixed throughout the year.
- Even young children should be encouraged to build their own understanding in the process of reading and writing. This is **constructivist learning** in which students gain or discover knowledge through active learning engagement.
- Regular print and electronic media are both important learning/reading tools.
- Informal assessments must be balanced with standardized test scores. You will collect samples of each student's work on a daily basis, knowing little instructional information of value is gained from standardized tests.

Research Based Reading

Assessment in Research Programs

A reading program based on scientific study initiates the process with individual assessments. Tests are provided along with detailed record forms. Based on results, children are grouped according to skill levels. In kindergarten, some children will be ready to begin early readers. Others will need instruction in letter name and sound recognition.

At regular intervals, children are re-tested to ensure appropriate progress. Assessment "drives" instruction. At any time during a school year, each teacher will have an understanding of how quickly and how successfully each child is learning. The ability to maintain records is critical.

What Does Research Indicate?

Benefits of assessment include accuracy in determining placements in learning materials. A challenge includes finding ways to use time wisely for the class while each child is tested individually.

No Child Left Behind (NCLB) mandates that following assessment, **research** or **evidence based** programs should be taught using strategies that have been scientifically documented to show evidence of value. The five components include: phonology, phonics, fluency, vocabulary and comprehension. A fundamental theory of research-based instruction is that learning to read is difficult and must be carefully taught. A description of the five basic components of reading is below.

Include Five Basic Components

The Reading Panel includes the following **five components** in the scientific approach to teaching reading.

- **Phonemic awareness** (understanding that sounds make up words and words are made of sounds) must be taught.
- **Phonics** instruction (matching sounds to symbols) is included.

- **Fluency** (words-per-minute or speed).
- **Vocabulary** (word identification along with definitions).
- **Comprehension** (understanding).

All components of reading are taught within core instruction, which is basic instruction. Response to Intervention is threaded through core instruction in an attempt to reduce needs for special education services.

Core Instruction with RTI

What Does Research Indicate?

Once initial assessment ends, reading instruction begins. In 2000, the National Reading Panel (NRP) published an approach to teaching reading that is based on data driven instruction and on individual assessments. Following individual assessment, groups are formed and are given **core instruction**, which is made up of systematic, scientifically based strategies that have shown evidence of successful application. After much research, the panel decided that in addition to core, a plan for intervention and prevention must be established for unsuccessful students. The intention was to provide enough support to avoid special education. The plan, Response to Intervention, was developed into three levels called tiers.

Description of Core and RtI

Core instruction, is provided to all students beginning in kindergarten and requires from 90 to 120 minutes a day. In addition to adopting core curriculum, states are mandated to participate in **Response to Intervention** (RtI). In RtI, all children receive **Tier 1** core instruction.

- Those students needing additional support receive **Tier 1 instruction with modifications**, which differentiates instruction by using adapted materials and practices.
- In addition, children who are not making adequate progress in Tier 1 add **Tier 2** Instruction. The purpose is to provide additional supplementary support.
- Those students that continue to struggle with combined Tier 1 with differentiation and assistance from Tier 2, replace Tier 2 with **Tier 3** remediation. Tier 3 lessons can be provided by a classroom teacher, a paraprofessional, or by a special education teacher. Tier 1 instruction continues.

Many experts share the belief that learning to read is a complex task that does not come naturally. Beginning readers must first understand connections of sounds, symbols, spoken language and reading. Many experts believe that reading must be taught early and that success is largely based on prior experiences with books and print. Children who learn to read successfully in first grade will probably read well in grades four and above. Those who enter school lacking print experiences will probably continue to struggle. Students who do not learn to read will not be able to use reading to learn.

Individualized Approach

What Is Individualized Reading?

In *Reading for Students with Special Needs*, Guszak describes a classroom based on individualized reading. In an individualized reading program, each child reads books at the appropriate independent and instructional reading levels each day. Collaborative learning is encouraged with **heterogeneous** seating arrangements. Children with stronger skills are encouraged to help those who benefit from peer assistance. According to Guszak, each room contains a library filled with trade books as well as a basal reading library, a writing center and additional learning centers. From a large supply of library and basal readers, children select books to begin reading. The teacher assists with selections when help is needed.

What Does Research Indicate?

Research on individual choices about what to read indicate that when students self-select, they read longer than when material is assigned to them. Amount of time spent reading makes the difference between slow, plodding reading and fluent, expressive reading. Research also indicates that independent reading builds fluency, increases vocabulary and builds background information (schema).

Independent Reading Description

The following description comes from the classroom of Mr. Johns. Each morning begins with 20 minutes of independent reading followed by 20 minutes of instructional reading. Comprehension follows reading for an additional 20 minutes as students write answers to comprehension questions over instructional reading. After lunch, the teacher reads aloud to the class. Early in the year, the teacher prepared the children to begin each day with independent reading. Although Mr. Johns initially rewarded table groups for starting independent reading at 8:00, the process now happens without a word or signal from the teacher. During independent reading, the teacher models by also reading. Children either read silently or use mumble reading. When the timer goes off, children exchange their independent books for texts at their instructional levels. During instructional reading, the teacher monitors and informally assesses.

Instructional Reading Description

Although the teacher moves from child to child during instructional reading, he rarely helps with unknown words. If unsure of a child's progress, the teacher will either listen to the child read orally for a short time or will ask for a quick retelling of what the child is reading. If the teacher feels a child is not making adequate progress, the child may be asked to read a book while listening to an accompanying recording. While moving among the children, the teacher updates each child's record for instructional reading. Once again, some children read silently while others mumble read.

Written Comprehension Questions

As the timer indicates the end of instructional reading, each child locates a question folder and begins to answer generic questions covering what was read. The teacher includes two rules for answering comprehension questions. First, the answer must use the question stem to form the answer. Second, the answer must be in a complete sentence. Although words from the question must be spelled correctly, unknown words may be circled.

Usually, children work in pairs to answer questions. They are expected to orally discuss the question and answer before each begins writing. Generic questions, called PLORE, usually include the following pattern of information.

- *Predicting Questions*: Typically, children are asked to make predictions made from examining pictures, titles and subtitles.
- *Locating Questions*: Locating questions can encourage students to scan for specific information, or to look for certain pages or paragraphs. A locating question could also ask for information about the author or reference material suggested in the text.
- *Organizing Questions*: According to Guszak in *Reading for Students with Special Needs,* organizing requires students to use information gained from reading in a new way such as to create an outline, identify the main idea, list the sequence, or create a graphic organizer.
- *Recall Questions*: Before one can organize, one must remember facts and details. Usually, teachers rely too heavily on simple recall questions. For this reason, Guszak suggests connecting recall to organizing activities.

- *Evaluating Questions*: When students are asked to evaluate, they are expected to make personal judgments. An internal evaluation asks whether a text is consistent throughout. External evaluations compare multiple pieces written on the same subject. In addition, use evaluative questions to prod in-depth, value-oriented thinking.

As children write, the teacher again rotates and checks as many answers as possible. By doing so, the teacher reduces the amount of grading. Even more important, the teacher can help with corrections at the time of the writing. A Writing Workshop follows answering comprehension questions. (See Writing section for a detailed description.)

Individualized Reading Programs also include time for skill instruction. Usually, skill lessons use inductive learning, in which children use what they already know to learn new words and generalizations.

Reading Workshops

A reading workshop builds on the values of independent reading. In *The Reading Zone*, Nancie Atwell argues convincingly that students learn to read by having time to read and enjoy books. She describes her style of Reading Workshop. Books are not assigned according to any benchmark test results. In spite of this and the fact that students do not complete worksheets, test results are good at the end of the year.

Following a 10 to 15 minute reading mini-lesson, students spend their time curled up on carpets and beanbags reading books of their choice. A few examples of brief lessons included at the beginning of each Reading Workshop are included below.

- Teachers help students choose books. A book that is too easy is one with very few words or one with all familiar words. If a book is too hard, many of the words are unknown. Some teachers tell students to sample a random page by raising a finger for every word on a page that is unknown. If all five fingers are raised, the book is too hard.
- Information about what good readers do (and do not do) is shared. For example, good readers predict and then check predictions. Good readers re-read if they become confused.
- Students are taught when it is appropriate to read different ways and at different speeds. For example, students learn how to read slowly, how to skim, and when to skip sections.

In addition to the brief mini-lesson, teachers record information about what each student will be reading. As students read, the teacher holds conferences. During the last 5 to 10 minutes of class, the students meet together on the carpet to share what they read. It is important to note that the majority of the time, the children are reading individually.

No external rewards are given. No special method or pedagogy is used. Students experience reading pleasure by enjoying individual book choices, which they read at individual rates.

Atwell's reading program stands in stark contrast to the "evidence based" instruction advocated by NCLB. Consider which program is most likely to meet individual needs, enhance reading proficiency and instill a love of reading.

At the end of independent reading, each child records progress and switches to a book at the instructional reading level. Children reading the same book are encouraged to sit together and help one another. Guidelines for instructional reading are posted.

1. "I can do most of the reading on my own."
2. "I can figure out unknown words and meanings."
3. "If I can't get the word quickly and it seems unimportant, I can skip it."

Advantages & Disadvantages of Self-Selecting

Individualized Reading and Reading Workshop are sometimes combined. In *Déjà vu*, Wassermann links Reading Workshop with individualized reading because both encourage students to choose their own reading material. Controversies rage today over whether to assign books for literacy or to allow students to choose their own. Advantages of allowing students to self-select include the following thoughts.

- Self-selections are more likely to fit individual reading abilities.
- Self-selected books hold more interest and personal relevance to individual students.
- Even though students are reading different material, the students can share what they are reading and learning with one another.
- Students can easily journal about self-selected books.
- Choice helps develop a life-long love of reading.
- Forcing each student to read the same material creates boredom for some and frustration for others.

Advantages of choices made by teachers include these thoughts.

- Books read by groups or by the entire class provide a common theme.
- All students are exposed to quality literature.
- The teacher will be able to point out important points and insights.
- Reading target books allows the teacher to emphasize skills that will be on state exams.

Many teachers are combining the two approaches with some assigned reading and some options for individual choice.

The Daily 5

Two teachers, who happen to be sisters, developed a system for structuring and individualizing reading instruction that seems to pull the best of everything together. Their program builds on individualization and self-selection, coupled with careful teaching, modeling and rehearsing. Their method of teaching new skills and procedures serves as a model for the introduction and mastery of all new concepts. Work done by children is **authentic** (real books and real writing) and **child centered** instruction, which is based on the needs of children. The plan is developed around the following five activities. In between each activity, children gather at the carpet for a teacher-directed lesson.

- *Read to Yourself*—Each child reads individually from a **book that fits**, which is a book the child can read at the independent level (99% word recognition accuracy). The purpose is to become a better reader by practicing.
- *Read to Someone*—Children work in pairs to read to one another. The purpose is to improve fluency and to check understanding.
- *Listen to Reading*—Listening to expert readers builds vocabulary and models fluency.
- *Writing*—Just as children learn to read by reading, they learn to write by writing.
- *Spelling and Word Work*—Working on words and improving spelling improve writing fluency and accuracy.

In the beginning of the school year, the teachers claim that they spend six weeks teaching expectations for procedures needed for independent work to be successful. The two sisters define successful independent behaviors as those that require no teacher re-direction and no continual positive reinforcement. That translates into time when a teacher can focus on teaching or assessing individuals and small groups while the remainder of the class stays engaged with meaningful work. No workbook pages are used. Children are reading real, authentic material with 99% competency and writing independently.

Building Stamina for Extended Independence

The sisters believe that just as the body builds up **stamina** by gradually increasing the difficulty and length of time for physical workouts, readers must build up stamina to read for extended times. Initially, a kindergarten class may not be able to stay focused on reading for more than one minute. When initiating *Daily 5* to children in first, second grade, or above, begin with 3-minute sessions for independent work.

Short, repeated practice sessions lead to success. In the beginning of the year, you may need to practice many times during one lesson. As soon as *one child* gets off task, give the signal, end independent time and return to the carpet (or an appropriate gathering place). Short, repeated practice sessions yield more positive results than extended sessions. Even later in the year, it may be necessary to end an independent session and return to the meeting area to review and re-teach as needed. Practices should be positive and even fun.

Individual Book Collections

Each child maintains an individual set of books, which the teachers refer to as book boxes or book bags. Collections of books can be presented in zip-lock bags, plastic boxes, or covered paper boxes. At the beginning of the school year, individual collections are arranged according to information from the previous teacher. Once lessons have been mastered on how to choose a book, children pick their own collections. Book choices come from the collection in the classroom as well as from the school library. Providing individual sets of books prevents children from spending the entire time searching for the right book. The search is limited and is immediately available.

Gain Attention and Self-Check

Once children are engaged in reading or writing, you will not want to jolt them with a strident bell or your own loud voice. The two teachers recommend using chimes, which create a different sound with a gentle tone. When the time comes to cease an individual activity and return to the gathering place, you want the process to move quickly and smoothly. This behavior, like all others, must be taught using a specific procedure described below.

One goal is for children to learn to self-assess. Once children return to the carpet after working independently, the teacher asks for those who were totally successful and focused to indicate with a thumbs-up signal. If a child needs to improve, the signal will be a sideways thumb. The teachers do not use a thumbs-down. A quick review may be all that is needed. Sometimes, the behavior skill needed for the activity must be taught again.

Teaching Read to Self—Day One

Initially, children must learn the following three ways to read a book: read pictures, read words, retell to someone else. First, model reading the pictures by describing and talking about each picture. Re-read the same book by reading the words. Use Think Aloud to emphasize thinking while reading. Finally, (usually the next day), review the first two ways to read and model retelling. While retelling, describe what happened on each page of the book. The next step is to develop an I Chart.

I Charts

The teaching process for "I Charts" begins with ideas from the children. Each I chart is written on a 24" by 36" poster. The purpose is to create a visual reminder of expected behavior. Creating the charts requires discussion, modeling and writing. Each chart remains posted for the remainder of the year to show a history of what children have learned and mastered.

On each chart, children's ideas will show value and will help supply words to describe the intended behavior. The teacher's behaviors will also be noted. A separate I chart is created for each of the five components of *Daily 5*. The one below is an example of a chart for reading to self.

I Chart—Read to Self	

Why Important?
     Reading helps us be better readers.
     Reading is fun.	

Looks Like • finding a book in my bag • reading entire time • holding a book • looking at book • staying in one place • fingers flowing under print	**Sounds Like** • low mumble voices in room • pages turning • rustle sound when getting new book
What is teacher doing? listening to individuals or small groups read testing individuals	

Discuss and Model

After completing the chart, ask if any child wants to model expectations from the chart. As a student demonstrates, comment and refer to the I Chart. When the child finishes modeling, ask the class to review behaviors.

Next, choose a child who frequently misbehaves to gain attention. Ask that child to model incorrect behavior. This provides an opportunity to lavish attention on the student. Pleasantly, review points being modeled incorrectly. Finally, ask the same child to demonstrate the correct procedures. Once again, provide attention and positive reinforcement.

Practice Reading to Self

For three minutes, allow all students to practice reading alone. Tell them you will only ask them to practice for three minutes. Initially, teachers take one child at a time to that child's individual book collection and then direct the child where to sit. Even if children want to read for longer than three minutes, keep the time short in the beginning to ensure success. According to the two sisters, you are teaching the children to develop "muscle memories" by practicing correctly. Once muscle memories are developed, children will automatically choose appropriate behaviors.

The teachers advise sitting in the assessment or group teaching location to observe. Teachers are advised to avoid using proximity, eye contact, or any form of correction or reinforcement. The goal is for children to read alone without needing guidance, correction, or praise from the teacher. This frees the teacher to teach or assess individuals and/or small groups.

Checking In & Self-Assess

After three minutes, give the chime signal and gather children in your chosen teaching space. Review the chart by reading the behaviors slowly enough for children to reflect. Ask children to self-assess with thumbs up or thumbs to the side. Determine if any behavior needs to be discussed or clarified.

Practice Again

In the beginning, repeat the three-minute practice. After three minutes, give the signal, meet on the carpet and review the chart again. Close the lesson with a final review of all that was learned and practiced on day one.

On day two and beyond, review three ways to read a book and continue the steps with increased time for reading to self. Continue to add a minute each day unless a child gets off task sooner. Cris Tovani, an author of adolescent literacy states, "Whenever an activity fails, it is because I haven't done enough modeling. Modeling gives students words and examples to frame their thinking."

Teaching Reading to a Partner

According to the sisters, research indicates that reading with someone else encourages collaboration and increases attention. Before children practiced reading to themselves, the group lesson focused on skills needed to read successfully alone. After mastering reading to self, the children are again gathered on the carpet. The new lesson will focus on skills needed to read to others. The authors recommend spending six days teaching students how to do this correctly.

- On day 1, teach EEKK (elbow to elbow, knee to knee) while sitting side by side on the floor. In addition, model voice volume and ask students to question one another about who, what, when, where, and why.
- The emphasis for day 2 is on sharing the same book and checking for understanding. Even if each child reads from a separate book, the listening partner will ask questions about what was read.
- On day 3, practice how to choose books with partners by considering both students' book bags. Teach students to use "rock, paper, scissors," to choose a book.
- Day 4 provides instruction and time to practice choosing a place to sit in the room.
- Teach students how to choose partners on day 5. Advise students who need a partner to raise their hands. Make eye contact and ask, "Do you want to be my partner?" Teach students to respond positively.
- On day 6, teach students how to coach one another if one student comes to an unknown word. Advise the listening partner to count to 3 and then ask, "Do you want some coaching?"

Each lesson follows the same procedures used for Read to Self by following the steps below. Teach an initial lesson for each new activity.

- Using students' words, develop an I-chart named for the activity. Discuss the chart.
- Ask two students to model reading together correctly. As they read, discuss their behaviors and refer back to the chart.

- Request that two different students model incorrect actions for reading together. After discussing, ask the pair to model correct actions.
- Allow pairs to practice for 3 minutes. In the beginning, take each pair to their book boxes and then suggest a location for the pair to sit and read.
- Give a signal, return to carpet, and review the chart. This is the time to allow students to self-assess.
- Allow an additional 3-minutes for practice. Resist interrupting to redirect or to give positive reinforcement.
- Bring the children back to the carpet for a final close and review.

Day 2 and Beyond

Once again, review lessons from the previous day. On day one, partners read from the same book and alternate by reading different paragraphs. A different oral reading strategy, called "I read, You Read" can be helpful for developing better fluency. In this new strategy, partner one reads a paragraph and partner two re-reads the same paragraph with an emphasis on fluency and expression.

In addition, use day 2 to model ways to read from separate books. To model, invite each student to choose a book from his or her individual collection. Follow the steps below.

- While partner one reads one page aloud, partner two listens with a finger marking the place to begin reading in a different book.
- After listening, partner two asks questions over the selection read.
- Partner two reads a page while partner one listens with a finger marking the place to begin again.
- Partner one checks the comprehension of partner two.

Partners will decide whether to read by taking turns, read in the same book repeating sections, or read in different books. A fourth way would be for both partners to read together from one another's books. Partners make decisions using "Rock, Paper, Scissors" to allow the winner to decide which reading plan to use.

An I-Chart for reading to someone else might look like the example below, which comes from page 66 in *Daily 5*.

I Chart for Reading to Someone
Value: Helps us be better readers Best way to improve fluency
Use EEKK. Read with quiet voices. Read the entire time. Stay in one place. Start quickly.
Teacher will work with students.

Listening to Recordings

Once students understand the process of reading together, they may choose to listen to recorded readings instead of reading with partners. Recordings over difficult texts can provide support until students can read the books alone. Listening to recorded books benefits fluency and is very helpful to ELL students.

Individual Headphones

Audio books require headphones. When shared, the headphones break frequently and threaten the danger of spreading head lice. To avoid problems, the two sisters included small headphones on the request list that went home to parents at the beginning of the year. When students bring their own headphones, they write their names on the equipment, place them in zippered plastic bags and store them in their individual book boxes. Listening to recordings will require the same preparation as all other *Daily 5* lessons. An example of an I-Chart in *Daily 5* provides the ideas below.

Listening to Reading
Value: Helps us be better readers. Helps us learn new words. It is fun.

Get out all materials. Listen to the entire story. May listen to another story if there is time. Stay in one place. Listen quietly. Start quickly. Put materials away neatly.
Teacher will work with students.

Writing in Daily 5

One part of *Daily 5* focuses on providing an additional time to write and hold writing conferences. This writing opportunity provides focused group instruction over specific writing skills in addition to the writing workshop, which is held in the afternoons. Students can choose what and how to write and can work individually or in pairs. Usually, during writing workshop, a specific topic or genre will be assigned.

As with all components of *Daily 5*, each lesson begins by setting a purpose. One of the first and most important lessons is to teach students what to do when they want to use a specific word in writing and do not know how to spell the word. The authors' tell children to spell the word according to sounds and to draw a line under the *word*. The line indicates that the writer is insecure about the spelling and will need to return to the word later. Encourage students to keep the writing flow going. A sample I-Chart provides the following example.

Writing
Value: Helps us be better readers and writers. People want to read what we write. We have choices about our writing.
Write the entire time. Stay in one place. Work quietly. Choose what to write about. Start quickly. Underline words we're not sure how to spell and move on.
Teacher will work with students.

Spelling and Word Work in Daily 5

The final component to teach in *Daily 5* is spelling and word work. In this section the focus is on spelling and building vocabulary. Although the authors of *Daily 5* do not recommend any specific strategies for spelling and vocabulary, you can refer to *Spelling* and *Vocabulary Modules*.

By now the procedures are familiar to students. They know how to brainstorm ideas for I Charts and how to practice using new behaviors. Depending on the age of students, a list for spelling might include the following: whiteboards, dry erase markers, magnetic letters, clay, letter stamps, colored markers and various types of paper. The two sisters provide ideas for a spelling and word work I-Chart on page 86.

Spelling and Vocabulary
Value:
Helps us be better readers, writers and spellers.
Spelling helps us write more clearly.
It is fun.
One person takes out materials and takes them to a quiet area.
Stay in one place.
Work on building stamina.
Start quickly.
Put materials away neatly.
Teacher will work with students.

Combining the Parts into Daily 5

Authors of *Daily 5* recommend introducing one of the five components at a time until all are mastered. Each day, the practice sessions will last longer and new components of *Daily 5* will be added. Also, the two authors advise starting with 3-minute practice times and building stamina to approximately 30 minutes for each area.

Once you have taught the procedures for each area, your teaching time will focus on skills needed for a lesson. For example, if students need a lesson over prefixes, you will use your direct-teach time on the carpet to teach that skill.

The entire program alternates between direct-teach times with the entire class gathered on the carpet and practice times for each of the specific areas. One added benefit is that children have the opportunity to get up and move to a new location throughout the reading language arts time.

Assessment in Daily 5

Although it is tempting to assign a few workbook pages to check understanding, this practice is not needed. Once students know exactly what to do during each of the five components, you will begin to conference with individuals. Conferencing will provide an authentic method to assess each student in each area. Not only are you avoiding busy work; hopefully you will not have stacks of papers to grade each evening. While students work independently, you will be teaching individuals and working with small groups.

You will only be able to teach and assess comfortably if you have taught students to ignore you. Teaching children when and how to ignore you begins during the introduction phase when you observe independent practice without correcting, redirecting or using positive reinforcement. Instead of interacting with individuals (or even giving the look), you will end independent practice when any one student gets off task. This is your cue to gather the class and re-teach and review the behavior expected for this section. Short, repeated, spaced practice is well researched as critical to teaching new skills. The first six weeks will determine the success of *Daily 5*.

Bibliography

Biddulph, Jeanne. "Guided Reading" *The Guided Reading Approach Theory and Research*. Huntington Beach, CA: Learning Media United. 2002. *<www.pacificlearning.com>*

Bookman, C. *Modeling Guided Reading FAQ* (video). Lawrence elementary.
<http://www.youtube.com/watch?v=txC-Qo_8GiU>.

Caro, M. *What is Balanced Literacy?* <http://mrscarosclass.com/balanced_literacy.htm>

Crawley, Sharon. *Remediating Reading Difficulties*. McGraw Hill: New York, NY. 2012.

DesBarres, A. and J. Pitman. *The Components of Balanced Literacy*. YouTube. 2010. <http://www.youtube.com/watch?v=8nhZ7g0955Q&feature=related>

Fountas, I., G. Pinell. "Guided Reading Programs—Guided Reading Leveling Chart" *Scholastic*. 2011. <http://teacher.scholastic.com/products/guidedreading/leveling_chart.>

Gunning, T. *Creating Literacy Instruction for All Children*. Pearson: Boston, MA. 2003.

Guszak, F. *Reading for Students With Special Needs*. Kendall Hunt: Dubuque, IO. 1997.

Pinnell, G., I. Fountas. "Research Base for Guided Reading as an Instructional Approach" *Scholastic*. 1996. *<www.scholastic.com/guidedreading>*.

"Matching Readers with Texts." 2011. *"The Lexile Framework for Reading. MetaMetrics,* Inc.

"National Reading Panel" *U.S. Department of Education.* Rockville, MD. 2000. *<http://www.nationalreadingpanel.org/ContactUs/contactus.htm>*

National Institute of Child Health and Human Development. *Report of the National Reading Panel.* (NIH Publication No. 00-4769). Washington, DC: U.S. Government Printing Office. 2000. *<http://www.nationalreadingpanel.org/ContactUs/contactus.htm>*

Wahlig, H. "Guided Reading Activities for High School World History." *eHOW*: University of Phoenix. 2010.

Swartz, S., R. Shook. *Using Guided Reading to Provide Direct Instruction in Phonics and Comprehension.* 2004. <http://www.stanswartz.com/ philippines.html>

Assessments and Problems

Assessing Reading

Formative and Summative

A **formative assessment** determines how well a child is progressing toward mastery of an objective. A **summative assessment** provides documentation for a grade or ranking. The current shift in reading instruction encourages ongoing, formative assessments in order to plan meaningful daily instruction. This emphasis on assessing for guidance rather than solely for a grade allows you to:

- Select appropriate reading materials,
- Individualize instruction when needed,
- Form skill groups when appropriate,
- Decide on an approach or strategy to use with each child.

As a teacher, you want to know if a child has strategies for decoding, whether he or she gets meaning from print, and what attitude the child has toward reading and writing. In addition, individual assessment reveals how quickly the child can demonstrate mastery of new skills and information.

Prior to Assessment

Visual and **auditory acuity** (physical ability) must be good for any child to succeed in reading. In addition, each child must exhibit good **receptive language** (ability to hear and understand) as well as strong **expressive language** (ability to speak the language clearly and easily). Further, freedom from emotional trauma, adequate nutrition, peaceful sleep and average intelligence all play important roles in learning to read and write. Therefore, in order to obtain accurate test results, make certain each of the following falls within the normal and expected range.

- Visual acuity,
- Auditory acuity,
- Competence with English language,
- Intelligence,

Barbara Frandsen

- Emotional stability,
- Physical health, diet, and rest,
- Previous instruction.

Assessing Phonemic Awareness

When assessing a child's phonemic awareness, avoid showing words or letters to children. You are not assessing letter name or recognition—only the child's ability to hear the **phonemes** or sounds.

Rhyming Words

Explain that when two words rhyme, they sound the same at the end. Speak slowly as you share the three examples below. The child will not see words during this assessment.

b**at** - h**at**

f**eet** - m**eet**

h**ear** - f**ear**

1) Before saying each word, remind the child to listen to the ending in order to think of a rhyming word.
2) Say one word at a time without allowing the child to see the word.
3) Ask the child to repeat the word.
4) Ask the child to say a different rhyming word.
5) Write the word said by the child in the space provided.

Target Word	Word Said by Child
lace	
boy	
sing	
rock	
met	
eat	
tail	
bet	
beat	
ten	

Each correct word = 1 point. Divide the number correct by10 to determine a % of accuracy.

Nursery Rhymes

In addition, check the child's ability to create words that rhyme by leaving the ending off of familiar nursery rhymes. Use the following example to explain and model. Read the example slowly. Add an emphasis when you say the word "wall."

> *Humpty Dumpty*
> *Sat on a **wall***
> *Humpty Dumpty*
> *Had a great _____.*

After modeling, ask the child to orally fill in the missing word in each of the verses below. Write the words said by the child in the blank spaces.

> *Jack and **Jill***
> *Went up a _____.*
> *To fetch a pail of water.*

> *Jack fell **down***
> *And broke his _____.*
> *And Jill came tumbling after.*

Matching Beginning Sounds

Demonstrate initial sounds by sharing the following examples. During assessment, the child will not see the words.

/b/, /b/, /b/ is the first sound you hear in the word *bear*

/t/, /t/, /t/ is the first sound you hear in the word *top*

1) Before saying each word, remind the child to listen for the first sound. (Do not separate or repeat the initial sound as you did in the examples.)
2) Say one word at a time without allowing the child to see the word.
3) Ask the child to repeat the word.
4) Ask the child to orally identify the beginning sound.
5) Write the sound given by the child in the appropriate space.

Word Said	Expected Phoneme	Phoneme Said by Child
kite	/k/	
hat	/h/	

tar	/t/	
mom	/m/	
dad	/d/	
seat	/s/	
bird	/b/	
up	/u/	
apple	/a/	
elephant	/e/	

Each correct phoneme = 1 point. Divide the number correct by10 to determine a % of accuracy.

Segmenting Sounds

Assess ability to segment (separate and count) the number of sounds in words. The child will not see the letters or words when segmenting. Slowly say each of the words below and demonstrate by separating the individual sounds.

Bat = /b/, /a/, /t/ = 3 sounds (number is for your benefit only)

Leak = /l/, /e/, /k/ = 3 sounds

Go = /g/, /o/ = 2 sounds

1) Before saying each word, remind the child to listen for the number of sounds.
2) Say one word at a time. (Do not say the individual sounds as you did when explaining the examples.) The child will not see the words during assessment.
3) Ask the child to repeat the word.
4) Ask the child to tell you how many sounds were heard.
5) Write the number in the space provided. (The number of sounds is provided for your benefit; not to be shared with child.)

Word Said	Number of Sounds	Number Heard
hat	3 /b/, /a/, /t/	
pet	3 /p/, /e/, /t/	
be	2 /b/, /e/	
gate	3 /g/, /a/, /t/	
wind (to wind)	4 /w/, /i/, /n/, /d/	
slow	3 /s/, /l/, /o/	

glide	4 /g/, /l/, /i/, /d/	
cup	3 /c/, /u/, /p/	
tea	2 /t/, /e/	
chip	3 /ch/, /i/, /p/	

Each correct number = 1 point. Divide the number correct by10 to determine a % of accuracy.

Blending

Assess ability to blend individual sounds into words. Provide examples by slowly saying the sounds and words below. The child will not see the letters or words.

/s/, /i/, /t/ = sit

/b/, /e/, /g/ = beg

/r/, /u/, /n/ = run

1) Before saying individual sounds, remind the child to think about the word made by the sounds.
2) Say sounds for a word one time without allowing the child to see the individual letters or the word.
3) Ask the child to repeat the sounds one time.
4) Ask the child to say the word made by blending the sounds.
5) Write the word in the space provided.

Sounds	Expected Words	Word Said by Child
/p/, /i/, /g/	pig	
/b/, /a/, /t/	bat	
/t/, /o/, /p/	top	
/d/, /e/, /s/, /k/	desk	
/l/, /a/, /p/	lap	
/l/, /a/, /m/, /p/	lamp	
/m/, /e/, /n/	men	
/m/, /i/, /n/, /t/	mint	
/b/, /u/, /m/	bum	
/b/, /u/, /m/, /p/	bump	

Each correct word = 1 point. Divide the number correct by10 to determine a % of accuracy.

Segmenting Syllables

Explain that when counting syllables, the chin drops each time a syllable is spoken. Demonstrate with the words below. The child will not see the words or syllables.

Win = one syllable

Win - dow = window = 2 syllables

Bet - ter = better = 2 syllables

1) Position the child with a hand under the chin.
2) Say one word at a time divided into syllables.
3) Ask the child to repeat the divided word without seeing the word.
4) Ask the child to state how many syllables in each word.
6) Write the child's number in the space provided. (The number of syllables is provided for your benefit; not to share with child.)

Divided Word	Number of Syllables	Number Stated by the Child
tag	tag = 1	
roos - ter	rooster = 2	
wa - ter	water = 2	
ba - by	baby = 2	
re - mem - ber	remember = 3	
gig - gle	giggle = 2	
chair	chair = 1	
un - hap - py	unhappy = 3	
run - ning	running = 2	
al - pha - bet	alphabet = 3	

Each correct word = 1 point. Divide the number correct by10 to determine a % of accuracy.

Assessing Emerging Literacy Concepts

Once you have determined that a child has grasped phonemic awareness, begin to assess print and book concepts that go beyond understanding sounds. The following informal assessments help you determine which concepts a child needs prior to actual reading.

Personal Name Writing

On a piece of primary paper, ask the child to write his or her first and last name. Use the rubric below to assess each item.

	0 = no attempt	1 = poor attempt	2 = good attempt	3 = very good
Spelled first name correctly				
Spelled last name correctly				
Used upper and lowercase				
Wrote on the line				
Held pen correctly				

All √+ = 15 points.

Assessing Alphabet Letters

Ask the child to recite the alphabet without seeing the letters and without singing. Circle any of the letters that are missed.

a b c d e f g h i j k l m n o p q r s t u v w x y z

Show the child a separate set of the following uppercase letters and ask him or her to name the letters. Write incorrect letter names above the ones printed below.

D Q A Z E R H V F X B Y G U I T J P K O N C W M

Show the child a separate set of the following lower case letters and ask him or her to name the letters. Write incorrect letter names above the ones printed below.

d q a z e r h v f x b y g u i t j p k o n c w m

Ask the child to write the following letters (lower or upper case). Note any letters missed.

d q a z e r h v f x b y g u I t j p k o n c w m

Place an index card under each line. As the child names the letters, circle mistakes on your copy.

D Q A Z E

R H V F X

B Y G U I

T J P K O

O C W M

d q a z e r

h v f x b y

g u i t j p

k o n c w m

Assessing with Running Records

Once children begin reading simple sentences and stories, your ongoing assessments will guide book choices for independent and instructional reading. **Independent reading** includes materials the child can read alone. **Instructional reading** requires your assistance. One of the easiest ways to assess reading regularly involves using running records.

Word Recognition Assessment

Although you will also check understanding, the primary assessment during Running Records is identification of words that the child recognizes during oral reading. **Word recognition** is the ability to decode a word using any one of the word recognition tools: sight word memorization, phonics, structural analysis, configuration clues, context clues, or dictionary skills.

By determining the number of words the child recognizes, you gain insight into whether a text is appropriate for you to use for instruction or if the material is a good fit for the child to read alone. Daily reading at a **frustration** level is one of the most damaging practices done in education. Below, you will read guidelines for independent and instructional reading. Anything lower than instructional reading is considered at the frustration level. Use your Running Records to carefully avoid giving a child a book that is too difficult. Frustration material is not challenging; it is humiliating, painful, discouraging and unkind.

Independent Reading

Guidelines for **independent reading** (reading the child can do alone) include 98 percent word recognition and 95 percent comprehension. In simple terms, if a child **misses more than one word out of 20**, the text is too challenging to be read independently.

Instructional Reading

For **instructional reading** (reading the child can manage successfully with guidance), the percentages include 90 percent word recognition and 75 percent comprehension. Any percentages below these are considered frustration reading and must be avoided. If a child misses **more than one word out of ten**, the text is frustration level reading. Set the material aside until word recognition skills are stronger.

Determining Word Recognition Accuracy

Determine percentage of **word recognition** (words read accurately) by following these steps.

- Subtract the number of **miscues** (mistakes) from the total number of words (except for self-corrections).
- Divide the remainder (number of words read correctly) by the total words in the passage.
- For example, in a 50-word passage, if a child had 5 miscues, 45 words were read accurately (45 ÷ 50 = 90 percent word recognition accuracy).

When questions are used to assess understanding, determine percentage of **comprehension** (basic understanding) by dividing the number of correct answers by the total number of questions. A child who correctly answers 4 out of 5 questions has demonstrated 80 percent accuracy (4 ÷ 5 = 80).

Codes for Running Records

Running Records are quick, oral reading assessments. Reading Recovery teachers complete running records without making second copies. (Reading Recovery is a one-on-one program. It is designed to lift the bottom reading levels in first grade through daily tutoring.) You will find the task easier if you make a copy of each child's reading selection so that you will be able to take notes as the child reads. Use √ marks (called **ticks**) to indicate each word read correctly. Listen to each child individually as you complete running records. Although during assessment, you do *not* assist with reading, you may read titles. In addition, you may state unknown words after waiting approximately seven seconds. Consider the following method of marking **miscues** (mistakes during oral reading). The term, "miscue" comes from the belief that mistakes in reading happen because one or more cues are missed.

Marking Miscues

Indicate accuracy by writing a tick (√) above each word read correctly.

√ √ √
The dog sat. (all words read correctly)

Indicate **substitutions** (wrong words) by drawing a line above the word missed and writing the word that the child says. If a child makes several wrong attempts, write each one.

√   √ <u>*sits* sets said</u>
The dog sat.

Indicate **omissions** (words or phrases left out) by a - (minus sign) above the omitted word or phrase.

<u>   – </u> √   √
The dog sat. (left out "the")

Show **insertions** (words or phrases added) by writing in the extra word or words that the child added.

√   √   √ *down*
The dog sat ↑.

Indicate **repetitions** of two or more words by drawing a line above the repeated section with an arrow showing where the repetition began. An uppercase R is written at the end of the line.

<u>   R </u>
The dog sat.

If a child repeats the same two or more words, write R and the number of times repeated.

<u>   R3 </u>
The dog sat.

Indicate **self-corrections** with (SC). Self-corrections do not count toward the total number of miscues.

      SC
√ <u>home</u> √ √ √ √
The house is full of light.

As you examine each error, ask yourself, "What **cue** (skill need) caused the child to make this mistake?" As you consider self-corrections, ask, "What skill enabled the child to make a correction?"

If you help a child during reading, create a large "T" and indicate the type of help given. If the child asks for help with a problem word and then responds accurately to your encouragement, write A (for appealed or asked) to the left side of the "T." If you voluntarily tell the child the word, write a T (for told) to the right of the large "T."

The house is big and dark.
(appealed/asked)   **A** | **T**   (told without being asked)

The major purpose of a running record is to determine a student's strengths. Noting strengths as well as needs enables you to plan the child's next learning steps.

Assessing Categories of Miscues

There are three major categories (called **cues**), which cause children to make miscues. See cues in *Slaying the Comprehension Dragon*. One category is the lack of ability to visually decode the grapheme and match it with the correct phoneme. This category is referred to as a visual skill, although it is more accurate to categorize the problem as a **graphophonic cue** (grapheme to phoneme) challenge. A second category that creates miscues is the lack of understanding about the meaning of words or ideas. A child who reads, "I rode a house to school," is not attending to the meaning of words. This type of miscue relates to meaning and is called an error in **semantic cues**. The third category that creates challenges for some children is the lack of understanding (or lack of attention to) the structure of the language. In English we say, "She is a pretty girl," but in Spanish, the structure is, "She is a girl pretty." A child who reads, "The running is running," has placed a verb where English requires a noun. This type of miscue in structure and grammar is called an error in **syntax cues.**

As you listen to a child read, note miscues. Later, determine the types of cues the child used and cues the child needed to use in order to be successful.

Name _____ Date _____

Miscue	Grapho phonic	Semantic	Syntax
house She rode a horse.	initial c same	√ - lacks meaning	√+ noun for noun
goat The horse got here.	initial c same	√ - lacks meaning	√ - noun for verb
dad His father helps him.	no matches	√+ same meaning	√+ noun for noun
gave She got an award.	initial c same	√ - new meaning	√+ verb for verb

If a child self-corrects, ask, "How did you know to change that? You were thinking as you read." **Self-corrections** occur when a reader notices a discrepancy between: 1) what was seen on the page and what was said, 2) what makes sense and what was read, or 3) language structure the child knows and the language stated during reading.

Determining Oral Reading Rate

Rate (speed or words per minute) presents an effective means of assessing the child's comfort level with print. Poor reading rate almost always results in lack of comprehension.

Using a stopwatch or a watch with a second hand, begin timing as soon as a child starts reading orally. When the time ends, indicate with a slash mark. Time for one minute and count all words read. You may also time for 30 seconds, count all the words read and multiply by two. A third option is to time for 15 seconds, count all words read and multiply by four to determine an average words-per-minute reading rate. The following chart suggests appropriate oral reading rates at various grade levels:

- First Grade 60 wpm
- Second Grade 70 wpm
- Third Grade 80 wpm
- Fourth Grade 90 wpm

Assessing Silent Reading Inventory

In order to assess a child's silent reading, you will need to locate or create a second set of graded reading passages comparable in difficulty to the set used for oral reading. Inform the child that after reading each passage, several questions will be asked orally. Discontinue silent reading once the child's comprehension drops below 80 percent. Following silent reading, you will have no word recognition to assess, only comprehension.

Importance of a Silent Reading Rate

There will be times when a child's oral reading rate is irregular and slow. The child will struggle with substitutions, omissions, insertions and repetitions. If the same child surprises you with better than average comprehension you will be wise to take a silent inventory. If a child's silent rate and comprehension are both good, the child may simply have a challenge with oral reading. Although you will help the child develop confidence when reading orally, remember that very few adults are called upon to read aloud very often.

Silent Reading Rate

With your stopwatch ready, indicate when the child is to begin reading. After a minute, ask the child to stop and point to the last word read. As during oral reading, you have three options for timing: one minute, 30 seconds, or 15 seconds. The numbers below suggest appropriate rates for silent reading at different grade levels:

- First Grade 80 wpm
- Second Grade 90 wpm
- Third Grade 100 wpm
- Fourth Grade 110 wpm

Notice that silent reading should be faster than oral reading.

What Doesn't Work—Reasons for Failure

Practices that Fail At-Risk Readers

In *Educational Leadership*, March, 2011, Richard Allington pens the following words, "We could teach almost every student to read by the end of 1st grade. So why aren't we doing it?" Allington claims that most children entering kindergarten know letter names. It is the few who do not know letter names who are most likely to struggle with reading. Consider the reasons Allington gives for the failures to reach these children.

Core Reading Problems

Core Reading is made up of "evidence-based" strategies with strong records of success. Although a major purpose of Core Reading is to meet needs of all children, problem can be found.

Some Children Need More Time for Mastery

In many cases, Core Reading Programs are failing to remediate struggling readers. Even though teachers are applying the strategies recommended by researchers, most teachers do not repeat a lesson enough times for struggling readers to gain mastery. Typically, a teacher will focus on a skill such as gaining the main idea for a week. When the researchers apply the same strategies, they spend much more time before moving to a new skill.

Lack of Time for Daily Reading

A second major reason for failure of struggling readers within Core Reading Programs is that the children spend very little time actually reading. Out of a 90-minute reading block, children may only read for 15-minutes. The remaining time is spent on skills and workbooks.

Teachers who add a little time for test preparation create even more difficulties for struggling readers.

Need for Independent Level Books

Allington also asserts that not enough time is spent on independent reading, which his article refers to as **"high-success reading."** The article claims that children do not improve significantly when they only engage in reading at their instructional levels. A key factor in how much success a student experiences is linked to the number of texts read at 98% or above accuracy.

Need for Self-Selected Books

Often, children are not given opportunities to read self-selected reading material. All children in a group read the same stories. When children are allowed to self-select, much more progress is noted.

Computer Instruction Problems

Research indicates that computer games and computer-based reading products do not work as well as a good teacher. The *What Works Clearinghouse* only indicated "strong evidence" for one commercial program. In fairness, there were many programs that had not been rated. (Allington is not attacking the altered texts that digital media can produce for students who learn differently.)

Paraprofessionals

"Students who work with teachers, as opposed to aides—**paraprofessionals**, read far more of these high-success texts." According to the article, paraprofessionals help but do not provide as much quality instruction as needed by struggling readers. Possibly, with additional training, paraprofessionals could improve the quality of their instruction.

Summary

In closing, our struggling readers in kindergarten are becoming our struggling readers in grade four. At-risk students require more instruction from experts—highly-educated classroom teachers. They must spend large amounts of time reading independently and reading self-selected materials. When learning skills, at-risk students need more time for mastery. Teaching fewer skills at the mastery level will benefit far more than surface learning many different reading skills.

How Eyes Contribute to Reading

Obviously, **visual acuity**, the physical ability of the eyes to see, contributes heavily to the success or failure of reading. In addition, more than physical acuity influences reading. Failure of any one of the following eye mechanisms causes reading problems. When the eyes are working properly for reading, they move together across the page with frequent stops that are called **fixations**. It is during fixations that visual information is absorbed. Most readers fixate once per word. Individuals who learn to speed-read increase the range of each fixation from 8.5 characters to around 18 characters. However, when this occurs, many words are skipped. Skipping words is appropriate when speed-reading since many words are "glue words," which are not critical to meaning.

Movements between fixations are called **saccades** (from the French word meaning to jump). The effect is rather like watching a slide show with time for movement before a new slide can be seen. During saccades, the movements are so fast that eyes do not process information. Perhaps the brain knows to ignore the visual blur that would be seen during eye movements. One theory claims that information before and after saccades masks the perception of information during the movement.

Approximately 10 to 15 percent of the saccades move the eyes backward rather than in a continuous forward movement. Although most **eye regressions** are automatic and harmless, in some readers, they indicate confusion. Backing up and re-reading is usually a good practice. If over-done, the regressions become a speed bump for good fluency.

Another important eye movement in reading involves the **return sweep** of the eyes at the end of a line. This return sweep is actually a complicated eye movement that frequently creates problems. Eyes must drop down to the next line while also moving from the end of a line on the right back to the left to begin again. Eyes of students with inadequate return sweep patterns may find themselves several lines below the target.

A teacher who understands the complexity of eye involvements during reading can support students by making several adjustments with print. The modifications suggested below should be offered to any student who wants to try something different. Those who need the modifications will continue; others will get bored and return to normal print.

Adjusting for Print Disability

Eye movements depend on **typographic features** such as letter size, font, and the length of each line. Even when visual acuity is good, children may exhibit problems with the ability to focus on small print. Larger letters and shorter print lines help some children who experience difficulty with reading. Adjusting letter size and length of the line puts the focus on the **print disability (PD)** described by David Rose. According to Rose, the problem lies with the print; not with the student.

Chronological age or grade does not ensure that the eyes are ready for small print reading. Expecting a child to read small print before eyes are ready may arrest developmental processes, creating lasting damage. According to Barbara Vitale, a national expert on learning disabilities, most children need large print (like the print size used in early primary grades) through grade four.

If you allow a child to read larger print, you may discover that, in time (approximately 21 days), the developmental need will be satisfied and the child will make a transition to reading regular type. Regardless of age, the student with problems will probably benefit from:

- Reading large print on the overhead screen, the chalkboard, or a chart,
- Reading large print books such as those provided for children with limited vision,
- Shortening the line of print,
- Propping handheld reading material at a 20 to 45 degree angle.

Sometimes changing the angle supports the eyes. Taking the time and effort to experiment with different types of print or angles will never damage a child and may create a significant improvement.

Scotopic Sensitivity Syndrome

Imagine the following situation. You request visual screening for a child who is unable to decode connected print. Results of visual assessment indicate that the child is within the normal range for **acuity,** which is the physical ability to see. Because you know something is wrong, you increase the size of the font, shorten the line of print, and place reading material at an angle for the child. The struggle continues. The child may even complain that letters move, turn upside down, or fall off of the page. After reading, the child's eyes look red and begin to tear. You notice the child attempting to read in dimmer lighting such as under a table. The child may want to turn the computer screen to a very dim setting. These behaviors and complaints may indicate a situation called **Scotopic Sensitivity Syndrome** (SSS). SSS is not dyslexia but often accompanies dyslexia.

Students with **SSS** suffer from the rays omitted by fluorescent lighting. Black letters on stark white paper increase the problem. Print does not "behave" as it should. Words may appear steady initially but begin to move as the child continues to read. The longer a student reads, the more difficult and painful the process becomes.

Various paper colors alter the light rays on the page. A student may read more easily if print is copied on light blue, pale green or beige paper. A few students require darker shades of color.

A related solution is to place transparent plastic overlays on top of the print. Ideally, the overlay will be at least as large as the page, if not larger. A color that works for one child may not help someone else. Depending on the amount of natural sunlight, a favorite color may work well on Monday but fail to help on Tuesday. Making glasses with tinted lenses will not work. Daily trial and error is required. When working with overlays or different colors, ask, "Which color makes the print sharper, clearer, easier for your eyes to see?"

What about the other children? As soon as you offer overlays to one child, the rest of your class will ask for the same opportunity. Solve the problem by purchasing enough overlays for every child in the classroom. Those who do not benefit will soon become bored and will discontinue use of overlays. The one or two children who benefit will gratefully use various colors the rest of the year. You can find a test on the Irlen web site. Go to <http://irlen.com/index.php.>.

Assessing Overlays

Some children benefit from placing a colored transparency over the text being read. To determine the usefulness of this practice, follow these steps.

- Cover half of a page with one transparency color and ask, "Which side is sharper, clearer, easier for your eyes to see?"
- If the child chooses the side with the transparency, move it to the opposite side of the page.
- Place a different transparency color where the first one had been.
- Ask, "Which side is sharper, clearer, easier for your eyes to see?"
- Continue to show different transparency colors to the child.
- Continue to alternate sides of the page. With each comparison, ask, "Which side is sharper, clearer, easier for your eyes to see?

Provide a variety of transparency colors and encourage children to experiment. Those who benefit will continue to use them.

Eye Tracking

Even students with perfect acuity may have trouble moving their eyes smoothly across a line of print. Fixations and saccades must move from left to right. At the end of each line, the eyes must make a return sweep to the next line down. If one's eyes are skipping around, the child will omit words, insert words, repeat lines or phrases and fail to locate the next appropriate line. The result will be erratic, jerky reading with pauses and many miscues.

Although it is necessary to mention concerns to a parent, you do not have the freedom to tell parents to seek help from a professional eye doctor. There is concern that a few parents will insist that the school pay for the formal assessment, which will create problems for your principal. Voice your concerns to parents by saying, "Some parents whose children have this problem have taken them to an optometrist who checks for **pursuit** (the medical name for tracking)." If money is an issue, your PTA may be able to help.

Assessing Eye Movements

Even if the parent refuses or is unable to take the child to an optometrist, you can do your own informal assessment by following the steps below.

- Sit directly in front of the child so you can observe eye movements. Watch for jerky movements, red, teary eyes, and long pauses followed by quick movements to catch up.
- Hold a pencil with an interesting eraser or topper in front of the child and ask that the child keep his eyes on the pencil topper. Tell the child you will be moving the pencil.
- The distance between the child's face and the pencil should be approximately the length of your arm from your wrist to your elbow.
- Move the pencil slowly from left to right. As you repeat the movement two or three times, watch for any jerk in eyes. Following each movement, encourage the child to close both eyes for one or two minutes before starting a different direction.
- After moving the pencil horizontally, move the pencil vertically. Finally, move the pencil diagonally from upper left to lower right. Reverse from upper right to lower left.
- Jerky horizontal movements are sometimes seen in a child who reverses, repeats, and omits words. Problems with vertical movements indicate challenges copying from a board or overhead onto paper. Those who have problems with the diagonal movement are often challenged by the return sweep.

If you identify erratic eye movements, it will be helpful for you to practice the movements two or three minutes each day. Ideally, the child's eye movements will improve. When you spot a specific jerk, slowly go over that spot several times. You may feel you are ironing out a wrinkle. Although practicing eye movements can be helpful, finding time to do so creates a challenge for a classroom teacher.

Sensory Causes of Reading Failure

The act of reading requires more of the eyes and ears than seeing and hearing. The following terms describe some of the intricate skills that must be in place for successful reading.

- **Visual acuity** is the ability to physically see the graphic symbols (graphemes).
- **Visual discrimination** is the finer visual skill of discerning subtle differences in letters and numbers. Children with poor visual discrimination skills frequently confuse letters such as (b) and (d).
- **Visualization** uses the ability to imagine pictures about the meaning of the text.
- **Auditory acuity** is the physical ability to hear different letter sounds (phonemes).
- **Auditory discrimination** allows the reader to recognize subtle differences in similar sounds. The sound of /e/ in elephant and /i /in igloo are examples of small differences in sounds that children with poor auditory discrimination skills often miss.

Home and School Impact

A child's current and past home environment sometimes creates hurdles for learning. A child who lacks meaningful life experiences is almost as disadvantaged as the child lacking physical nutrition and care.

- **Schema** or **prior knowledge** (background experience and information) is necessary in order to link new ideas to personal understanding. Without numerous life experiences, children come to the reading task with very little prior knowledge, which is often called schema. Television provides some vicarious experiences, but because television viewing lacks interaction, the experiences remain superficial. Nothing replaces real life, hands-on experiences with firsthand seeing, hearing, and doing.
- Diet, nutrition, adequate sleep, and basic health play important roles in learning any skill. Hungry or sick children find it difficult to concentrate on the intricate job of reading.
- Parents' attitudes also play a critical role in building interest, motivation, and personal value for learning to read. Children

from homes where learning is not valued often present challenges for motivation and relevance.

Appropriate Instruction

Good teachers model every aspect of learning. In addition, good teachers share examples of good literature and demonstrate reading and writing thought processes. Although some children thrive as readers and writers with almost any type of instruction, most depend on a good teacher and appropriate learning conditions. Adequate and appropriate levels of text must be available. A healthy classroom environment requires the following:

- Chairs and desks that fit the children's bodies (including standing desks and bean bag chairs),
- Natural light,
- Quiet times and places to study and think,
- Living plants,
- Music played at appropriate times,
- Computers with up-to-date, quality software,
- Numerous opportunities to move and interact through the day.

Language Dominance

Children whose primary or dominant language differs from English often face challenges learning to read and write in English. These children are English Language Learners (ELL). One strategy, found in the Fluency Module, is designed to support English acquisition. It is called the Language Arts Mastery Program (LAMP). Many children benefit from strategies that are designed for ELL students. In all situations, build on strengths by acknowledging cultural values and language skills.

- Develop vocabulary in spoken English by reading aloud and helping children connect spoken language with print.
- Strengthen vocabulary by attaching word meanings to concrete objects and actions. This practice is called "**realia.**"
- As ELL children transition from a primary language to English, encourage use of words from both languages when speaking or writing. This practice, called "**code-switching,**" provides support for oral and written **expressive language**. Familiar words in the child's first language are substituted for unknown words in English. The resulting sentence is a combination of two languages.

- Respect and acknowledge the cultures of all children in your classroom.
- Communicate with families and encourage family members to support language development.

Intelligence

No one wants to admit that a child has low or below average intelligence. However, there are children who simply learn more slowly and require more repetition of tasks. Children who are cognitively challenged demonstrate several characteristics.

- Mastery of all tasks takes more time than for most children.
- Use of easier learning material often reduces frustration.
- Repetition ultimately brings mastery and is not found to be boring.
- Understanding does not significantly improve when you read material to the child.
- Oral language skills are usually consistent with reading and writing ability.

Most cognitively challenged children can and do learn to read and write. In time, and with patient teachers, they succeed but will do so at a different rate than children with normal learning abilities.

Dyslexia & Related Disorders

The following definition of dyslexia is from the Texas Education Code (state law): "**Dyslexia** means a disorder of constitutional origin manifested by a difficulty in learning to read, write, or spell, despite conventional instruction, adequate intelligence, and socio-cultural opportunity." Broken down, dyslexia is a condition originating before or during birth that makes reading, writing and spelling difficult to learn in spite of instruction, intelligence, or home environment.

Dyslexia is a specific type of disorder under the large umbrella of learning disabilities. Dyslexia focuses on decoding, fluency, reading comprehension, written composition and spelling. Learning disorders may extend beyond reading and language arts to other areas. Learning disabilities may include:

- **dyslexia** (disability with letters),
- **dysgraphia** (disability with written symbols),
- **dysphasia** (disability with **expressive**—spoken and written language and **receptive** language—language heard or read and understood),

- **dyscalculia** (disability with math calculations)

Most physicians and teachers now believe that dyslexia manifests as a result of a medical condition in the brain. Research using magnetic imaging techniques (such as MRI and PET scans) documents that the left and right brain hemispheres in individuals with characteristics of dyslexia are symmetrical. Normally, the left hemisphere, the part that processes most of our language, appears larger than the right side of the brain. Though you lack qualifications to diagnose this medical disorder, characteristics of dyslexia include:

- Difficulty with **phonological awareness**—understanding that sounds make up words and words are made of sounds *plus* the ability to determine how many separate words are in a sentence and how many syllables in a word,
- Difficulty decoding nonsense or unfamiliar words (**pseudowords**),
- Difficulty with words in isolation,
- Poor fluency,
- Weak reading comprehension,
- Difficulty learning names and sounds of letters,
- Difficulty learning to spell,
- Difficulty with composition,
- Difficulty with learning the alphabet,
- A family history of similar problems.

Before Labeling

Before applying the dyslexic label, consider prior and present instruction, intelligence, and home environment. Problems with the following conditions must be ruled out as causative factors before a diagnosis of dyslexia can be applied:

- Vision,
- Hearing,
- Speech and language,
- English language proficiency,
- Intelligence,
- Emotional problems.

Part of data gathering also includes past report cards, daily observation records, parent conferences, formal reading assessments and the results of accommodations and efforts to remediate.

Texas Teaching Requirements

Guidelines help schools and teachers determine appropriate programs for children with dyslexia. Consider the following Texas requirements when designing dyslexia remediation.

Requirement	Definition
Direct Instruction (by the teacher rather than through inquiry/discovery)	Instruction is delivered in a structured and sequential manner. Instruction must fit the alphabetic principles.
Individualized Instruction	Both materials and methods must meet specific learning needs of individual children.
Graphophonemic Instruction	Letter names and sounds must be taught using synthetic or analytic phonics. (**Synthetic phonics** instruction puts individual sounds together to create words. Analytic phonics instruction looks at words and analyzes parts and sounds.)
Language structure	Language instruction must include **morphology**—study of parts of words, **semantics**—study of meanings, **syntax**—structure and grammar, **pragmatics**—relationship of language and real-life environment.
Linguistics	Patterns of language, **phonograms** (word families) or **rimes** (word families), are used to develop fluency.
Meaning based	Reading must be purposeful and must emphasize comprehension.
Multisensory	Auditory, visual, tactile, and kinesthetic processes must be used simultaneously (at least two senses at the same time).
Phonemic awareness	Instruction must ensure that students detect, segment, blend, and manipulate sounds in spoken language without seeing print. (Understanding that sounds make up words and words are made of sounds.)
Process oriented	Processes of **word recognition** (decoding words using various skills), and **comprehension** (understanding) must be integrated to accomplish true reading.

Barbara Frandsen

Acceptable Accommodations in Texas

Even when taking state tests, accommodations are available to any student as long as changes do not alter test results. It is important to note that a student does not have to be diagnosed in order to take advantage of the following accommodations. It is, however, important to document that the same measures are used on a daily basis for instruction.

- Instructions may be given orally.
- Colored transparencies may be placed over the test.
- A place marker may be used with the test. (Instead, encourage use of fingers to guide eyes.)
- An individual test may be given in which the student may read aloud or may read test items into a tape recorder to play back while working.
- Braille or large-print versions of the test may be used.
- A hearing-impaired student may have an interpreter to sign directions.
- A student may respond orally to test items. The test administrator must record the child's answers verbatim on a standard answer sheet.
- If unable to write, a student may dictate a composition to a test administrator by spelling all words and indicating capitals and punctuation.
- If unable to write, a student may use a computer but may not access the spell-check feature.

Challenges & Practical Suggestions

Ideas in the following chart can be helpful for a child with dyslexia at any age. Many of the following suggestions are for older students with characteristics of dyslexia.

Reading Characteristics	Possible Solutions
Word sequence is reversed during oral reading. Parts of words are reversed (flutterby for butterfly).	Practice horizontal eye tracking. Place a green dot next to the first part of a word or put removable green tape over the beginning of a word.
It is easier to talk about a subject than to read about it.	Allow the child to gain information through discussions, videos, and audiocassette tapes.

Reading speed is slow.	Break the reading task into short sections. Ask the child to reread several times with quick breaks after each reading. Read titles, subtitles, and questions first to set up expectations. Enlarge the print. In addition, try dimmer lighting or use of colored transparencies.
When reading orally, many words are repeated.	Use two fingers to gently push the eyes *across* the page. Practice horizontal eye tracking.
Reading comprehension is poor when reading silently.	Encourage visualization during reading. Teach students to monitor self-talk. "Am I seeing the pictures? What am I thinking about while reading?" Allow the child to read technical or difficult sections aloud.
Comprehension is poor when reading orally.	Encourage visualization. Set a purpose for reading a very short section. Stop. Check comprehension. Ask the student to actively do something: write, act out, discuss, or draw after each short section.
The child ignores context clues.	Highlight all context clues or cover them with colored removable tape so they stand out.
The child is unable to use phonics as a decoding tool.	Use flash cards with pictures. Color-code the most difficult word parts.
The child cannot recall the alphabet.	Teach visualization of alphabet sections using 3 to 5 letters per section.

Dysgraphia

Dysgraphia is a writing disorder under the overall topic of learning disabilities. "Dys" has to do with inability. "Graphia" relates to creating printed symbols (**graphemes**). Although different from dyslexia, which focuses on reading, dysgraphia sometimes accompanies dyslexia.

However, dysgraphia can exist alone without other problems. Writing difficulties that do not disappear by the middle of second grade may indicate dysgraphia. Use checklist items to support requests for additional testing by special education teachers or school diagnosticians. Your job includes knowing which characteristics to observe and record. Along with observing the following behaviors, you will be expected to rate their frequency and intensity.

- Does the child reverse letters or words when writing?
- Is the child awkward or uncomfortable when writing?
- After mastering a spelling word for a test, does the child write the word incorrectly on daily work?
- Can the child copy from a book or paper on the desk?
- Can the child copy from the chalkboard or overhead projector?
- Is it more difficult for the child to write about an issue than to talk about it?
- Is the child confused about hand dominance?

    To assess hand preference, hand the child pencils, scissors, and other items at the midline and notice which hand the child uses to take each item. The midline runs down the middle of the body.

- Does the child have a hand preference on one side of the body and an eye or foot preference on the opposite side?

    To assess eye preference, roll up a piece of paper and hand it to the child at midline. Ask the child to pretend the paper is a kaleidoscope to look through. Notice the child's eye choice.

    To assess foot dominance, roll an imaginary ball to the child and notice which leg the child uses to "kick" it back to you.

Frequent Writing Problems

The following writing problems are common to emerging writers as well as those with dysgraphia:

- **reversals** from horizontal mirroring:

    b and d,
    q with p,
    s and z.

- **rotations** from vertical mirroring:

b and p,
d and g,
q with d,
n and u,
6 and 9,
5 and 2,
m and w.

- **transposals** (entire words or numbers written backward):

dog and god,
was and saw,
235 and 532.

- **closure** (leaving letters or figures unfinished),

- **directionality** (confusion when going from left to right or top to bottom),
- **position in space** (inability to place letters or numbers on the line),
- **size constancy** (inability to keep numbers or letters the same size on a given task),
- **omissions** with writing, such as "help" written as "hep,"

Remedial Activities & Materials

Use the following materials to help develop fine motor coordination.

- Chalkboards/whiteboards or vertical surfaces provide excellent transitional activities linking gross to fine motor skills.
- Clay or Wikki Stix offer ways to help children develop fine motor control.
- Personal desk copies of appropriate models of upper and lowercase letters facilitate writing.
- Pencil grips sometimes ease the discomfort for beginning writers and students with dysgraphia.
- Paper with raised lines (Meade) can help.
- Frequent breaks from writing ease the stress of writing.
- Computers and word processors are important.

Encourage students by saying, "Can you see your improvement? You are making progress. You should feel good about your hard work."

Strengthening Hand Control

Each of the following exercises is designed for young, emerging writers as well as for students with dysgraphia. Use as "break-time" activities with the entire class. Guide children to do the exercises daily and to hold each position for a count of five. After each exercise, ask the children to release and shake out their hands.

- Press palms and fingers together at the midline (center of the body) with elbows close to each side. Press hard to the count of five.
- Touch the fingers and thumbs of both hands together and press to spread the fingers apart. Repeat five times.
- Interlace fingers behind the back and extend the arms as high as possible. Take five breaths, exhaling slowly.
- Stretch the fingers by interlacing the fingers of both hands at the midline and pushing hands out with palms facing away from the body. Repeat five times.
- Make a fist with one hand. Use the other hand to cover the fist and tighten. Repeat three times and change hands.
- Hold the arms out in front of the body. With arms extended, touch right and left thumbs to the fingertips of the same hands. First, touch thumbs to index, middle, ring, and little fingers. Reverse the order. Movements of left and right hands occur at the same time.
- With arms extended, keep one hand motionless as the thumb on the other hand touches each finger (as described above). If a child cannot touch the thumb and fingers of one hand without the second hand moving slightly, the child is not developmentally ready for fine motor writing.

In order to support hand control, teach children to lay the palm of the non-dominant hand on the arm of the dominant hand while writing.

Behavior Problem Letters

All rounded letters curve toward the left margin (that is the starting place)—with the exception of two behavior problem letters. You guessed it, (b) and (p) stubbornly curve toward the stopping point (the period).

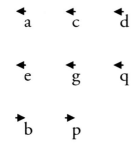

a   c   d

e   g   q

b   p

behavior   problem

Challenges and Common Sense Ideas

Many of the following suggestions provide ideas for emerging writers as well as those with characteristics of dysgraphia.

Writing Characteristics	Possible Solutions
Words and letters are frequently reversed.	Teach the memory aid called "Behavior Problems." Instruct young, emerging writers to create whole body letters on the floor. Guide children to sky-write body-size letters or numbers using clasped hands.
Body language is awkward when writing.	Provide writing grips. Teach the child to place the non-dominant hand over the arm that is writing to help stabilize writing. Allow a student to alter body positions by: • Sitting on a pillow, • Lying prone on the floor, • Standing to write on a vertical surface, • Standing to write horizontally at a tall desk.
Copying from the board or overhead produces problems.	Give the student copies of all board or overhead work at the student's desk. Guide the student to practice vertical eye tracking for two minutes a day.

Copying continues to be difficult even when material is on the student's desk.	As you teach, record your lessons so the child can listen again later.
Writing about a topic is much more challenging than talking about it.	Encourage the child to type on a word processor. Allow the child to dictate to an adult. Allow the student to record ideas about a topic. The student will then take dictation from his or her recorded message. Reduce the length of writing assignments. Use study-buddies who write together. Encourage use of writing frames (graphic organizers).
Letters and numbers lack closure and contain open spaces.	Encourage the child to trace over large (1-inch) tactile letters. • First trace with two fingers. • Trace with felt markers. • Trace with pencils. Practice writing on a chalkboard or vertical surface.
The child indicates a problem with position in space by ignoring the lines on a page when writing.	Allow the child to use tactile paper with raised lines. Practice on a whiteboard or vertical surface.
Letters and numbers are inconsistent in size.	Allow the child to use tactile paper (Meade) with a raised line between two solid lines. Practice on a chalkboard or vertical surface. Ask children to trace one-inch tall letters and numbers using: • Two fingers, • A marker, • A pencil
The child switches back and forth from manuscript to cursive letters.	Place a preferred model of either manuscript or cursive letters on the child's desk. Encourage the child to be consistent.

Bibliography

Anderson, Wilson, and Fielding. "The Effects of Independent Reading on Reading Achievement." Boston, MA: Hourghton Mifflin Co., 1997. <http://www.eduplace.com/rdg/res/literacy/in_read1.html>

Atwell, N. "The Pleasure Principle" *Scholastic Instructor*. Edgecomb, Maine, 2011.
<http://www2.scholastic.com/browse/article.jsp?id=8132>

Chen, K. and G. Carper. "What is Code-Switching?" *Code-Switching and Identify.* 2007

Coyne, M.D., E.J. Kami'enui, and D.W. Carnine. Research on Beginning Reading. Boston, MA: Pearson, Allyn Bacon, Prentice Hal, 2006-2011.

Elmhurst Public Library. Elmhurst, IL 2011.
<http://www.elmhurstpubliclibrary.org/Kids/HighInterestLow VocabBooks.php#Grade_One_Lexile_100_400

Frandsen, B. *Yes! I Can Teach Literacy.* Austin, Texas: Family School, 2006.

Fitzsimmonr, Mary. "Beginning Reading." Education.com. 2006-2011.

Guszak, F. *Reading for Students with Special Needs.* Dubuque, Iowa: Kendall Hunt, 1997.

Irlen, H. "The Irlen Method." *Irlen.* 1998.
<http://irlen.com/index.php>

Irlen, Helen. *Reading By the Colors.* Garden City Park, NY: Avery Publishing Group, 1991.

Index

Barbara Frandsen

Y

CPSIA information can be obtained at www.ICGtesting.com
Printed in the USA
LVOW031212130712

289865LV00001B/6/P